THE CHURCH OF
THE CLASSICAL AGE:
THE GREAT CENTURY OF SOULS

VOLUME 2

THE CHURCH OF
THE CLASSICAL AGE:
THE GREAT CENTURY OF SOULS

VOLUME 2

Henri Daniel-Rops

Translated from the French
L'Église des Temps Classiques: Le Grand Siècle des Âmes
by J. J. Buckingham

CLUNY
Providence, Rhode Island

HENRI DANIEL-ROPS

THE HISTORY OF THE CHURCH OF CHRIST

CLUNY MEDIA EDITION, 2023

This Cluny edition is a republication of Chapters IV–VI of the 1963 edition of
The Church in the Seventeenth Century, a translation of *L'Église des Temps Classiques:
Le Grand Siècle des Âmes*, published by E. P. Dutton & Co., Inc.

············

For this Cluny edition, citation and reference styles
have been updated and developed, as needed,
for the purposes of clarity and accessibility.

For more information regarding this title
or any other Cluny Media publication,
please write to info@clunymedia.com, or to
Cluny Media, P.O. Box 1664, Providence, RI 02901

❧ VISIT US ONLINE AT WWW.CLUNYMEDIA.COM ❧

ISBN (paperback) | 978-1685952686
ISBN (hardcover) | 978-1685952709

NIHIL OBSTAT: Joannes M. T. Barton, S.T.D., *Censor deputatus*
IMPRIMATUR: Georgius L. Craven, *Epus Sebastopolis Vic. Cap.*
WESTMONASTERII, DIE 15 MARTII, 1963

The *Nihil obstat* and *Imprimatur* are a declaration that a book or pamphlet is considered
to be free from doctrinal or moral error. It is not implied that those who have granted the
Nihil obstat and *Imprimatur* agree with the contents, opinions or statements expressed.

Cover design by Clarke & Clarke
Cover image: Gregorio De Ferrari, *Moses Striking the Rock
for Water* (detail), late 17th century
Courtesy of Google Arts & Culture

CONTENTS

CHAPTER IV

Louis XIV: "Most Christian King"

1. THE SUN KING

A French historian may be forgiven if he allows a little sentiment to appear in his approach to the study of Louis XIV—the man and his reign. For never, in the thousand years that wove the thread of her history, had France been as strong, as glamorous, as radiant as she became during that long reign when, under the rule of the thirtieth Capetian, she attained the pinnacle of her fortunes.

The image of this monarch is so colourful that the mind, somewhat dazzled by the splendour, is inclined to admiration rather than to an impartial judgment. Louis XIV was Versailles: Versailles with its palace, its parks, its glassy lakes and its masterpieces—an unparalleled *ensemble* which the world would copy but never equal. Louis XIV evokes military glory obedient to French arms, strongholds captured by Vauban, the crushing campaigns of Condé and Turenne, captured enemy flags hanging in the cathedral of Notre Dame, and Europe anxious to recognize and accept a new order based on French standards. Louis XIV represents order of another kind and a model which French genius created and proclaimed, and which Europe accepted without hesitation—the language of Molière and Racine spoken henceforth by kings and ambassadors; a French conception of creative form compelling recognition by western civilization and blossoming into an unprecedented magnificence. France's debt to this man and to his reign is so vast that it would be unjust and even absurd to deny it. He gave her fifty years of firm rule, an effective structure embodying many ideas that have

234 survived to the present day, a language, a literature, an art, and above all a feeling of greatness born of a noble sense of urgency. The expression which Perrault used to characterize this period, "the century of Louis XIV,"[1] was undoubtedly the expression of a courtier, intended to flatter his master by comparing him with the Emperor Augustus; but it stated a reality which history has acknowledged.

Since Christianity is unquestionably associated with that glory and achievement, to what extent may a Christian historian share this admiration? The part played by Christianity is especially evident through the official documents which assign to the Catholic religion a fundamental position within the State—through the customs and practices accepted by the mighty king himself and the majority of the French people, through the liturgical ceremonies which year after year, from the crowning and anointing of the sovereign at Rheims to his funeral at Saint-Denis, give character and rhythm to his own life and that of the nation. The century of Louis XIV, in so far as it concerns the things of the spirit, was not merely the century of Molière and Racine, La Bruyère and La Fontaine, Mansart and Le Vau; it was also the century of Bossuet, the fearless apologist, of Fénelon, whose heart was enamoured of God; of Bourdaloue, Fléchier, Mascaron, Massillon and a group of preachers who have never perhaps been matched in any age. It was the century of St. Margaret Mary Alacoque, St. Louis-Marie Grignion de Montfort and St. Jean-Baptiste de la Salle.

But more essentially the Christian religion was linked with everything that stood for solidity and grandeur in France during that period. It bound together members of society; it was the code of morals, the key to institutions, and it embodied the meaning of life itself—"the whole of man," as Bossuet remarked. To fail to recognize the part played by Christianity is—as Nisard said of Voltaire, historian of Louis XIV—"not to reach the heart." On the other hand, to study the reign from the Christian standpoint is to probe the spiritual depths of the epoch, for there only its genius lies revealed. The triumph of order and authority over the forces of crisis and

---

1. Also used later by Voltaire.

disintegration, to which the classical era ultimately tended in every domain, 235
was achieved through the reawakening of a spiritual allegiance having its
roots in time immemorial; that allegiance had been restored to life by the
admirable upsurge of the preceding period, and the whole nation was prepared for the contest. If the century of Louis XIV honoured the man even
more than it honoured France, it was because its foundations were those of
the Cross.

When we consider, however, the events of this glorious epoch, too
many of them appear to be out of tune with a Christian conception of life
and the world. This glittering reign contains many dark patches, and the
detractors of Louis XIV, among them Michelet and Lavisse, have not had to
seek far for a bill of indictment. The facts are there to hand; there is no need
to search for them. They are apparent in the policy adopted towards the
Protestants and the Jansenists, but especially in the ghastly methods used
to secure victory by force of arms. Other examples, still more surprising,
are to be found in the relations between the Catholic King of France and
the Sovereign Pontiff, whom a Catholic must acknowledge as the Vicar of
Christ. And how is a Christian to assess that apparent indifference to the
misfortunes and sufferings of the lowly, hardly compatible with the tradition established by a former Louis—Louis XII, the "Father of his people"?

We are evidently faced with a kind of indwelling contradiction. This
appears even more manifest when we consider together the two forms of
title in general use during the reign. Since the time of Louis XIII it had been
the custom to distinguish the king of France by the additional title "Most
Christian King." Paul II first used the title in 1469 in a letter to Louis XI.
When Louis XIV reached the apogee of his glory his flatterers persuaded
him that he was comparable with the sun itself, and they urged him to have a
medal struck to confirm this humbug. To what extent can the "Roi Soleil"—
the Sun King—also be called a Most Christian King? Are not the two titles
incongruous? There is, in any case, no doubt whatever that the Sun King
would find it very difficult to be "most Christian" in the manner of St. Louis.

The events of the reign did, in fact, demonstrate the antithesis between
the two titles. It would be unjust, and contrary to historical fact, to disregard

the solid Christian basis on which the reign of Louis XIV rested; but it would also be unjust to gloss over the serious faults of which the king and his regime were guilty towards religion, its precepts and its rights. It seems that a real paradox existed between Christian principles, which neither the king nor his servants treated lightly, and the contingencies—necessities perhaps, but certainly inevitabilities—that appertain to government. Monarchical absolutism, indispensable during that period and demanded by peoples themselves as a means of controlling crises and preventing a return to chaos, was attaining its zenith, its acme of perfection. Was it reconcilable with the Gospel, the religion of humility and poverty and its ideal of justice and love? All the great religious discussions of the reign were to converge upon that question.

But the man mostly concerned with that question was he upon whom everything depended and from whom everything proceeded; he embodied the regime so perfectly as to be inseparable from it, bearing both the burden of responsibility and the glory of his reign. In many ways he was as much the prisoner of the system as he was its master. Where does pride begin and end in a king who declares, as Louis did, that love of glory held the highest place in his sentiments, and convinced himself by that very fact that he served a cause that reached infinitely beyond its scope? A leader who knows well that firm discipline is indispensable to the security of the country entrusted to him must find it difficult to decide where charity begins and ends, especially when an occasional act of injustice is the price to be paid for the maintenance of order. Every event that occurred, including those that affected religion, touched the depths of the man in Louis XIV; they influenced his attitude towards faith, towards God and the Church. Raised up by the regime itself to such an eminence that he was scarcely permitted to remain a man, would Louis XIV discover within himself sufficient moral strength, born of humility and submission to the divine will, to resist the temptations resulting from his lofty position? Could he possibly strike a balance between the demands of the high office he assumed and his obligations as a poor sinner?

When describing the "century" of Louis XIV historians repeatedly use such words as reason, order, light, unity, discipline and balance; but in every

case the words appear to skim the surface of reality. They are especially inadequate and inaccurate when used to deal with the religious aspect. The truth
is to be sought among the crises that rent the long reign, and not so much
in the atmosphere of solemnity that surrounded the Masses celebrated at
Versailles and the eloquent funeral orations; it will be found in the conflict
existing between the rigid demands of a doctrine requiring detachment,
purity and humility of heart and the infinite charity of a saint, and the poor
human nature of the man who had to apply it.

2. GOD'S VICEROY

ON the day following Cardinal Mazarin's death Harlay de Champvallon, at
that time president of the Assembly of the Clergy and Archbishop of Rouen
(later of Paris), said to Louis XIV: "Your Majesty instructed me to approach
M. le Cardinal in all matters of business; but the cardinal is dead. To whom
does your Majesty wish me to address myself in future?"

"To me," replied the king. "I shall dismiss you shortly."

This was the first occasion on which the king expressed his determination "to be his own first minister in future," a decision which he repeated
to the Chancellor Séguier, to Fouquet, his superintendent of finance, to Le
Tellier and Hugues de Lionne, all of whom showed great surprise.

The king's *Mémoires* suggest that his decision was by no means made
on the spur of the moment. For years he had been signing the documents
presented to him by Mazarin without reading them, but he had pondered
things over in his mind more than he appeared to be doing. "I continually
tested myself secretly, without confiding in anyone," he wrote, "meditating
upon every occurrence." The old cardinal was not mistaken when he said
that his pupil "will be a late starter, but he will go further than anyone."

What were the profound motives that decided this burly lad of twenty-two, hitherto more interested in horses and pretty girls than documents
and affairs of State, to assume the burden of responsibilities that went
with power? What psychological evolution brought about this change of

attitude; what sentiments, what men, what reading influenced him? None of the king's biographers has asked himself that question; yet it is perhaps the key to the whole reign. Was it merely pride, a thirst for power or distrust of men, that determined the most dictatorial of kings to refuse to share the direction of affairs with anyone? Few appear to be aware that a copy of Godeau's *Catéchisme royal* (Godeau was Bishop of Grasse), which appeared in 1659, was given to the king immediately on publication. He acquired from this work a theory of royal power that was particularly prone to excite in a young mind a passion for absolutism, though the work was based upon a genuinely Christian theology. At the very commencement of a reign that lasted more than half a century, and during which the king never swerved for a moment from his decision to be "his own first minister," he most certainly recognized the Christian obligations of this "trade of king." In assuming personal authority he considered that he was obeying a command from heaven.

On reaching his legal majority eight years earlier—fourteen years of age in the case of kings—he was crowned in the brilliantly lit cathedral at Rheims, its arches and pillars adorned with magnificent tapestries. Everything in that wonderful ceremony compelled his mind to seize upon the religious and sacramental significance of his office. The ancient liturgy, its rites, music and symbolism, had undergone little change since the time of King Pepin the Short; everything reminded him again and again that as king-priest, the anointed of God, successor to the Scriptural kings, Saul, David and Solomon, he occupied a positive position in the world under God's will and ratified by the Church. The tunicle, the dalmatic and the cape which he donned in turn reminded him of the three Orders of the priesthood. During the singing of the litanies he lay prostrate on the ground, just as a priest does at his ordination and a bishop at his consecration. The holy oil rubbed on his forehead, breast and shoulders was the same as that used in the administration of the sacraments. More hallowed still were the words of the antiphon: "Almighty and eternal God, it was Your Will that the kings of France might receive the holy anointing with the balm sent by heaven for that purpose to the saintly Bishop Remigius." Even more impressive was the Church's acknowledgment of the king's supernatural powers, for it confirmed the rite of "touching for scrofula" (king's evil) and recognized that he possessed the miraculous gift of healing sores by his touch. Indeed, the pomp of the ceremony, the firing of guns, the ringing of bells, the cheering of the people, those priceless adornments, his crown and sceptre, the hand of Justice, the great purple mantle decked with golden fleurs-de-lys were all tangible tokens of an authority that proceeded direct from God, having nothing to do with earthly values. To add emphasis to the young king's conviction, jurists had perfected throughout the centuries the doctrine of kingship by divine right,[2] and this had been further developed during the reign of his father and grandfather. The doctrine had now reached a state of perfection. "Kings are made by God," wrote Councillor Le Bret; Coquille, Duchesne, Bignon and Savaron went even further. Soon Bossuet, the most powerful Christian voice of the age, produced his *Politique tirée des propres paroles de l'Écriture sainte*, in which he made a definite break with the tradition of Ballarmine and Suarez. He developed and defined the idea when he wrote: "A king's throne is not the throne of a man, but the throne of God Himself.... Royal power is sacred: God raises up kings as His ministers and reigns through them over nations.... Obedience to princes is therefore an obligation of religion and conscience.... One should not consider how princely authority was established; it is sufficient that it exists and governs.... An inherent holiness exists in the character of a king, and no crime can efface it."

Such were the theories that Louis XIV read and heard repeated in all manner of ways, not only by jurists (e.g., Domat in his *Droit public*) but by bishops in their theological writings. He must also have read, again from the pen of the Bishop of Meaux, these words, which transcended everything that had gone before: "According to the Scriptures princes are gods, and they participate to some extent in the independence of God."

How could the king fail to absorb such doctrine? Ideas such as these occur time and again in his own writings (the *Mémoires* and *Testament*)

---

2. See Volume 1 of this work, p. 220.

under different forms. "Here below kings fulfil a function that is wholly divine. It is the will of God that whoever is born a subject shall obey without discrimination." And again, more precisely: "Because a king takes the place of God he participates in His knowledge."[3] The doctrine of kingship by divine right was therefore put into practice in a systematic and awe-inspiring manner throughout the entire reign. The king's golden rule of life was based upon what he had read in Bishop Godeau's *Catéchisme royal*: "May your Majesty remember at all times that he is a Viceroy of God."

A conviction such as this, rooted in the conscience of a prince, was not without its advantages. Undoubtedly it contributed towards determining the atmosphere of the reign, an atmosphere of incomparable majesty maintained for half a century—an air of solemnity, perhaps artificial and tiresome, but which none the less provided a dignity scarcely known during other Capetian reigns (the succeeding one, for instance). It produced a continual and instinctive gravitation towards an ideal of grandeur. Indeed, the king's person appears to have been stamped with these qualities. All observers are unanimous in agreeing that such an air of majesty emanated from Louis XIV that it impressed everyone who came into his presence. "Everything about him," said Mme. de Motteville, "inspired respect and fear, and those upon whom he looked intently could not escape this feeling." And Saint-Simon adds: "No man ever inspired such awe; one had to begin by getting accustomed to seeing the king if one were not to stop short suddenly when speaking to him." Needless to say, this conviction that he was the trustee of God's power and majesty had its dangers; but the fact that he entertained a great respect for his trust was a point in his favour.

In some respects the consequences of the king's conviction that he was God's Viceroy were favourable. By taking his role seriously, not merely on account of the rights it conferred upon him but also because of the obligations it imposed, he was drawn to assume the duties of his state in an extremely steadfast and conscientious manner. The gravity of the doctrine

---

3. Jacques Pirenne has compared these words with those used by the ancient Egyptians. The pharaohs of the fifth dynasty (the twenty-fifth century before our era) were declared to possess all knowledge "from their mother's womb."

of divine right lay in the fact that it imposed on its recipient demands worthy of the power it granted him. Never did Louis XIV seek to escape them.
His *Mémoires* and his *Testament* deal admirably with his conception of his
mission and the manner in which he desired to discharge it. He regarded
the "trade of king" as "great, noble and delightful"; but he wished to feel
"worthy to acquit himself well of everything he undertook." This illustrious
man was, therefore, the most hard-working of kings. "That is how a king
reigns," he said. "That is why he reigns." He had no desire for power without
work. "To wish for the one without the other implies ingratitude and presumption towards God, and injustice and tyranny towards men." Throughout his entire life Louis XIV devoted many hours a day to public affairs,
either alone or with his secretaries of State. He continued to preside over
the council until the eve of his death, and conformed to a discipline whose
purpose, whatever one might say, went beyond furnishing an opportunity
to exalt his kingship through court etiquette.

The actions of a king here below, in his capacity of God's Viceroy, must be
providential in the sense that they reflect God's work. The king must ensure
the reign of "justice, the precious trust that God has placed in the hands of
kings, and through which they participate in His wisdom and power." The
king must "show towards peoples subject to him the same marks of paternal
goodness that we receive daily from God," and have "no greater desire than
to safeguard the weak against the oppression of the strong, and relieve the
destitute. He must also guarantee to maintain Christian order which is the
foundation of society, defend those virtues which Christianity demands of
men and, in short, protect the faith, its dogma and the Church." Such were
the duties of a king, and Louis XIV was fully conscious of them. There is no
evidence that he sought to escape them. "He is charged with a great burden"
said Bossuet; and he knew.

Such a conception was genuinely Christian. "How can we possibly
imagine," writes Pierre Gaxotte, "an absolute monarchy separated from the
commandments of God?" It is precisely to the extent to which Louis XIV
strove to remain loyal to such principles that he deserved the title "Most
Christian" bestowed on him by diplomatic custom. But just how much

242   did he really strive? The doctrine had to be applied by a man made of flesh and passions like every other, ceaselessly beset by temptations and no more immune from sin than anyone else. Can a Viceroy of God permit himself certain weaknesses without creating scandal? What is more to the point, this earth-bound representative of heaven runs the risk of forgetting occasionally that his most trifling act is responsible to a higher Justice; he is liable to confuse the delegated authority vested in him with an entirely temporal authoritarianism. Between monarchy by divine right and an absolutist system of State control collusion would be almost inevitable, and that was the tendency of the age. Between the conviction that one represents God on earth and the illusion of being something more than a man there exists an incline down which it is very easy to slide. Did Louis XIV manage to avoid confusing the issue?

3. THE HEART OF A KING

IT is a fact beyond dispute that Louis XIV was a believer. He spent the whole of his youth in an intensely spiritual atmosphere, under the influence of a Spanish mother of great piety and the memory of a devout father. He had been constantly told that his birth was an answer to prayer, that he was indeed Louis the "God-given."

In 1650 he solemnly renewed the dedication of his realm to Our Lady made by Louis XIII, and instructed "all institutions to admonish each and every one to have a special devotion to the Holy Virgin." One of the first acts of his personal rule was to take part in the Stations of the jubilee solemnized in 1661. He walked in the processions to show, as he said, "that it was through God and His grace rather than by his own efforts that he hoped to accomplish his aims."

Throughout the reign the practice of religion played an important part in the schedule and time-table that governed court etiquette. Morning and evening prayers formed part of the ceremony of the *lever* and *coucher*—when the sovereign rose from or retired to bed. The king assisted at Mass every day,

respectfully kneeling from the *Sanctus* until the priest's Communion. At   243
nightfall he never failed to take part in the evening service. He attended in
person a number of processions—at Corpus Christi, for instance, and those
arranged three times a year by the Order of the Holy Ghost (on January 1,
February 2, and the feast of Pentecost). He also followed in the procession
of February 10, to commemorate the dedication of France to Our Lady. In
Advent he listened to the Sunday sermons, and sometimes on Wednesdays
and Fridays; during Lent he attended them all, and scrupulously obeyed the
Church's laws relating to fasting and abstinence. He publicly warned the
court that he expected everyone else to do likewise. He attended the offices
of Holy Week regularly, even during the years when his personal difficulties
with the sixth and ninth Commandments prevented him from making his
Easter duties. On Maundy Thursday he washed and kissed the feet of thirteen poor children in the presence of the Chaplain-General; afterwards he
served them a meal, and the princes of the blood, headed by the Dauphin,
acted as waiters and cup-bearers.

All this clearly constituted a splendid and steadfast homage to the
Christian religion. It is difficult to say to what extent these ceremonies were
an expression of the king's faith. From what we know of his practices we
cannot regard him as extremely devout. He received Holy Communion five
times a year at the most: "At the parish church on Holy Saturday," Saint-Simon tells us, "and in his private chapel on other days, such as the eve of
Pentecost, the feast of the Assumption, the eve of All Saints and Christmas Eve." We know of no recorded instance of his having felt impelled to
approach the altar out of a personal desire or to satisfy an interior need.
During Divine Service he was reluctant to use a prayer book; even Mme. de
Maintenon was often unable to persuade him to do so. When he had one
he scarcely opened it and contented himself with saying the Rosary, which
seems to have been his favourite devotion. All his life he kept the beads he
had inherited from his father, and which had previously belonged to Henri
II and Henri IV. It was, in any case, a peculiar Rosary: the beads were tiny
skulls in ivory. There seems to be no record either of any spontaneous desire
to read spiritual books, a practice which his father and his cousin, Philip IV

of Spain, always followed. His father had been a fervent admirer of Loren-
zo Scupoli, and Philip of Maria d'Agreda. Mme. de Maintenon often complained to the king that he paid little attention to the books she read to
him. There is no mention anywhere of his having made retreats, as did St.
Louis, who was accustomed to withdraw frequently to some monastery. All
the evidence suggests that the spiritual tide of the century of saints did not
sweep the great king's soul towards mystical heights.

It has often been said, and perhaps unjustly, that the religious practices
of Louis XIV were simply a matter of form, a way of showing his sincere
respect for the religion of his forbears. The king might have read in a letter addressed to him by Fénelon,[4] if indeed it ever came to his notice, this
unsparing criticism of his faith: "You do not love God; you only fear Him
with the fear of a slave. Your religion consists of nothing but superstitions
and petty superficial practices. You resemble the Jews whom God accused of
honouring him with their lips and not with their hearts. You are scrupulous
in trifles and obstinate in things that are dreadfully wrong." It is difficult to
know to what extent the Archbishop of Cambrai was right; to judge properly one would have to probe the depths of a heart that was never inclined
to be prodigal with its secrets, but strove rather to conceal its innermost
thoughts.

We do know, however, from certain characteristic traits and from what
the king has said, that he possessed a faith that was anything but formal.
When he was eighteen he confided to an intimate friend that he could not
understand how anyone in a state of mortal sin could sleep at night with an
easy conscience. "On great feast days," said Mme. de Caylus, "he experienced
twinges of conscience because he could not pray, or prayed badly." And the
Abbé de Choisy aptly commented: "More than once, despite official whis-
pers, the king preferred to abstain from the sacraments than approach them

---

4.   The letter was written to the Duc de Chevreuse, but intended for the king. It is
included in Fénelon's *Oeuvres complètes* (t. 7, pp. 321–25). No one can say whether
the king read the letter or not; but it seems that some passages regarding the necessity
for signing a peace must have had some influence on him. Traces of this influence may
also be found in the conversations that the king had with Maréchal de Villars.

unworthily." This was a source of scandal to the common people, but of edification to the wise and enlightened. In 1704, on the brink of old age and consequently very much wiser, he admitted to Massillon after one of those dramatic sermons in which the celebrated preacher was so proficient: "Whenever I listen to you, Father, I am displeased with myself." Those are not the words of a man whose religion is a matter of mere routine, decorum or policy.[5]

There were no spiritual complications attached to the faith of the Roi Soleil. The reassuring simplicity of his beliefs sheltered him from the insidious subtleties of Jansenism and Quietism, and certainly held him aloof from disturbing ideas such as those of Pascal, from anxious searchings and shattering revelations. Yet he was not a man whose conscience was easily satisfied, contenting himself with a few superstitious practices and assuming that he was thereby saved; it was not as simple as that. Through the outward show of splendour we get a glimpse of a man like ourselves, face to face with his soul, and like us, wrestling with the Angel.

For this king who loved court etiquette was well acquainted with those human passions that play havoc with the soul and endanger eternal life. He yielded to some and vanquished others, as all men do. His life appears to have been a conflict of the will. In his youth he was subject to fits of violent anger; he eventually succeeded in curbing them so that he always remained supremely master of himself. He never allowed anyone to notice that he was in pain, either morally or physically; he did not even allow himself to be ill, and above all to appear so. In the face of death he displayed a praiseworthy strength of mind.

In other matters he was undoubtedly less exemplary. Historians, in an attempt to prove that he was, as one has said, "unacquainted with the refinements of Christian morals," have strongly emphasized his waywardness where love was concerned; and certainly the picture is hardly edifying. He wrote in his *Mémoires*: "If it is true that the heart, unable to reject its

---

5. Saint-Simon relates that he was deeply impressed by the eagerness with which the king inquired, on being informed that Louis XIII was dead, whether his father had received the Last Sacraments.

natural weakness, experiences despite itself these common emotions, reason at least should conceal them." It must be admitted that Louis did not succeed very well in putting this precept into practice. His display of mistresses and legitimized children was offensive; but was the conduct of his Catholic Majesty, Philip IV of Spain, any better? The Most Christian King's resounding, and sometimes simultaneous, love affairs present a rather disagreeable picture resembling that of a sultan with his harem—the tender Mlle. de la Vallière, the disturbing and attractive Mme. de Montespan and other beautiful but less famous women, such as Mlle. de la Motte Argencourt, Mlle. de Marivault, Mme. de Ludre and Mlle. de Fontanges. Does this picture suggest that, as a slave of violent passions, he did not suffer in consequence? On several occasions, as the feast of Easter drew near, he was seen to make an effort to return to the right path in order to receive Holy Communion. There were one or two moving incidents. On Maundy Thursday 1675, a courageous priest refused Mme. de Montespan absolution, and the king, far from punishing the bold man, admitted that the fact perturbed him and ordered his mistress to leave the court. This she did—though it was only for a short time. What is also remarkable, and indeed to the king's credit, is that he allowed Bossuet, Bourdaloue, Massillon, Dom Cosme and other preachers to lecture him from the pulpit. The precision and violence of their censure were astonishing. We have only to read the devastating attack Bourdaloue made in his sermon on impurity, uttered in the very teeth of the culprit! No twentieth-century dictator would endure such a castigation. Louis XIV was a great sinner, a public sinner, and he was fully aware of the fact; the sense of sin can be profoundly beneficial to the soul.

Furthermore, we must remember that about halfway through his reign the king put an end to these violent love affairs once and for all.

This may have been due to the decisive influence of Mme. de Maintenon and her devout circle, for we must not underestimate the qualities of this good and clever convert, grand-daughter of Agrippa d'Aubigné and widow of the paralysed poet Scarron. She became governess to the king's illegitimate children by Mme. de Montespan, gradually won her master's favour, and ended by secretly marrying him. She was no common sycophant, playing on the king's scruples in order to secure him for herself. "Lord God," she wrote, as though making a confession, "all my life I wish to adore whatever Your Providence ordains for me; I submit to it without reserve. Let me be of service to the king in the salvation of his soul.... Let me be saved with him!" These words were written with sincerity; and equally sincere were the king's spiritual impulses, his disgust with his past and his weariness of repeated sin. The alleged conspiracy between Mme. de Maintenon and Fénelon to worry and beset the king does not entirely explain his attitude. Even when respect and a strong tinge of boredom were the only feelings he retained for his wife, Louis XIV still did not return to his former excesses. He was forty-six when he married Scarron's widow, and he led an absolutely upright life during the last thirty years of his reign. The approach of old age is not sufficient to explain this victory over himself.

One aspect, however, of Louis XIV's character must appear distressing to a Christian: we might call it pride, egoism or hardheartedness, for all three are usually found together. He was naturally proud, but the defect was intensified by the education he had received. As a mere child he had been the object of a form of flattery which might have turned anyone's head. His mother prostrated herself before him, declaring that the "respect in which she held him was greater even than her love." His first lessons in handwriting consisted in copying the words: "Homage is due to kings; they do whatever pleases them." The doctrine of divine right could only emphasize this tendency towards pride, and there is much to suggest that what he had been told about his "miraculous" birth might easily have driven home the conviction that he was entrusted with a superhuman mission.

The danger of excessive pride was therefore inevitable, and no doubt Fénelon was right when he said: "You love only your glory and your comfort. You view everything in terms of self as if you were the god of earth, and everything had been created to be sacrificed to you." Bossuet expressed himself more prudently, but he evidently thought the same when he spoke of the dangers of unlimited power, and referred to Nabuchodonosor and Balthasar. Saint-Simon went further, referring to the king in stinging terms as "loving and valuing only himself and having no purpose outside himself."

Indeed, the amazing thing is not that the great king should have been proud in view of the upbringing he had received and the worship with which he was surrounded,[6] but that a prince so flattered did not yield to hysteria. It has very often been said that "only the fear of hell prevented him from demanding adoration," but this is pure malice. He was too clever to lose sight of the precariousness of things human and the fear of judgment. Bossuet called this "the remedy God Himself has prescribed to kings against the temptations emanating from power." Mme. de Sévigné relates that some members of the Order of Minims dedicated a thesis to the king in which they likened him to God, as though God were but the copy of the king. Bossuet had no difficulty in convincing him that such praise was indelicate, and Louis XIV, of course, rejected it.

It is none the less true that on many occasions he was severe and indifferent to the point of inhumanity. Despite many acts of spontaneous kindness, especially towards the young, there were too many occasions when he proved to be sadly lacking in the most elementary kindness. That might not be regarded as serious if his harshness were merely a principle of government. Olivier d'Ormesson quoted the king as having said: "I know I am not loved, but I am not bothered about it, for I wish to reign by fear." He could hardly be condemned on these words alone, for one may argue long as to whether the use of gentleness or force is of more value in the management of men. Even his reputed cruelty, that quiet cruelty towards the women he loved, may easily be excused on the sensible principle, which he stated in his *Testament*, never to allow love to interfere with politics. But it is very distressing to think that this hardness, pride and egoism seemed to enclose his heart in steel, rendering him insensible to great suffering, heedless of flagrant wrongs and somewhat lax where justice was concerned. We are painfully surprised to see a young king bring pressure to bear on the judges in the trial of Fouquet, his superintendent of finance, in hope of securing

6. Bearing in mind the persistent and fulsome praise showered on Louis XIV there is some excuse for his pride. The Abbé Dangeau, brother of the memorialist, even produced a *Dictionnaire des bienfaits du roi*.

his execution; and to read of the brutal and irrevocable disgrace of Olivier d'Ormesson because his conclusions in his report on the affair were not in the king's favour. Even more painful is the fact that in his old age the king went so far as to imprison Vauban for his moving appeal on behalf of social justice. And what are we to think of a military leader whose armies laid waste the Palatinate, of a king who organized the *Dragonnades* in Languedoc? France's "Great King" lacked the very qualities which would have made him a really Christian king; the quality that was also wanting in that other great Catholic king, Philip II of Spain—the fragrant spiritual bloom of mercy—the charity of Christ.

4. THE KING AND THE CHURCH

THE oaths taken by Louis XIV during his coronation ceremony were many and elaborate. He swore "to protect the Church in his kingdom, as it is the duty of every king to do," "to safeguard peace at all times" within the Church, and to prevent the Church from falling victim to disorder and evil. Such was the basis of that alliance between the Crown and the Church, which had been the foundation of French monarchy since the time of Clovis. One of the oaths taken by the king was even more precise: to preserve "the canonical privileges, rights and jurisdiction of the Church"; and those who officiated at the ceremony replied in a prayer which resembled a warning: "As the clergy stand nearer to the holy altar than the rest of the faithful so must you endeavour to ensure that the clergy are treated with the greatest respect and maintained in suitable places, that God's mediator on behalf of men may make you mediator between the clergy and the people." The recognized position of the clergy as the first Order of the realm was thus clearly defined.

It goes without saying that Louis XIV did maintain that ancient alliance between the Altar and the Crown. He maintained it as a believer, wishing to remain loyal to the vows made at Rheims. But it was also good policy; he appreciated that it provided his throne with its most solid foundations.

There are, however, many ways of interpreting that alliance. In principle it meant a collaboration between two authorities working together in the best interests of the people, but each having its own sphere of activity, the one spiritual and the other temporal. In actual fact this collaboration, founded on equality of authority, almost ceased to exist as time went on. Sometimes the Church sought to bring the lay power into subjection; at other times, and especially after the great theocratic ventures had run their course, kings strove to control the Church. As far as appearances went that was the underlying, if not expressed, purpose of Louis XIV. The question was bound to arise sooner or later whether the Church, honoured, flattered, its hierarchy surrounded with marks of esteem, could avoid becoming a part of a system, a cog in the machinery of government under a regime that tended more and more towards centralization and dictatorship.

The exclusion of ministers of the Church from positions of authority was a hard and fast principle of the regime of Louis XIV, and one to which there was no exception. Doubtless the king remembered the power of Richelieu and Mazarin. Saint-Simon relates that when someone expressed surprise to Louis XIV that he did not place on the Council a certain cardinal whose services he commended, the king replied: "I have made a rule, to which I adhere, never to have a minister of the Church on my Council, especially a cardinal." And in his *Testament* he stated explicitly and with a touch of humour his reasons for this ostracism: "because ecclesiastics are a little too inclined to take advantage of their profession, and sometimes make use of it to minimize their rightful duties...."

But if the king did not wish the clergy to interfere in his affairs he did not by any means think that he should abstain from interfering with the business of the Church. Quite the contrary: the collusion of the spiritual and the temporal, and unfortunate consequence of the 1516 Concordat which did so much harm to the Church and against which the Council of Trent failed to take a strong stand, became a factor of government during the whole reign of the *grand monarque*. Louis XIV used to the full his right, recognized in the Concordat, of nominating candidates for bishoprics and abbeys. That the Pope reserved to himself the right of canonical investiture was a minor consideration to the king. In actual fact it was he and he alone who appointed the higher clergy.

It must be appreciated that in the king's eyes this was a task of some importance: "The most hazardous part of his duties," as Bossuet said. And Louis had every intention of performing it worthily. He even wished, as he assures us, "to observe in the sacred army" the same rules that he applied to the promotion of his military officers, and admit "to the bishoprics and other high positions only those who have served the Church in missions or in carrying out the functions of parish priests or curates." The Council of Conscience was available to assist him in his choice. The king himself presided over the Council and, especially from about 1682 to 1684, was very concerned with what took place at its meetings. His confessor (Father La Chaise[7] at first, and above all Father Le Tellier) occupied a prominent place in the Council as representative of the French clergy, dealing with religious affairs and disposing of titles and benefices. But Mme. de Maintenon, after her marriage to the king, managed things over the heads of the Jesuits, and eventually became a kind of minister for ecclesiastical affairs.

The king's good intentions and the influence of those who assisted him did not lead to really satisfactory results. The very system of control which Louis XIV exercised, his gradual isolation in the restricted environment of Versailles where active control became more and more centralized, inevitably resulted in the majority of bishops and other Church dignitaries becoming minions of the court, the government and the administration. Le Tellier, Archbishop of Rheims, Jean-Baptiste Colbert, Bishop of Montauban, and

---

7.   A well-known cemetery named after Father La Chaise or de la Chaise (1624–1709) now stands to the north-east of Paris on ground which at that time belonged to the Jesuits. Father La Chaise exercised a considerable influence over the king. He was not, as Rébelieu stated in his *Lavisse* (viii. 1), "Secretary of State for religious affairs, sole representative of the Church of France to the king, chief treasurer and paymaster of the royal bounty," but he did advise the king as to the disposal of benefices. Every Friday after Mass Louis XIV spent many hours with him either working or discussing matters affecting his soul. La Chaise courageously endeavoured to avoid nominations which might have given scandal, despite the flood of applications he received. An article by Father Guitton entitled "Le père de la Chaise et la feuille des bénéfices" appeared in the *Revue d'histoire de l'Église de France* (1956), p. 29ff., and dealt with La Chaise and the promotion-hunters.

André Colbert, Bishop of Auxerre, were the sons, brothers or cousins of ministers. The former chaplain to the Queen Mother was appointed to Saint-Malo and the king's chaplain to Auch. Mme. de Maintenon had her beloved confidant the Abbé Godet des Marais (who was none the less a very pious priest) installed at Chartres. Still more surprising, many bishops were taken into the king's household: Valot and Daquin, Bishops of Nevers and Fréjus respectively; Sanguin, Bishop of Senlis, whose father was a *major-domo* at Versailles—all "cads in purple," to use the words of Saint-Simon. The most ridiculed prelate of them all was Ancelin, Bishop of Tulle, whose mother had been one of the king's nurses.

Abbots and abbesses were appointed in the same arbitrary manner. The competition was lively, for these posts yielded a good income. The *in commendam* system, denounced by all reformers during the preceding period, was practised more than ever. Abbesses transferred from one Order to another to acquire a wealthier convent; bishops would offer some abbey in their diocese to a highly placed minister. Both Mme. de Montespan and Mlle. de Fontanges obtained from the king splendid convents for their sisters. We have the famous story, told by Saint-Simon, of the little Comte de Toulouse, a natural son of Louis XIV, asking for a bishopric for his valet Picard to compensate him for the fact that the valet's brother Vexin had been given some profitable abbeys. To crown all, the king took it into his head to seek a dispensation from the Holy See in order that one of his legitimized sons might enter the Church.

It was surprising that this state of affairs did not infect and corrupt the episcopate under Louis XIV. Although it was not generally up to the standard of its counterpart in the time of Louis XIII and Richelieu it was, in fact, not bad; it even included some splendid personalities who had either survived the previous epoch or had simply remained loyal to the duties of their state.[8] But members of the higher clergy, the worldly minded bishops and commendatory abbots, were absolutely devoted to the king, zealous in his service and dazzled by his splendour.

8.   See below, Chapter V, on the qualities of certain bishops.

That was a serious matter. Even Bossuet and other bishops who pos- sessed the most brilliant qualities as churchmen allowed themselves to be captivated by Versailles, the court and the fact that they came under the king's notice. "Whatever will you do at Rheims?" a lady of fashion asked Le Tellier when he was returning to his diocese. "You will be bored to death there!" Racine satirized the "petite assemblée" of fifty-two prelates who followed the court around. For ambitious priests who wanted to make headway Versailles became the object of their pilgrimage *ad limina*. Bishops and important Church dignitaries were certainly no longer employed in official lay positions to the same extent as in the past, but one or two were diplomats and administrators. An archbishop, for instance, occupied the post of King's Lieutenant and Governor, and Henri de Sourdis was at the head of the Admiralty. But by all appearances they were as much a part of government machinery as they were a means of enhancing the king's glory. When Colbert met with resistance in his attempt to bring production under his control there were bishops in several localities who shouldered the responsibility of making the working class conform. The subordination of the episcopate was such that, when the Bishop of Agen openly criticized Colbert's policy the powerful minister rebuked him before the whole court, and threatened to have him taken back to his diocese under guard. Needless to say the bishop made no reply, terrified lest the punishment might be carried out.

One of the most unhappy consequences of this subjection of the higher clergy was that it became practically cut off from Rome. "To write directly to the Pope, to his ministers or to anyone representing him in this court," said Saint-Simon, "or to receive any letter whatever without the king or his Secretary of State knowing the reason for it and permitting it, was an unpardonable crime against the State. The practice was punished and therefore ceased entirely." Thus, at a single stroke, attachment to the Holy See, if not loyalty to Rome, disappeared. "Osmosis exists between the universal Church and a particular Church; they are distinct but not separate. They open out into one other, the interests of the one being bound up with the interests of the other. When their relationships become strained it does harm to the very life of both."[9] The Gallican crisis showed in a painful manner the consequences of this factual and spiritual separation. And there is no doubt that the evident slowing down of the spiritual upsurge noticeable at the beginning of the reign of Louis XIV must be seen in relation to this separation.[10] The laws made by the Council of Trent were not officially accepted in France during the reign of Louis XIV any more than they had been under his predecessors; they were not even taken into account in the assemblies of the Clergy, where henceforward only Gallican freedoms were considered.[11]

We must not overlook the fact that, although the king's subjection of the clergy to his will was part of a broad policy, he could not have failed to consider other very material advantages. His idea of ownership was strictly totalitarian. "Everything within our realm, of whatever nature, belongs to us.... Kingship implies the right to dispose absolutely of all property possessed by churchmen and laity." In the view of Louis XIV everything that had been said about the object of Church property and the intention of the founders was merely a groundless scruple. "The principle will not, in fact, be invoked unless it be to thwart any tendency on the part of the clergy to elude their public duties." In his *Testament* Louis even attempted to demonstrate under five heads that as ecclesiastics are not burdened with heavy expenses they should pay more taxes than the other orders of society. But what justification had the government to encroach upon Church property by so disposing of benefices that the proceeds found their way into the ever-empty Treasury? The affair of the *Regale* (the king's right to receive revenues of vacant bishoprics) was the occasion, if not the cause, of the serious

9. From Father Broutin's *La Réforme pastorale de France au XVII siècle*, II, 52.

10. See Volume 1 of this work, Chapter II, p. 153.

11. We can see that Gallicanism was a cast of mind common among the French clergy of that day, and quite distinct from the question of doctrine. There were, moreover, degrees in this tendency towards moral particularism and ecclesiastical chauvinism. They could be recognized in the cassock worn by the bishops: the deeper the blue the more closely was the wearer inclined towards Gallican ideas. Saint-Simon speaks of the "blue patch" of bishops; and Rigaud's celebrated portrait of Bossuet (in the Louvre) shows the bishop dressed in a violet cassock with a very definite tinge of blue.

controversy that arose between the Most Christian King and the Holy See. Even though the royal treasury might not have gained a great deal from the *Regale*, the fact that the trouble seems to have originated as a question of pounds, shillings and pence is typical of the *modus operandi*.[12]

Thus, in every sense, collusion between Church and State was flagrant. This fact is recognized even by historians who are not inclined to condemn the mistaken ideas of caesaropapism. "Was there ever a close union of Church and State?" asks Cardinal Baudrillart. "The Church of France was closely bound to the king and almost merged into the State," says Pierre Gaxotte. And Gabriel Hanotaux is even more categorical: "Religion was nothing other than the State." A Catholic mindful of the lessons of history cannot wax enthusiastic over this type of identification. How can a national Church remain loyal to the principles of which she is the guardian if she is to be subject to the State whose interests are mainly temporal? Since the time of Constantine and Byzantium the Church has learned to distrust sovereigns who are "bishops from without." There was some ground for Fénelon's burst of indignation: "Abuse of our rights and usurpations no longer originate in Rome. The king rather than the Pope is the master of the Gallican Church, and the king's power over the Church has passed into the hands of laymen who lord it over the bishops!" Had that been all, the situation might not have been so bad; but once the king had become master of the national Church, he might seek to intervene in more restricted fields. At a very critical phase of the Jansenist *débâcle* the Attorney-General d'Aguesseau threatened that the king might establish a new article of faith when he thought it desirable, and enforce it upon his bishops. There was much wisdom in the prayer uttered by Bossuet: "May God prevent our Most Christian Kings from aspiring to sovereignty over things sacred."

In short, this confusion between Church and State determined the religious policy of Louis XIV throughout his reign. His intervention in things sacred moved steadily towards absolutism and caesaropapism,

---

12. Despite appearances the origins of the *Régale* affair were spiritual rather than financial. See below, p. 277.

striving to achieve that totalitarian unity which was his evident purpose in every other field, whether it concerned economy, intellectual life or the fine arts. The result was a series of crises and catastrophes ending in downright failure.

5. DEFENDER OF THE FAITH AND OF MORALS

THE religious policy of Louis XIV did not, in fact, assume at once the emphasis and ruthlessness that characterized it during the crises arising out of Protestantism, Jansenism, Quietism and even Gallicanism, until after the period from 1680 to 1685. In many ways these years marked a turning-point in the reign. By 1682, when the king was finally installed at Versailles, he had reached the height of his glory. The medal comparing him with the sun had just been struck, and Paris had recently bestowed on its master the title of Louis the Great. In 1684 the Peace of Regensburg marked the apogee of the French Sun over Europe. By that time the king was a widower and in his forty-fifth year; he had abandoned his youthful indulgence, married Mme. de Maintenon and was on the way to a sincere conversion. Henceforward his religious policy and interior development were closely related, and to some extent intermingled. Having become devout without being any less dictatorial, Louis XIV would intervene in religious matters in the role of defender of the faith and of morals and protector of the Church, a Church whose powers were in his view strictly subordinate to his own.

He had never in the past failed to insist on respect for the Catholic faith and the Commandments, even when his personal conduct ill qualified him to play the role of Father of the Church. It seems hardly probable that Louis XIV applied to himself those words in Molière's *Tartuffe*, which Cléante hurls at devout people of every type: "Why do you take upon yourself what is Heaven's responsibility?" One of the first acts of his personal rule was to republish an edict under which blasphemy was punishable by death. In 1661 Parliament ordered the arrest of two men under that edict: the first a blasphemer who was condemned to the galleys; the other a skittle-player who could not cure himself of the tiresome habit of taking the name of God in vain when his ball missed the skittles, and was duly hanged. When three years later, in 1664, the nuns of Port-Royal refused to submit to the authority of their archbishop, they were actually disbanded by the police. Such was the solicitude of Mlle. de La Vallière's lover in defence of the faith.

As time passed he went still further. About the middle of the reign several decrees were issued to safeguard the holiness of the Sabbath and all feasts preceded by a vigil fast. They amounted to seventy-eight days in the year and, if we are to believe La Fontaine's mischievous cobbler, they caused some inconvenience to artisans and craftsmen. A royal ordinance reminded generals that their troops were obliged to fast during Lent; when military leaders objected that it was difficult to comply with such orders during a campaign they were told that their Quartermaster-General's department should apply to the bishops to obtain the necessary dispensation.

When Louis XIV himself returned to a more rigid practice of religion he used his authority to ensure that his *entourage* followed his example. Dangeau's *Journal*, dated Easter Monday, April 3, 1684, contains the following entry: "On rising, the king spoke severely about courtiers who failed to make their Easter duties. He said he had a high opinion of those who made them well and urged everyone to think seriously about it, adding that he would be grateful to them if they did so." This certainly suggested a great improvement on the sentiment expressed by Cléante in *Tartuffe*. Whether pressure of this kind resulted in any spiritual improvement in the court is perhaps doubtful. A joke played by the Marquis de Brissac on some of the "devout" ladies of the court caused a great deal of amusement at Versailles. One evening the Marquis said loudly that the king would not be present at prayers. On hearing this some of the lovely ladies hastily blew out their candles and hurried from the chapel, but were very upset to learn later that the august worshipper had attended after all. The irony of La Bruyère in his famous *Caractères* is very much to the point: "Nowadays piety consists in... knowing your way about the chapel, being acquainted with the position of seats which allow you to be seen or not seen. A devout person would just as soon become an atheist if the king were one."

Louis XIV was evidently not content to "defend" the faith at Versailles merely by urging his courtiers to approach the confessional. When difficulties arose over doctrine he again intervened with the same enthusiasm. He appeared more anxious than the Pope himself to revive animosity in the Jansenist dispute.[13] The nuns at Port-Royal were forbidden to accept novices, and four or five obscure Jansenists were thrown into the Bastille. Later, when the affair took a turn for the worse, the king intervened personally, and urged the Spanish authorities to have Father Quesnel arrested. In conjunction with Mme. de Montespan and Father La Chaise he examined the documents relating to the suspect, asked the Pope to condemn unequivocally a number of harmful clauses, decided on the demolition of Port-Royal-des-Champs, and "at his express command" had the Bull *Unigenitus* accepted by his stubborn Parliament. By the time Louis XIV died, over two thousand people had been imprisoned on account of Jansenism.

He dealt similarly with Quietism. In his handling of the *Maximes des Saints* and the *Nouveau Testament en français* he acquitted himself like a theologian; and, when the authorities in Rome were divided and hesitant in their examination of Fénelon's theories, the king submitted a memorandum of his own opposing the supporters of the Swan of Cambrai, as Fénelon was called. Another example was the arrest of Father Lacombe by the king's police. Imprisoned for a while in the Bastille and on the île de Ré, he afterwards spent nine years in the château at Lourdes and fourteen at Vincennes, and was eventually declared insane and sent to Charenton,[14] where he died.

Saint-Simon, referring to the king's behaviour, caustically observes that as Louis grew older he imagined he was doing penance when he did it on

---

13. Chapter VI deals with the history of Jansenism and Quietism.

14. As "defender of the faith" Louis XIV must also be credited with having re-established Catholicism in Alsace, whence it had been wellnigh eliminated by Protestantism. The annexation of Alsace was advantageous to the Catholics. On October 21, 1681, three months after the surrender of Strasbourg, Mass was celebrated in the cathedral the first time for a hundred and twenty-two years. Two days later Bishop Fürstenberg, a German well disposed towards France, received Louis XIV at the portal. The Jesuits of the province of Champagne immediately set to work. It was they who suggested the colonizing of Alsace by Catholics.

the backs of other people. The irony is perhaps not altogether fair. It is just as reasonable to believe that as Louis XIV returned to a stricter observance of the faith he became more conscious of the duties to which he was bound by his coronation vows, and that he sincerely wished to assume the role of "God's sergeant"—a role which his ancestor St. Louis regarded as the primary duty of kings. If such were the case, Louis XIV would naturally have discharged that duty in a manner recognized and understood at that period. Moreover, under a regime of thorough-going absolutism such as he intended to establish those who deviated in the matter of religion were regarded as rebels, destroying that national unity of which the Catholic religion constituted the bond. Doctrinal deviation, let alone heresy, was utterly incompatible with the principle "one king, one law, one faith." The greatest religious drama of the reign was to prove this abundantly.

6. THE REVOCATION OF THE EDICT OF NANTES

WHEN Louis XIV assumed personal control the problem of Protestantism was already a complex one.[15] The "religionnaires," as the Calvinists were usually called, numbered over a million adherents; they had one hundred and thirty-six pastors and six hundred and fifty temples. Their members included sailors (among then Duquesne) along the coasts of Normandy, Aunis and Poitou, manufacturers and merchants at Montauban, Nîmes, Montpellier and Grenoble, and peasants in the Cévennes and the mountains of Dauphiné. On the whole they were peace-loving people, only too anxious to be left alone. Deserted by their leaders, who had merely taken advantage of disorder to seek fortune and adventure, they were favourably reported upon to the king by Mazarin in 1652. Perhaps that was an astute stroke of diplomacy on the cardinal's part. "The pasture may be rank," he said, "but at least the little flock does not wander away." Colbert, whose influence was growing, appreciated the hardworking qualities of the Protestant population. That

15. See Volume 1 of this work, Chapter III, p. 218.

illustrious soldier and champion of the throne, Turenne, had not yet been converted. There was nothing to suggest that peace would not continue.

But the fanatics, whether Catholics or Protestants, did not lay down their arms. Wherever the "reformed" were most numerous they continued to harass the "popish" population in every possible way; and, if the authorities shut their eyes to their activities, they strove to expand, shamelessly violating the provisions of the Edict of Nantes. In the district of Gex alone twenty-three new temples were opened in fifty years. The Catholics on their part regarded the pacificatory edicts imposed by Henri IV as a truce that might be revoked at any time. Even though the Protestants no longer existed as a political party, there still remained the deeply rooted memory of the state within the state and the dangers the country had recently faced as a result of Protestant power. "England and the northern Protestant countries," said the discerning Jacques Bainville, "had set an example by suppressing what remained of Catholicism, and excluding Catholics from employment." If the king of France decided on action similar to that which had taken place in England public opinion was certain to approve.

There is no doubt whatever as to why Louis XIV adopted a policy so radically different from that of Richelieu and Mazarin. Religion was the main reason; but a religion too narrow in conception and indeed hardly Christian. It was, however, the religion of the vast majority of the people. On the day of his coronation the king had sworn to exterminate from his realm and all places under his jurisdiction any whom the Church declared to be heretics. He therefore deemed this to be a duty to which he was bound by conscience. Bossuet reminded him of it in his *Politique tirée de l'Écriture sainte*: "The king should use his power to destroy false religions within his State." Louis XIV was certainly sincere when he wrote: "I do not doubt that it is God's will that I endeavour to lead back to His ways all my subjects."

Needless to say, this psychological motive was reinforced by the political incentives we have noted. There is no doubt whatever that the whole country was convinced that diversity of religion within the State was incompatible with perfect law and order. "If uniformity of external worship and interior faith are not maintained among the king's subjects," said

Fléchier, "they will always be as different races at war within the bosom of   261
the Church and the country; they will be two bodies instead of one." This
inflexible Catholic totalitarianism was echoed by certain Protestant voices.
Élie Benoist, for instance, declared that "diversity of religion disfigures the
State"; and Turenne: "The independence of pastors is incompatible with
order." The unifying character of absolutism as expressed in such sentiments
was desired by the whole country, and it tended towards the elimination of
differences in religion.[16]

From the very beginning of the king's personal rule his coldness towards
Protestants bordered upon hostility. When the representatives of corporate
bodies presented their customary congratulations at court he declined to
receive the Protestant ministers, and Pastor Vignoles, sent by their chamber at Castres, was expelled from Paris. The Assembly of the Clergy had
complained of a number of infringements by the Calvinists, and the king
ordered a court of inquiry to be set up in every province under the joint
presidency of a Catholic and a Protestant. In every case a lukewarm Protestant was chosen. Sixty-four temples were demolished in Poitou; in the
Gex district only two remained. Another edict (1662) went still further.
By applying *stricto sensu* Article 28 of the Edict of Nantes, which permitted Protestants to have schools without stipulating the number of teachers allowed or taking account of educational requirements, it was decided
that there would be one teacher to each school. At Marennes, for example,
one teacher was allowed for six hundred Protestant children! In June 1662
a number of Huguenots who failed to remove their hats when a procession was passing were sent to the galleys. One might have expected a little
more tolerance at a time when the court was applauding Molière's *École des
Femmes, Tartuffe* and *Don Juan*.

---

16. In 1657 the delegates of the reformed Churches met in Paris, and passed a somewhat
surprising resolution assigning a theological basis to royal absolutism: "Our opinions
in relation to politics and religion are identical. We believe that a subject may never
merit a reward from his sovereign, even though he render him the most outstanding
service. Any favour granted by the sovereign should be regarded as an act of grace on
his part; a subject who expected a reward would be guilty of insolence."

There were good Catholics who strove by other methods to lead the straying Calvinists back to Catholic unity. Nicole and Arnauld, who published three works refuting Calvinist errors, were among the Jansenists who had recently become reconciled under the Clementine Peace, and endeavoured to convince the Protestants. Bishops, among whom was Hardouin de Péréfixe de Beaumont, at that time Bishop of Rodez and later Archbishop of Paris, espoused the cause in their pastoral letters. There was, among others, the Jesuit Raimbourg, assisted by secular priests and laymen who worked together in the Compagnie du Salutaire Entretien. The young Bossuet outshone them all with a handbook, admirable for the precision and depth of its doctrine: his *Exposition de la doctrine catholique* which was approved by Innocent XI and followed soon afterwards by the *Histoire des variations des églises protestantes*. The Protestant reply is to be found in the writings of Jean Claude (1619–1687), Aubertin, Jurieu (1639–1713) and Basnage. In 1678 Mlle. de Duras organized a debate which brought Claude and Bossuet face to face in a verbal duel, and the Catholics declared that their champion had crushed his opponent.

These controversies were to some extent fruitful. They resulted in a few sensational conversions that were largely due to the arguments of Bossuet, Montausier and Dangeau. Mlle. de Duras herself was converted; but the most outstanding event was the conversion of Turenne, who in 1668 returned to the faith of his fathers with the dignity and sincerity of a soldier. It is probably true to say that his conversion had a more beneficial effect than any other of that day. Some embraced Catholicism to win the king's favour, but the motives of others were even more worldly. Pellisson, a former clerk to Fouquet and himself a convert, invented a kind of "conversions account," maintained from the revenues of extremely rich abbeys to which the king had not appointed an abbot. It also derived its income from a third of the *régale* under a statute of 1676. A commoner who recanted would receive six *livres*, a trooper thirty and a sergeant forty. Compensation to a member of the nobility might take the form of a yearly pension up to three thousand *livres*. Whatever the motives of the people concerned, the conversion of nobles such as the Duc de la Trémouille and the Duc de la Force

had some effect; though the latter's conversion remains uncertain.[17] They
led the king to believe that the return of all Protestants to Catholicism was
a possibility, and thus contributed towards an intensification of his efforts
in that direction.

Pressure came from every quarter. Whenever the Assembly of the Clergy met, its members reiterated their complaints against the transgressions
of the Protestants. Following a military victory in 1675 the coadjutor to the
Bishop of Arles exclaimed to the king: "Are you not indebted to God for
this glorious victory? It now remains that you show your gratitude by using
your power to exterminate heresy completely." What was there to prevent
Louis XIV from becoming another Theodosius or a new Charlemagne?
"All Catholics regard freedom of conscience as a dangerous precipice," the
Assembly emphasized; "a trap set to ensnare simple minds, a door leading to
libertinage. Take it from them, Sire; remove this deadly freedom!"

Undoubtedly Mme. de Maintenon whispered similar ideas into the
king's ear, and with increasing insistence as his power developed. Did not
this grand-daughter of Agrippa d'Aubigné say in 1679: "If God spares the
king there will not be a Huguenot left in twenty years"? Louvois, whose
prestige was growing, spared no effort to achieve the same ends; not only
on account of his hatred of Colbert, who offered protection to Protestant
and Catholic manufacturers and work-people alike, but because he had no
wish to allow his enemy Mme. de Maintenon the satisfaction of success.
The sanctimonious set at court were in favour of strong measures. And we
cannot exclude the possibility that some courtiers, jealous of the commercial and industrial prosperity of the Huguenots, may have used their influence to pursue aims that were anything but apostolic. At the very moment
when the persecution was being intensified Mme. de Maintenon wrote to
her brother: "Now is the time to buy Protestant estates; they are going for
a song." We can hardly avoid a feeling of discomfort at this undisguised
expression of sentiments.

17. Another Duc de la Force, a descendant of the above, has written a book entitled *Louis XIV et sa cour* (Paris, 1956). See p. 58 of that book.

"In order gradually to reduce the number of Huguenots in my realm," wrote Louis XIV in his *Mémoires*, "I decided to refrain from imposing further restrictions and to ensure that they enjoyed the privileges allowed by my predecessors. I determined to grant them no more, but rather to maintain existing privileges within the narrowest limits that justice and propriety permitted. I would allow no personal favours whatever, so that they might be compelled to ask themselves whether it would not be in their best interests to become Catholics." This was precisely what had been suggested by Councillor Bernard of the Présidial at Beziers in his *Explication de l'Édit de Nantes* (1666) and by the Jesuit Meynier in his *Édit de Nantes exécuté selon les intentions de Henri le Grand* (1670).

The Protestants were thus subject to all kinds of vexatious measures— and in the name of the Edict! Whatever had not been formally authorized was forbidden. For example, there was nothing in the Edict to the effect that Protestants could bury their dead by day; they were therefore compelled to bury them at night. It was not stated that they could invite their friends to weddings; attendance was therefore limited to twenty persons. There was no formal statement in the Edict giving them the right to be judges, notaries, bailiffs, royal secretaries, lawyers, doctors, booksellers or printers; they were therefore driven from all the professions. Rarely has the art of textual misrepresentation been used to better advantage. Mixed marriages were prohibited, and children born of them were declared illegitimate and snatched from their parents to be brought up in the Catholic religion. Occasionally tragedy was softened by comedy, as in the case of an old man of eighty when someone called to take him to the catechism class! It was decreed that Protestant children could become Catholics on reaching the age of seven, and their parents were required to make an allowance towards their education in the Catholic faith. These measures resulted in a flood of emigrations. An edict was therefore promulgated under which captured fugitives were sent to the galleys, and sales of real estate executed by them during the previous two years were rendered void.

Such measures led to conflicting results. The weak and lukewarm yielded and recanted; people of strong convictions resisted. Disorders broke out

in Dauphiné, Vivarais, Languedoc, and even on the outskirts of Bordeaux;
and a number of Protestants, among them a pastor, were broken on the
wheel. When Colbert died in 1683 Louvois gained considerable influence,
and the situation became more serious.

Either Louvois or Marillac, governor of Poitou, invented the loathsome
method of winning converts known as the *Dragonnades*. Soldiers, especially
dragoons, from whom the *Dragonnades* derived their name, were billeted
in the houses of Protestants with authority to do whatever they wished. It
is not difficult to imagine the excesses of which these booted missionaries
were capable. An engraving of that period shows a dragoon, a sword at his
side and in his hand a musket levelled at a kneeling Protestant about to sign
his recantation. They committed the most abominable crimes; there were
thousands of cases of looting, torture and rape. They roasted the feet of men
and children; they dragged women through the streets by their hair; they
flogged old men in the presence of their children. Their atrocities were such
that Catholics frequently gave shelter to Protestants who were visited by
the king's dragoons. Bishop Le Camus at Grenoble, Cardinal de Coislin at
Orleans, the Bishops of Gap, Lescar, Tarbes, Saint-Pons and others protested publicly and opposed the sending of troops into their dioceses. In 1685
the Assembly of the Clergy passed a resolution condemning the use of force.

It would be surprising if, as some historians have suggested, Louis XIV
knew nothing about the *Dragonnades* and the tragic state of affairs that
existed. It is difficult to believe that the protestations of the clergy, of several
bishops, of the Maréchal de Vauban and others were never brought to his
notice, especially in view of the fact that he eventually removed Marillac
from office. He may have thought that these excesses were the work of a few
extremists; but he was more impressed by the results obtained, the news
that reached him every day of mass conversions. They were a source of great
joy to him, as Mme. de Maintenon said. Indeed, Protestants were being
converted in large numbers: in the district of Nîmes alone sixty thousand
in three days. At Montauban and Bordeaux the whole population became
Catholic under a resolution passed by the municipal council. Castres,
Montpellier and Uzès followed their good example. In many places the very

266   news of the arrival of the dragoons was sufficient to awaken an intense zeal for abjuration. The more discriminating Catholics questioned the value of such conversions; and Mme. de Maintenon was anxious about the spiritual condition of all those unhappy people who recanted without knowing why. But they themselves knew only too well.[18]

Louis XIV was led to believe that there were scarcely any Protestants left in France; that those who had not fled had been converted or were on the point of conversion. Almost every day Le Tellier, Louvois and Father La Chaise informed him of mass conversions, the news of which was brought by special courier. On October 18, 1685, an edict drafted by Le Tellier was presented at Fontainebleau for the king's signature, and registered by Parliament on the twenty-second: it was the Revocation of the Edict of Nantes. "Whereas the greater part of our subjects of the so-called reformed religion have embraced the Catholic faith, the enforcement of the Edict of Nantes is no longer necessary.... We have therefore decided to efface the memory of the disorder, confusion and evil which the development of this false religion has occasioned in our realm, and nothing can be more to the purpose than to revoke absolutely the Edict of Nantes."[19]

All the temples were demolished. Protestant assemblies, even in private houses, were everywhere forbidden. Pastors were given two weeks in which to leave the country. Children born of Protestant parents had to be baptized by priests and brought up as Catholics. Persons who remained loyal to the new religion or attempted to emigrate were condemned to the galleys. These

18. Not satisfied with their activities at home the king's administrators intervened in Savoy, where the twenty-year-old Duc Victor-Amédée II was experiencing a temporary attraction towards everything French. The persecution of the Waldenses which had commenced thirty years earlier (see Volume 1 of this work, pp. 204–205) had abated slightly, but now broke out again with greater fury. The Waldenses of the Briançon and Pignerol districts fled from France and took refuge in the valleys of Piedmont. Savoyard troops gave chase, assisted by French soldiers from Catinat. This was not war but butchery; three thousand women and children were massacred in a meadow, and the prisons of Savoy were packed.

19. The revocation did not apply to Alsace, which was administered under the provisions of the Treaties of Westphalia, but the province did experience some pressure from the *Dragonnades*.

measures were in every respect comparable with those taken against Catholics in many Protestant countries.[20] That such methods should have been adopted by the grandson of Henri IV is lamentable, for France was thus stooping to the level of countries where intolerance had become the rule; Louis XIV was breaking completely with the policy of his wise predecessors.

We are tempted to describe the revocation of the Edict of Nantes as "something worse than a crime—a blunder!"[21] Public opinion welcomed it none the less with deplorable enthusiasm. It fired the imagination of poets, and inspired artists and writers. Six medals were struck to commemorate the event, and seven engravings were made. The French Academy set a competition on the subject of "Apollo victorious over the serpent Python," and the prize was won by Fontenelle. It inspired the painter Le Brun and the sculptor Coysevox. The measure won the approval of the most brilliant intellects of the day: Racine, La Bruyère, La Fontaine, and also Mme. de Sévigné, who wrote: "It is the greatest and finest thing that has ever happened." The Abbé de Rancé called it a miracle, "a miracle we might never have hoped to see in our time!" Such was also the opinion of Bossuet who, in his funeral oration on Michel Le Tellier, praised to the very skies "this new Constantine, this new Theodosius, this new Marcianno, this new Charlemagne!" Though Vauban expressed his doubts on the efficacy of the measure, as did Saint-Simon later, it would have been difficult to find anyone sufficiently courageous at that time to express disapproval. Public opinion was unquestionably with the king.

Pope Innocent XI's attitude was ambiguous. He declared publicly to Christina of Sweden that "the use of force propagates heresy; it never conquers it." He asked James II of England to show consideration towards the Protestants who took refuge in his country, and he endeavoured to persuade Louis XIV to mitigate the severity of his measures. None the less he congratulated the King of France officially, and a year later caused the *Te Deum*

---

20. See Volume 1 of this work, pp. 205ff.
21. The words were first used in connection with the execution of the Duc d'Enghien; they have often been attributed to Fouché or to Talleyrand, but were in fact used by Boulay de la Meurthe.

268   to be sung to dispose of rumours concerning his attitude. It seems likely that the Duc d'Estrées, French ambassador to the Holy See, was exaggerating when, in his desire to flatter his master, he told the king of the Pope's "joyous outburst" on hearing the news. In fact the words used in the Pope's congratulatory letter might have had several meanings: "It is a deed," the letter said, "that will endure for ever in the annals of the Church." Political events, such as the Gallican dispute, which was at its height, perhaps explain the Holy Pontiff's attitude of reserve.[22]

It cannot be denied, however, that this general enthusiasm for what constituted a crime against conscience was lamentable. It may be interpreted as an expression of the intolerance of the age, the desire for national unity and the conviction, especially among the more enlightened, that many of the "reformed" had indeed returned to the Catholic Church of their own volition. The attitude of Bossuet was above all significant. We have referred to his enthusiasm over the revocation of the Edict; but he was also among the bishops who rejected violence in their dioceses, and condemned the abuse of power. He stated publicly that it was wrong to force recent *réunis*—converts from Protestantism—to receive Communion and assist at Mass; he claimed that they should be treated with tact and instructed with gentleness. He even undertook soon afterwards to revive the work of *rapprochement* between opposing religions. The position adopted by this great Christian prompts us to be wary in our criticism of what may appear to us a dreadful and repugnant measure, but which, in the eyes of its contemporaries, seemed politically wise and justified on religious grounds.

According to the judgment of history the revocation of the Edict is seen to be a glaring error. It involved France in grave material loss. Despite royal injunctions, a great number of Protestants were reluctantly compelled to flee the country rather than recant. The estimated numbers involved vary from sixty thousand to two million, though the latter figure is obviously absurd. The number was probably between three and five hundred thousand. The

---

22. An illustration of the Pope's attitude is suggested by the fact that he raised Le Camus, Bishop of Grenoble, to the dignity of cardinal when he fell into disgrace for having opposed the violent persecution of the Huguenots (September 8, 1686).

distressing flight of the refugees resembles many we have known in our time.   269
They fled by sea in stormy weather from the coasts of Aunis and Brittany;
they made their way at the height of winter across the precipitous passes of
the Alps and the Jura. Many fugitives died *en route.* Those who were captured
by the police were sent to the convict ships; the more fortunate were struck
down on the spot. Most of these emigrants were sailors, soldiers and teachers; good craftsmen and excellent people, energetic and hardworking. The
wealth in men and money lost in France in this way was enormous, for many
of the refugees succeeded in taking out of the country considerable sums in
gold. Many countries willingly offered asylum to the French Protestants. The
Grand Elector populated Berlin and Brandenburg with them. The Dutch
welcomed all the intellectuals and the savants, among them Pierre Bayle,
Jurieu and Claude, who taught in Holland. Sweden, the English colonies
of America, Ireland and South Africa also accepted them. These emigrants
took with them French technical skill hitherto unknown to the countries
in which they settled. Thus Ulster developed the linen trade for which Bel-
fast has become famous; Germany developed the culture of the artichoke;
the Cape began to grown the vine and the olive tree. Denis Papin, who
found refuge in Marburg, invented a boat with wheels that were turned by
a steam engine (1707). Wherever French Protestants settled they occupied
all the important posts; their departure weakened their own country and
strengthened France's opponents. So great was France's error that Christina
of Sweden aptly compared her with "a sick man who cuts off his arms and
legs." Perhaps the greatest tragedy of the emigration was that French Protestants served against France in hostile armies. At the battle of the Boyne the
Huguenot Armand de Caumont, Marquis de Montpouillan, was in command against his Catholic cousin de Lauzun. In 1914 five hundred officers
of French origin and bearing French names fought in the Prussian Army.[23]

23. An excellent survey of the present position of the Huguenots may be found in the
    magazine *Réforme*, November 9, 1957. Apart from the actual Protestant emigration
    of the period, mention must also be made of several hundreds of Waldenses who were
    hunted throughout France and Savoy. Most of them settled in Odenwald, Taunus and
    Württemberg, where villages may still be found with such names as Grand-Villars,
    Petit-Villars, Pérouse, Pinacle and Serres.

270   Meanwhile in France itself the Protestant problem was a long way from being solved by the revocation of the Edict. Nobody quite knew how to dispose of the fugitives' property. Should it be sold to the advantage of the State, or sequestered? Or should it be passed on to the nearest Catholic heirs? The handling of these concrete and definite problems was the source of much confusion and many malpractices.[24]

As for the *réunis*, it soon became evident that they were "converted" in name only. The priests of Normandy admitted that the old Huguenots were more zealous than ever in their Protestant convictions. Claude Brousson and other heroic pastors returned, and preached everywhere. The Catholic Church replied by sending its best preachers to the provinces where the converts were most numerous; Fénelon went to Saintonge and Bourdaloue to Languedoc. But the Church lacked an enlightened and dedicated clergy capable of winning hearts.

The formative training of the seminaries made very little impression. Fénelon, writing from the town of Saintes, said that his teaching had moved the people's hearts, but that his new converts tearfully complained: "As soon as you leave us we shall be at the mercy of monks who preach Latin at us, and talk of indulgences and confraternities. No one will speak to us without threats." The truth was, no one really knew how to handle the situation. An inquiry set up by the Council in 1698 revealed a rapid rise in Protestantism. How was it to be met? One governor recommended gentleness and another coercion. Bossuet and five other bishops protested strongly against certain disgraceful practices, such as the dragging of corpses of Protestants in the mud and throwing them on refuse dumps. In 1699 the king commanded the use of moderation, and district governors were deprived of their powers in religious matters; but it was almost impossible to curb the fanaticism aroused by the revocation. In many places government agents and parish priests pursued suspects, and forced the *réunis* to make at least a show of

---

24. Mlle. Hélène Delattre has made a special study of the subject in her thesis at the École des Chartes presented in January 1936: *L'aide financière aux protestants convertis. Étude sur le tiers des économats et la régie des biens des religionnaires fugitifs, des origines à 1724.* See *Position des thèses de l'École des Chartes,* 1936.

being Catholics. Time tended to fan the passions rather than allay them.
Loads of anti-Roman pamphlets arrived from Holland, England and Lausanne, and were distributed secretly. Many of them were written by Jurieu, who announced that the hour of deliverance was at hand.

A Protestant resistance movement was organized in the mountains of Dauphine, Lozère and Languedoc. In these secret communities an extraordinary atmosphere of emotion developed: women and children prophesied, among them "la Belle Isabeau," a wool carder from Grenoble. Uprisings broke out near Castres, at Velay and other places. In 1690 Lieutenant-General de Broglie crushed the first rebellion, but failed to halt the Protestant movement. The Assemblées du Désert met the more frequently. They gathered on the moors, usually at night, where their pastors or chosen leaders spoke to them words of faith and hope. Claude Brousson was caught and broken on the wheel at Montpellier, but nothing could dishearten those fierce "Children of God."

In 1702 the decisive upheaval occurred in the diocese of Mende. A priest known for his anti-Huguenot zeal managed to organize the arrest of a small convoy of fugitives; but the peasants of the district set them free, butchered the jailer-priest and two others, and burned a number of castles. A veritable war had commenced.

Wherever Protestants were fairly numerous they rose up at the call of their preachers—Séguier, Mazel, Espérandieu, Ravanel, Couderc, Pierre Esprit, Gédéon Laporte—and revolution broke out. The Church which had gone to ground in the desert marched off towards conquest, like the chosen people about to enter the Promised Land. Everywhere their prophets predicted crushing victories. Those who were taken by the police marched to their execution with cries of joy. "My soul is a garden of pools and shady trees," replied the preacher Séguier when the judge condemned him to be burned alive. They produced splendid leaders: Gédéon Laporte, a blacksmith built like a Hercules, Jean Cavalier, a twenty-year-old baker's boy who proved to be a strategist of genius in guerilla warfare, and Roland, his able lieutenant, a youngster of seventeen. Operations were undertaken against presbyteries, churches and convents. In order to recognize each other at night the partisans wore white shirts over their clothes. Soon the whole of France and Europe were talking of the exploits of the *Camisards*—the "white shirts."

While France was being attacked on all sides by foreign enemies and had insufficient forces to cover her frontiers, trained armies commanded by Broglie and Montrevel were indulging in savage suppression of rebellion. The letters of Fléchier, Bishop of Nîmes, present a frightful picture of the degree of violence resulting from the civil war between Frenchmen.[25] The best generals available, Villars and Berwick, had to be sent to suppress the rebellion. For three successive years (1702–1705) the fighting and destruction continued, and nearly five hundred villages were destroyed. Villars tricked Cavalier into leaving his camp by granting him a commission as a colonel, and giving him a vague promise that he would be free to practise his religion. Roland was killed in battle. Little by little the fever subsided, and the opposing sides discussed an amnesty. But the Protestant Church was not vanquished; it emerged from the conflict strengthened and tempered by its trials. It gravitated back to the countryside and the people where its real roots were to be found.

A few days before Louis XIV died he signed a new edict that reintroduced the old repressive measures. At about the same time Antoine Court,

---

25. "You are right to pity me in the unhappy situation which has obtained for nearly two years now...the practice of our religion has almost ceased in three or four dioceses. More than four thousand Catholics, including eighty priests, have been butchered in the neighbourhood, and nearly two hundred churches burned.... As for ourselves, we have neither rest nor recreation; in this town we are bereft of all consolation. When the Catholics are stronger the others are afraid they will be massacred; but when the fanatics are numerous in the district, the Catholics in their turn are afraid. I have to console and reassure them all in turn. We are shut off here and dare not move fifty paces beyond the town without risk of being killed. From my windows I have seen all the houses in the country round about burned down with impunity. Hardly a day passes without my learning in the morning of some fresh misfortune that has happened during the night. My room is often filled with people who have been ruined, poor women whose husbands have just been killed, fugitive priests who tell me of the unhappy plight of their parishioners. It is horrible. I comfort some and calm others, trying to help and succour them all as their father and shepherd. A large band of these rebels has recently been routed, and people think that it is all over. But they are mistaken; their minds are so distraught that they can think of nothing but their losses."

a preacher from Languedoc, assembled the first synod in a disused quar-
ry near Nîmes, marking the reconstruction of French Protestantism. As
always where religion is concerned, the policy of force had served no useful
purpose.[26]

7. THE MOST CHRISTIAN KING VERSUS ROME

WHEN Louis XIV struck at the Jansenists and the Protestants he did so
on behalf of the Catholic faith, in the interests of Church unity, which he
was unable to distinguish from national unity. We find it hard to believe
that during the very period when he was imprisoning the supporters of
Port-Royal and his dragoons were carrying out their "missions" against the
Protestants, the Most Christian King was engaged in a violent conflict with
the Apostolic See, playing a dangerous game with schism and even running
the risk of excommunication. But that is exactly what was involved in the
Gallican dispute, the episodes of which had such a shattering effect on the
minds of contemporaries.

Unpleasant incidents began to occur at the very commencement of the
reign. The king was then in the full pride of his youth, determined to use
every opportunity to manifest his pomp and power. His teacher Mazarin
had accustomed him to adopt a free and easy manner towards the Holy See;
he threatened to "examine closely the conduct of the election" of Innocent
X; and he abused Alexander VII for having given asylum to his foe the Cardinal de Retz. Hugues de Lionne, who had previously failed in his efforts
to get the irrepressible cardinal interned, endeavoured to worsen relations
between Paris and Rome, whereupon the king sent to Rome the Duc de

---

26. It is necessary to add that the repressive measures referred to had also a disastrous
effect on France's foreign relations by clinching the alliance of all Protestant countries
against her. The effect was just as disastrous from another point of view: Michelet
regards the revocation of the Edict of Nantes and the resulting episodes as a kind of
incubation period of the Revolution, and Albert Sorel remarks that "the jurists of the
Terror had only to dig into the miscellany of decrees against the Protestants to find
weapons for their own use."

Créqui, "a high-ranking soldier with extensive powers and great arrogance, but lacking in tact." The purpose of his mission was to wipe out by a display of sumptuousness the impression of failure bequeathed by the Retz affair. The duke followed his instructions to the letter. His manner was abrupt; in matters of protocol he was haughty and overbearing. His entire *entourage* resembled a miniature court, and every member copied his manner. Things reached such a pitch that in August 1662 the Corsican Guard, too often provoked by the ambassador's footmen, took advantage of a quarrel to avenge themselves. They besieged the Farnese Palace, and a bullet whistled past the nose of the ambassador's wife, killing one of his pages. Louis XIV treated the affair with an arrogance that amazed Europe. He sent an insolent letter to the Pope, had the Papal Nuncio escorted to the frontier, recalled his ambassador from Rome and sent troops to occupy Avignon. An army of fifteen thousand men threatened the Papal States. It was really a storm in a teacup, but the young king intended to make it clear that he would suffer no opposition to his will. Unfortunately some of the French bishops supported him. Alexander VII had to give in: he agreed to send a cardinal to France to present his apologies, to disband the Corsican Guard and, for good measure, to erect a monument in Rome to commemorate not only the offence but the atonement.[27]

Disputes of this nature had nothing to do with doctrine; other incidents, however, were much more significant though less resounding. As absolutism gathered momentum it could hardly be expected to tolerate any authority in France but that of the king, whether it came from the Pope or anyone else. Pierre de Marca died in 1662, but his learned treatise *De Concordia sacerdotii et imperii*[28] continued to furnish abundant polemic material to the enemies, avowed or otherwise, of papal authority. The State counsellor Le Vayer de Boutigny popularized this method in a small manual which ran

---

27. For a true appreciation of the psychological atmosphere and the reactions of public opinion, the reader is recommended to consult Father Mortimort's "Comment les Français du XVIIᵉ siècle voyaient le Pape," which appeared in Bulletin No. 25, *XVII siècle* (Paris, 1955).

28. See Volume 1 of this work, p. 225.

to many editions. He compared the State with a ship controlled by a captain and a pilot, the captain exercising full authority as to the ship's progress, its safety and the discipline of the crew, and the pilot being in charge of navigation; but de Boutigny reasoned that the king was the captain, and the Pope merely the pilot. It went without saying that the captain had the right to supervise the pilot, and even to reprimand him if he flagged!

Thus developed a trend of thought which, as we have seen,[29] began during the time of Pithou and Richer and which we today call Gallicanism, though its contemporaries were unacquainted with the term. Such expressions as Gallican Church, Gallican precepts and Gallican freedoms were for ever on the lips and in the writings of people of the Great Reign, in a jungle of bitter debates and arguments. Not that Gallicanism ever attempted, as Anglicanism did, to establish itself seriously as a national Church, taking schism for granted; nor did it constitute a homogeneous body of doctrine, still less a sect. Gallicanism was a complex blend of theories, traditions, interests, susceptibilities and disappointments, all of which embodied the common but definite purpose of limiting the power of the Pope and his interference in matters affecting France. That fact alone was quite sufficient to win the sympathy of Louis XIV, and dispose him to personify the fusion between the parliamentary and the ecclesiastical aspects of Gallicanism.

Furthermore, to understand the Gallican dispute and to appreciate the daring required to oppose the authority of Rome—an idea quite inconceivable today—it must be remembered that the dogma of Papal Infallibility had not yet been defined by the Vatican Council; it was not, in fact, defined until two hundred years later. Despite proposals put forward by the Jesuits, the Council of Trent had not stated the doctrine categorically. That the Pope possessed supreme authority was clearly understood; but so did the Ecumenical Council, which had stated the solid truths on which the Church had been reconstituted. At that time it was not absolutely clear which of the two authorities took precedence over the other, and it was permissible to hold either opinion—*in dubiis libertas.* On the evidence of the

---

29. See Volume 1 of this work, end of Chapter III, p. 223ff.

jurist Domat, a well-known Gallican, "the Regulars had spread the doctrine of papal infallibility to such an extent that the common people, not well versed in such matters, regarded it as Catholic doctrine and the contrary opinion as heresy." Enlightened people, however, were not inclined to adopt that view.

Within the first few weeks of the king's personal rule an incident occurred which clearly suggested his attitude in the matter. The Jesuit father Coret of the Collège de Clermont supported a thesis claiming that the Pope, having received the gift of infallibility from Christ, was indeed infallible. The battle was on. The Jansenists, only too pleased to get the Jesuits into trouble, let loose their wrath. Arnauld launched two vigorous pamphlets in defence of Gallican freedoms; and the king, although a determined enemy of Jansenism, flew into a rage over the Jesuits' thesis. Thanks to the pleading of his confessor Father Annat and the suppliant letters of Pierre de Marca, the king resisted the impulse to seize the thesis and imprison its rash author.

Two years later another incident occurred, again arising out of a thesis. A young Breton student, Gabriel Drouet de Villeneuve, was preparing to present his thesis at the Sorbonne when it was rumoured that the paper contained "Roman" theories that were unacceptable to the free Gallican Church. There was, in fact, very little in it: a mere statement to the effect that the privileges of certain churches had been granted by the Popes, and that Councils, however useful "were not indispensable." Another uproar; and again Arnauld and his friends intervened. At that time the affair of the Corsican Guard in Rome was at its height. Louis XIV was furious. "Humiliate Rome by every possible means!" he thundered. Parliament therefore censured the unfortunate student, forbade him to present his thesis, and the Sorbonne, after making a show of protest against this intrusion into its affairs, abode by the decision.

There is no doubt that incidents such as these were deliberately stirred up. Every opportunity was seized upon to foment and increase tension. When a Cistercian named Laurent Desplantes happened to write that "the Pope has authority over all Christians and full jurisdiction over the whole Church," Parliament was indignant that anyone should thus strike a blow at

its authority. And when the Sorbonne was again called to account it replied   277
by stating its tenets specifically in a *Déclaration en six articles* (May 4, 1663).
The paper was extremely cautious in tone, but maintained none the less that
papal infallibility was not officially taught in the learned *penetralia* of theology; upon which the king warmly congratulated the Sorbonne.

These incidents among many others reveal a state of mind. Gallican
influence developed in proportion to the growth of royal power. All sorts
of people were Gallicans: politicians set on absolutism and national prestige; bishops so closely associated with the regime that they were prepared
to follow ministers "blindly like flunkeys," as Bossuet said; prelates of irreproachable character (among whom Bossuet himself), utterly devoted to
the Church, its unity and its hierarchy, though perhaps a little too opportunist; and parliamentarians who had inherited the theories of Pithou
and were anxious to retain their privileges. A large number of Jansenists,
whose hostility to the Pope arose out of their hatred of the Jesuits, were
also Gallicans. "Scratch a Gallican, and beneath you will find a Jansenist,"
was a popular saying. Naturally enough the king's *entourage* and most of the
courtiers were Gallicans; they were only too eager to flatter his pride by provoking his wrath against the one rival who dared to challenge his authority.
The quarrel between the Most Christian King and the Holy See continued, with an occasional truce, for many years. Every possible pretext was
used to prolong the conflict—a controversial thesis at the Sorbonne, the
publication in France of a book by a Spanish Jesuit, an edict by Colbert to
reduce the number of religious and so provide more labour for agriculture,
the annulment of the marriage of Marie de Savoie, a ridiculous story about
the administration of Extreme Unction to a nuncio in circumstances which
the French clergy regarded as irregular. Finally, in 1673, came the affair of
the *régale*—the king's prerogative of enjoying the revenues of vacant sees—
which brought the conflict to a head.

In its early stages the cause of the trouble appeared to be merely financial; but the root of the problem lay in the king's claim to control and direct
the Church in France as though he were the Pope. It must be remembered
that Louis XIV believed that Church property was entirely at the disposal

of the king. Although in principle ecclesiastics were exempt from tax, it had become an established custom to vote a *Don Gratuit*—a free gift—every five years, and the money went into the treasury. In 1661 the *Don* amounted to two million *livres*, and in 1675 four and a half million. In addition to this, from about the time of the Merovingians the king had possessed the *droit de régale* under which he was entitled to receive the revenues of all bishoprics and some abbeys from the moment a See became vacant until the new incumbent was installed (*régale temporelle*); he even had the right to make appointments to ecclesiastical livings in a diocese where conferment depended upon the Ordinary (*régale spirituelle*).[30] The question that still remained undecided was whether the king's right extended to the southern dioceses where it did not exist at the time those areas returned to French rule. The bishops, supported by the Pope, opposed the king's claim, and they invoked the authority of a council held at Lyons in 1274. The ministers and the Paris Parliament supported the king, and they traced their case back to Philippe le Bel.

The question was reopened in 1608 and was debated for more than sixty years. Early in 1673 it was settled out of hand by an edict which decreed that every diocese in France without exception was subject to the *régale*. The extent of the king's control over the clergy then became evident. Of one hundred and thirty bishops, one hundred and twenty-eight accepted, while fifty-nine were affected by the measure. The only two to protest were Pavilion, Bishop of Alet, and Caulet, Bishop of Pamiers, highly respected and upright men who were in no way influenced by personal interests. Caulet appealed to the Assembly of the Clergy at its meeting in 1675, but the Assembly cautiously declined to get mixed up in the business. Rome

30. The *régale temporelle* was not valuable to the king from a financial point of view. Since 1676 two-thirds of the revenue were used for pension purposes and the balance was allocated to the "New Converts." Some of the buildings fell into a bad state of repair while the appointments remained vacant, and a special financial grant known as économes-sequestres was made for restoration. The *régale spirituelle* (which came into existence in the twelfth century) was extremely valuable to the king, for it enabled him to accommodate his minions (cf. C. Laplette, "L'administration des évêchés vacants et la règle des économats," *Revue d'Histoire de l'Église de France* [1937], p. 161ff.)

could not let the matter pass without a protest. When Pavilion died the Bishop of Pamiers continued to fight alone, determined to prevent the king from appointing anyone unworthy of the office to his See after his death. Although he was accused of Jansenist sympathies, the Holy See gave him its full support. Twice the Archbishop of Toulouse condemned him, and each time the Pope quashed the decision. When he was condemned a third time and deprived of his See he appealed to Rome. Thus began an intensely violent crisis which continued for fourteen years after the death (in 1680) of Caulet.[31]

The atmosphere in which the crisis developed was much more depressing, and the circumstances very much more complex than is generally supposed. Superficially the question at issue was whether the King of France was entitled to assume control over the Church's property and spiritual prerogatives. But quite apart from the legal aspect Rome was also concerned with Gallican theories as a whole and the fact that Louis XIV was

---

31. One of its episodes was known as the "schism of Pamiers." On the death of Caulet his spiritual son Jean Cede was appointed Vicar Capitular, against which the king reacted energetically. Four companies of cavalry were sent to Pamiers and billeted on the king's opponents—a repetition of the *Dragonnades* methods. Jean Ceric had to flee; he led a wandering life, but exercised his episcopal authority *by right and in fact*. On April 16, 1681, he was condemned to death *in absentia*, and he retaliated by excommunicating the *régaliste* canons. Public opinion was on his side, and the Pope supported him, though feebly. Under a brief dated January 1, 1651, the diocesan administration set up as an expedient by Montpezat, the Metropolitan of Toulouse, was condemned as illegal and a trespass. Hence the schism. There were two opposing groups of clergy: those who were loyal to Cerle and those who favoured the measures taken by the king and the Archbishop of Toulouse. In 1681 fourteen priests of the diocese who had gone over to the *régaliste* principle solemnly retracted their error. The seriousness of the schism is emphasized by the fact that the Holy See gave to priests loyal to Cerle power to validate marriages which had been performed by the *régaliste* priests. Carle died in hiding on August 16, 1691. He was a splendid figure who remained courageously loyal to the See of Peter, though unknown to the public generally. Despite the fact that he was hunted by the king's agents he had a high regard for the principle of royal authority; the language he used in his pastoral letters when referring to the king was very similar to that used by the bishops at Versailles. On the downfall of James II he was the only bishop in France to prescribe prayers and expiatory fasts. Monsignor Vidal has given an excellent account of this schism, which very few historians apart from Lavisse mention. See the résumé of "Le schisme de la régale au diocèse de Pamiers" (Paris, 1938), published in the *Revue d'Histoire de l'Église de France* (1939), p. 505.

280   inclined to favour them. Furthermore, his foreign policy was a cause of scandal. The anti-French clique did not lack arguments which might arouse the Holy Pontiff's anger: the king's desire for supremacy, his wars against other Catholic powers, his alliance with the infidel Turk and his annexations of territory without formal declaration of war. What strikes one as remarkable, however, throughout the episodes of the dispute is the extraordinary docility of the Pope, his reluctance to deal severely with the king, and the magnanimity with which he endured grievous wrongs. Innocent XI had been Pope since 1676.[32] He was a wise and prudent man, of stable character rather than of vast intellect. His was a truly priestly soul, overflowing with the virtues of justice and charity—a saintly figure whom the Church would canonize. Far from despairing of the "eldest daughter of the Church," who was acting like a stubborn child, he allowed her a great deal of latitude. He seized every opportunity to declare his desire to maintain "a very close relationship" with the Most Christian King, and refrained from using pressure against him until it became impossible to avoid doing so any longer. Louis XIV on his part treated him with great respect, even at the height of the conflict when the official mood was at its worst. His personal relations with the Pope remained good, and he declared that "it behoved him to kiss his hand." The king's attitude was not entirely based upon his need of support in his policy towards the Protestants and the Jansenists. At that period he was returning to a more earnest practice of religion, and under the influence of Mme. de Maintenon and Bossuet he could never have accepted the idea of schism; it would have been inconceivable to him to act like Henry VIII.

In 1687 Innocent XI wrote to Louis XIV on three occasions to put him on his guard against "those whose only desire was to curry favour by their flattery" and to draw his attention to the effective spiritual weapons at his disposal. Months went by and the king did not reply. The most astonishing rumours were current: it was said that the king was about to be

---

32. On Innocent XI, see Chapter V. The relations between Innocent XI and Louis XIV have been exhaustively studied by J. Orcibal in *Louis XII et Innocent XI* (Paris, 1949).

excommunicated, and that a French army of two hundred thousand men was preparing to march on Rome. In 1680 the French Assembly of the Clergy signed a declaration of complete and unreserved loyalty to the king "from whom nothing could possibly separate them."

The temperature was rising. The situation was aggravated still further by an incident connected with the convent at Charonne. Under the 1516 Concordat the king had the right to submit to the Pope nominations for the office of abbess, but he had no power to appoint. When the Augustinian nuns of Charonne were suspected of slight Jansenist tendencies the Government appointed a mother superior from the convent of the Order at Citeaux, without referring the matter to Rome. The nuns refused to accept her, barricaded themselves in their convent and elected another superior. The police finally closed the convent and disbanded the nuns—a use of force against which the Pope protested indignantly.

To gain support in his resistance to the Pope, Louis XIV then appealed to the clergy. The atmosphere was tense. "The Pope has pushed us too far," exclaimed Harlay. "He will regret it." The obsequious and worldly Archbishop of Paris who led the opposition to Rome held a meeting of a few members of the Assembly at his palace, and it was decided to convoke a General Assembly of the clergy of France, composed of two bishops and two priests from each province. Harlay acted as their spokesman. Opposing him was Bossuet, the new Bishop of Meaux, a much more colourful figure whose influence would soon be felt in France. The Assembly's discussions consisted mainly of a tussle between these two men: one was a zealous supporter of the king's authority, a finished courtier and a Gallican extremist; the other, infinitely more prudent and restrained, just as devoted to his king, but a respectful son of the Church, dominated by a desire for unity and an open supporter of papal authority. Bossuet began with an able speech in which he endeavoured to reconcile both points of view; he held that the Holy See alone was the pivot of the Church, to which the faithful are united through their bishops and the king, who are the trustees of divine power on earth. For a while it seemed that a solution might be found to the problem of the *regale*, but the Gallican extremists increased their pressure. Spurred on by

282   Colbert, who was fanatically hostile to Rome, Louis XIV asked the Assembly to determine the official doctrine of the Gallican Church and to define the spheres of authority as between Church and State.

This gave rise to lively discussions. Choiseul-Praslin, Bishop of Tournai, made a long statement on Rome's transgressions and shortcomings; the Assembly argued heatedly for or against papal infallibility, and the problem of the *régale*, was completely forgotten. Some members of the Assembly even mentioned schism, and Bossuet, torn between his loyalty to king and Pope, again endeavoured to keep the Assembly within the bounds of moderation; he drew up his *Déclaration en quatre articles* (1682), which the seventy-two members of the Assembly unanimously approved. The first article confirmed that the temporal power was absolutely independent of the Church; the second, that the authority of the Council was higher than that of the Pope (reference to this had been made at the Council of Constance); the third stated that the Gallican Church enjoyed special privileges because of its tradition of "rules, customs and constitutions"; the last article rejected papal infallibility outright. It acknowledged that the Holy Pontiff was "the highest authority in matters of faith," but held that "his decision is not irrevocable until it is confirmed by the judgment of the Church."

As soon as the *Déclaration des quatre articles* had been passed by the Assembly it was registered by Parliament and promulgated as law.[33] Naturally enough Innocent XI condemned it outright, "with a shudder of disgust." Even in France one or two theologians made a feeble attempt to oppose the declaration, and the Sorbonne, furious at not having been consulted, did likewise; but the king had no difficulty in disposing of all opposition.[34] It was not such an easy matter to get the better of the Pope. Not that Innocent XI used any of the weapons at his disposal; he neither excommunicated

---

33. The Four Articles remained law for a long time. The *Codes de la législation française*, by Napoléon Bacqua, may still be found in use in many French courts of justice. They were the fore-runners of the famous *Codes d'audience Dalloz*. This work contains a chapter dealing with ecclesiastical matters, beginning with the 1682 *Déclaration*. The Bacqua *Codes* were republished in 1843.

34. In any case, Louis XIV dismissed the Assembly. He probably regarded it as even more royalist than the king!

the king nor placed the country under an interdict; but he firmly refused to confer canonical investiture on the bishops nominated by the king. He remained deaf to all appeals, and allowed the vacant sees to grow in number until they reached thirty-five. It seemed as though the Catholic Church in France might eventually be deprived of legitimate leaders.

Louis XIV alternated between resignation and wrath. At first he complained that the Pope had become "hard-hearted." He instructed his ambassador, Cardinal d'Estrées, to say that the Declaration of the Four Articles was "merely a formality." This provoked a smile in Rome. Then the king changed his attitude; troubled maybe by doubt and remorse he played the bully when a rather trivial incident brought the dispute to a head. Embassies in Rome had enjoyed certain privileges which gave them immunity from police supervision. The privilege was abused to such an extent that it gradually included the whole neighbourhood in which the embassy was situated; in consequence the police had become almost powerless in half the city. Innocent XI wished to discontinue the custom. All the ambassadors agreed to surrender the franchise, in so far as it affected the neighbourhood of their embassies, but Louis XIV haughtily refused. When the Duc d'Estrées died the Pope warned the King of France that he would not receive his new ambassador unless he agreed beforehand to surrender the franchise. Louis XIV replied by sending the Marquis de Lavardin with an escort of six hundred armed men. Innocent XI excommunicated the French ambassador, but that did not prevent priests, and even bishops, from giving him the sacraments at the church of Saint-Louis-des-Français. A well-organized campaign rallied French public opinion to the king's side. French forces occupied Avignon at once, and the nuncio was placed under house arrest. There was even some talk of appealing to a council. The patience of Innocent XI was exhausted, and he assumed the offensive by excommunicating the king on November 16, 1687. However, as a supreme gesture of trust and affection, he refrained

---

35. The secret excommunication of Louis XIV was overlooked by historians for many years. Father Dubruel discovered the fact while preparing his work on the *Régale* dispute. It was first made known in an issue of *Études*, dated December 5, 1913. Cf. Dubruel, *En plein conflit: la Nonciature de France sous Louis XIV* (Paris, 1927).

284   from publishing the fact, and the king was informed privately.[35]

In truth, Louis XIV had grown weary of this squabble which, as a Christian, he found distressing. Mme. de Maintenon, who had been decorated with the Golden Rose, the highest papal distinction, was striving for a reconciliation. The Jansenist troubles were going from bad to worse, and they could not be resolved without the aid of Rome. The death of Innocent XI in August 1689 simplified matters, for the king pretended that the dispute was a personal one between himself and the late Pope, and the new one, Alexander VIII, met him halfway. The Pope allowed it to be known at Versailles that he was disposed to "settle the affair of the *régale* to the satisfaction of the king and the Holy See"; whereupon Louis XIV withdrew his troops from the Comtat Venaissin. But Rome did not intend to yield in the matter of principles; the Bull *Inter multiplices*, drawn up by Innocent XI, was published in 1681, declaring that the conclusions of the 1682 Assembly were "all invalid and without authority." Moreover, from his deathbed the Pope addressed a letter to the king in which he appealed to his conscience.

It was quite easy for Innocent XII to take advantage of the king's conciliatory attitude, which was accentuated by the fact that France was at war with the League of Augsburg. An understanding was reached in 1693: in exchange for a retraction in due and proper form the Pope approved the canonical investiture of all the bishops nominated since 1682, and extended the right of *régale* to the whole of France. Louis XIV gave instructions that the Four Articles were no longer to be regarded as legally binding, a retraction which the Parliaments in most cities declined to register. In any case, the Gallican quarrel ended with the undoubted victory of the spiritual power over the temporal.

Not that Gallicanism really disappeared. It became very closely associated with Jansenism, and remained a source of trouble to the Church in France long after the death of the Great King—almost until the outbreak of the French Revolution. When Louis XIV signed the *Édit des cinquante articles* in 1695, prescribing, "in pursuance of the rights of the Holy See," the organization of the Church of France, the authority of the crown over the clergy, the system of ecclesiastical jurisdiction, and even the fees of parish priests and other clergy, he may have been attempting to pay off old scores. But by that time the quarrel was over, and Rome let the matter pass. The document had a strong Gallican flavour, but its provisions remained the basis of Church policy in France until 1789.

8. "I HAVE BEEN TOO FOND OF WAR"

THE pride of Louis XIV was at the root of every distressing event that marked the relations between him and the Holy See; a pride so dominating that for many years it silenced the voice of conscience and maintained in the king an attitude of mind that should be foreign to a Catholic.

Moreover, we cannot fail to recognize this pride in the continual bloody wars that stained the great reign; and in the objects and methods of the king's foreign policy which undoubtedly contributed much to his personal glory, but brought discredit upon France.

On several occasions Louis XIV had very good reasons for entering into war. His father's aims had not been achieved, and France did not by any means possess all the territory which she might have legitimately claimed on the principle of language and population. Her frontiers to the east and to the north were badly protected; the ambitions of the Hapsburgs had not diminished; across the Channel England was developing rapidly, and resented the presence of a great power under her very nose. In many European capitals, and even in Rome, anti-French feeling was so strong at that time that a king who was solicitous of his country's interests had to be careful. Louis's assaults against Europe were therefore far from being entirely unjustified.

But there is also no doubt whatever that in numerous cases Louis XIV flung himself into the fray a little too lightly, without even attempting to negotiate in the hope of securing results by peaceful means. "I have been too fond of war," he admitted on his deathbed. When he was a child his teachers used to talk to him of conquests and victories; and, surprisingly enough, Bishop Godeau's *Catéchisme royal* had set before him the examples of the greatest butchers in history—Tamerlane and Genghis Khan. We can hardly be surprised therefore that Louis XIV should write: "The attributes of a conqueror are deemed the most noble and most lofty."

Did he knowingly aspire to world supremacy? Did he dream of establishing a French monarchy over the whole of Europe? We cannot find in his *Mémoires* any trace of such aims, or even a policy of "natural frontiers"; but he conveyed the impression that he cherished these ambitions, and it is possible that his fawning courtiers put into words what he pondered in his heart. He certainly did not prevent Aubery (though later he imprisoned him for two months) from publishing a Latin treatise on "the king's rightful claims to the Empire" (1667), in which he referred to France's claim to "the patrimony and ancient heritage of her kings," that is, all the territory which had been "in the possession of Charlemagne as king of France." Jacques de Cassan's book, *La Recherche des droits du roi*, was republished in 1670. This precursor of geopolitics affirmed the rights of the French Crown to Navarre, Naples, Sicily, Majorca, Milan, Genoa, Flanders, the Low Countries, Ravenna and Avignon. The document aroused feelings in the king similar to those awakened by previous theses: insolence in his relations with other monarchs, an offensive boasting of his successes, a desperate desire to humiliate opponents and (more important) a contempt of right and an often repeated conviction that one need not abide by treaties—that force should decide everything. In a way this was the broadly realistic policy established by the Treaties of Westphalia. But in view of the principle of balance of power in Europe such a policy could end only in catastrophic failure and the weakening of France. Much worse, it led the country to discard its noblest traditions. The Spanish writer and ambassador Francesco de Lisola published a satirical work entitled *The Shield of State and Justice*, in which he criticized the aggressions and transgressions of the king. "The fate of Europe is at stake," he wrote, "and sentence must be passed as to its freedom or enslavement." Even if we allow for the extravagance of language natural in controversy, it is depressing to see such words applied to an heir of St. Louis.

This aggressive policy of Louis XIV was not the only one possible at that time; others had, in fact, been suggested. The one put forward by

Claude Fleury in his *Lettre sur la justice* was bold enough to proclaim that "the same spirit of justice should exist between states as between individuals," that "most conquests are unjust," and that a policy devoid of ethics can end only in tyranny. The one proposed by Fénelon was perhaps too idealistic. It claimed that all Christian princes should restore their unjust conquests, and compensate peoples for whatever losses they had sustained. The same theory was developed by Saavedra Fajardo. It was unquestionably Utopian, but it embodied a genuinely Christian ideal of which Innocent XI had quite rightly reminded Louis XIV. The diplomacy of the Holy See was neither very skillful nor very far-seeing; it failed to discover in time the Protestant peril in the person of William of Orange, and made no attempt to reconcile the great Catholic powers; but it had at least the merit, especially under Innocent XI, of having courageously pointed out to the mighty King of France that even in the field of politics he had obligations as a Christian, and that the day must come when he would appear to answer for his actions before a tribunal that did not depend upon the power of the sword.

One matter on which the Holy See had occasion to reproach Louis XIV was his Eastern policy: his hesitation and ultimate refusal to join the crusade against the Turks which the Papacy longed to see organized. Not that the idea appeared anachronistic and absurd to the King of France, for the cycle of events since the beginning of his reign remained a continual reminder of the dreadful reality. In 1663 the Grand Vizier Köprili, who had reorganized the Ottoman Empire, flung against the West an army of one hundred twenty thousand men, composed of janissaries, Tartars, and Cossacks. Their hordes swept across Moravia and Silesia laying waste the country; more than eighty thousand Christians were sold in the slave markets of Constantinople. In every town in Germany the *Türkenglocken*—the bells of the Turks—were rung at noon every day. With this danger threatening the West, Louis XIV was torn between his duty as a Christian and the alliance which had bound France to the Sublime Porte since 1536. He decided eventually in favour of the Christians, and sent six thousand men, the flower of the French nobility, to help his brother-in-law, Leopold I. The Turks called these young heroes "The Maids," on account of the customary wigs they

288   wore. Their arrival decided the victory of St. Gothard on the island of Rab (1664). Despite this intervention Louis XIV carefully avoided destroying his connection with his Turkish ally.

Although the Ottoman threat had been temporarily removed, it had not been entirely disposed of. Twenty years later the Grand Vizier Kara-Mustafa proved just as aggressive as his predecessor Köprili, and openly began preparations for a new offensive against the Empire. It was then that Innocent XI, ignoring the existing quarrel with Louis XIV on the subject of the *régale*, tried to interest his conscience in a vast scheme to effect peace and unity among all Christian peoples and to stem the assault of the infidel. For a moment he nearly succeeded, but discord again developed among the Christians. The annexation of Strasburg by Louis XIV caused the Pope the greatest sorrow. In 1683 a new Turkish offensive by two hundred fifty thousand men threatened Vienna. A special messenger was sent by the Holy See to beg the King of France to think of the safety of Christendom. The Nuncio himself approached the king. "War against the Turk is God's will," he said, "and He will severely punish all who oppose or distract from it." The Most Christian King remained deaf to these appeals. No Frenchmen fought at the battle of Kahlenberg (September 12, 1683), when the heroic Polish expeditionary force under John III Sobieski cut down the Turks; neither did they take part in the Sixteen Years War (1683–1699) during which the armies of the West drove the Crescent from Hungary. The Nuncio wrote to Louis XIV in 1687: "If Your Majesty, having rid your own country of heresy, were to be favourably disposed towards the barbarian and the infidel, the whole of Christendom would stand amazed. You cannot do this without serious injury to your glory and, which is more important, without grave detriment to your conscience, of which you will one day have to give the most strict account to God." Yet the Franco-Turkish alliance became even stronger.

One hesitates to pass judgment on a policy which appeared so remote from the traditional Christian ideal. Might it not be justified on the principle of European balance of power, the desire to retain an ally capable of attacking the Empire from the rear? Events seem to suggest that the diplomacy

of Louis XIV was the right one; the eventual Turkish defeat, which French
support could not prevent, resulted in an enormous increase in Hapsburg
power, followed by the ruthless subjection of Hungary to the throne of
Vienna, the mass executions at Eperies and the defeat of Francis II Raköczy,
a friend of Louis XIV. Prince Eugene created a veritable empire from the
mountains of Bohemia to Serbia, a formidable power which might have
threatened France. Who can say whether all these events might not have
happened even if *the grand roi* had placed himself at the head of the Holy
League, as the Pope wished him to do, led the crusade against the Turks,
and built a peaceful Christian Europe around the French throne? These are
prospects with which the imagination may play; but other schemes lay concealed behind the foreign policy of Louis XIV.

We may indeed ask ourselves what were the objects of the continual
wars waged for thirty years of his long reign of fifty-four years; or whether,
in fact, this foreign policy based on force really did embody a coherent plan.
Was the purpose dynastic, as in the War of Devolution (1667–1668) and
the disastrous War of the Spanish Succession (1701–1714), which sealed
the ruin of France and put an end to her supremacy? Was it a question of
commercial interests, as in the war against Holland (1672–1678), or the
need to stem the ambition of the Hapsburgs, as seems to have been the case
in the War of the League of Augsburg (1688–1697)? But in this painful and
fruitless struggle France confronted not only the Protestant coalition (led
by William of Orange), roused to indignation by the revocation of the Edict
of Nantes, but even the Catholics of the Empire. One might well wonder
whether France's acquisition of Franche-Comté and a part of Flanders was
adequate compensation for the dreadful sacrifices in men and materials that
were the evident consequences of all this bloodshed. And from a Christian
point of view there was absolutely no justification for them.

Above all, how can we explain away the methods employed to execute
that policy? At the very commencement of the reign France occupied the
southern Low Countries on the controvertible principle of Devolution; this
was a clear demonstration of Louis's lack of respect for international law.
Then came the plan of "reunion," whose purpose was to reintegrate with

France all territories which had at any period (even from the time of King Dagobert!) belonged to regions recently acquired by France. Europe regarded this demand as an intolerable provocation. Montbéliard, the Saar, Deux-Ponts and most of Luxembourg were successively occupied. The annexation of Strasburg (September 28, 1681), which was an open city, was universally condemned as an act of unpardonable aggression, though the action might have been excused on the grounds that the city had allowed armies hostile to France to pass through it on three occasions. The Pope was horrified, and the incident may have caused the failure of the scheme outlined at that time by Spinola to reunite the Protestants to the Catholic Church.[36] The whole of Europe shuddered with anguish at the prospect of a universal French dictatorship. France's old friends abandoned her. Towards the end of the reign she stood alone, haughtily alone, facing a dangerous threat of opposition. "Alone against all," cried Louvois proudly. But the consequences had yet to come.

The methods adopted by Louis XIV during the course of his wars were quite often discreditable. Perhaps the Dutch pamphleteers exaggerated (as may be expected in this kind of propaganda) when they denounced "the unheard-of cruelties which the French have perpetrated"; but what we know of the occupation of Franche-Comté and Alsace by the troops under Condé and Turenne respectively can hardly excite our admiration. The event which, however, more than any other has left an indelible stain upon the "great century" was the dreadful invasion and devastation of the Palatinate, carried out by the order of Louvois at the beginning of the War of the League of Augsburg. Its object was to create a barren region extending along the whole frontier, and the leaders Duras and Tessé executed the task with dreadful zeal. Vineyards and orchards were utterly destroyed; towns and villages were razed to the ground or burned; rare and beautiful castles—among them the Château of the Electors, one of the wonders of Europe—were demolished; Mannheim, Spire, Oppenheim, Frankenthal, Bingen, Landenburg and Heidelberg were set ablaze. The unhappy populations fled through the snow, and those who survived hunger and cold described the

36. See Chapter V, section 12: "An Unfulfilled Hope."

kind of war waged by the King of France. It was little wonder that Europe in those days regarded Louis XIV as a madman.

When Innocent XI learned of these events he wrote a touching letter to his Nuncio concerning the brutality of the French troops in Flanders and the despicable burning of the town of Tongres, urging him to inform the king "how badly His Majesty is served by those who perpetrate sacrilegious and inhuman crimes in his name, drawing down upon his arms the hatred of Christian peoples; how the extermination of so many innocent people offends the honour of God, who has granted the king such prosperity and so many victories, and could, by a flick of the finger, reverse the situation and punish the authors of such dreadful massacres." In vain the supreme voice of the Church reminded Louis XIV of "the moment of death from which the sovereigns of the world, however great and victorious, are not exempt." In reply to this moving appeal a curt note from Father La Chaise stated that such incidents were inevitable in war, but that the King of France would see that the churches destroyed were rebuilt. Reminded of the charity of Christ and clemency towards innocent populations, Louis XIV, no doubt in good faith, thought to allay the Pope's sorrow by promising to rebuild walls!

9. "RELIEVE THE DISTRESS OF THE PEOPLE"

WHEN the old king was giving his last words of advice to his great-grand-son, the future Louis XV, having referred to the liking he had always had for war, he added: "Try to relieve the distress of the people—a thing which I unfortunately have not been able to do." An expression of belated regret, but also of sad truth. This final aspect of the reign remains to be discussed. It casts a shadow over the picture, for the splendour of Versailles, its luxury and its magnificent festivities, cannot obliterate the misery and suffering discernible in the background. It is a spectacle no Christian can contemplate without emotion.

The circumstances of the common people of France seem to have been wretched during the period. La Bruyère was perhaps exaggerating the condition of the peasantry when he wrote in his *Caractères*: "wild animals can be seen, male and female, roaming about the countryside, dirty and ghastly.... They appear to be able to talk, and when they rise to their feet they are seen to have human faces.... At night they disappear into dens where they live on black bread, roots and water...."

We like to think that this language is hyperbolical, and that today we would use the word "vegetables" instead of "roots." There is, however, abundant evidence to confirm the truth of this melancholy picture. In 1675 the district governor of Berry reported that in his province "the peasants are more wretched than slaves in Turkey." The same year the Duc de Lesdiguières drew attention to the fact that in Dauphiné "the greater part of the population had lived entirely on acorns and roots, and were reduced to eating grass and the bark of trees." And Mme. de Sévigné wrote in 1680: "Everywhere I see people who have no bread." A royal commission sent into Maine and the old province of Orleans described a very similar situation. "The common people," Vauban wrote in his diary, "eat meat scarcely three times a year. Three-quarters of them are dressed in rags, winter and summer, and they wear clogs over their bare feet." This state of things, which gradually worsened towards the end of the reign, when trade and industry had been ruined by wars and excessive taxation, provoked dreadful peasant risings which were even more dreadfully suppressed. The revolt of twenty-five thousand peasants in Brittany has become famous for the cruelties which the province endured when the uprising was crushed. The ten thousand soldiers let loose over the country committed countless crimes. "They do nothing but kill and rob," wrote Mme. de Sévigné. "A few days ago they put a little child on a skewer."

Would it be right to say that Louis XIV was personally responsible for such a situation? To a great extent he was probably not even aware of it. Versailles was a long way from the provinces, and neither his ministers nor the courtiers would have been anxious to keep him in the picture. Were the governors' letters laid before him, and the evidence of such courageous men as Vauban, Fénelon and the Bishops of Montauban and Mende? Louis XIV has been described as a kindly prince, happy to have an occasional chat with

a peasant. It is possible that if he had known the truth he might have wished
to do something about it; but he was a slave of the very system he had created and which did not permit him, absolute though he was, to know and act
except through an intermediary.

Furthermore, as we survey the details of this long reign we are impressed
by a decline in what was perhaps one of the most attractive moral phenom-
ena of the preceding epoch—what we might call the spirit of St. Vincent de
Paul. People had certainly become less anxious to fight against destitution
and the abuse of law. Of course, the great charitable works established at the
beginning of the century still survived: hospitals were opened; confraternities of charity, successors of the Company of the Blessed Sacrament, still
strove to do good. The king himself was well aware of these institutions and
frequently encouraged them by his gifts; but there is no doubt whatever that
he did not regard such activities as a major interest, as Louis XIII and Anne
of Austria had done. In short, he did not experience the anguish of Christ's
charity. When Fénelon, in his *Plan de gouvernement*, pointed out that the
king should examine his conscience according to the heart of God, begging
him to "relieve those who are at the last stage of exhaustion," to give bread
to the unemployed, to "have every convict set free at the end of his term of
punishment as fixed by the courts," he could not expect the right kind of
response from a sovereign like Louis XIV. That sense of social sin which is
one of the highest achievements of twentieth-century Christianity did not
exist in the seventeenth, except in a few rare and privileged souls.

In contrast, however, with these permanent departures from charity there were some men who spoke a truly Christian language. Bossuet's
resounding words, uttered in 1659 in his celebrated sermon on the eminent dignity of the poor within the Church, will echo through the world
for ever: "The poor you so despise were set by God as his treasurers and
collectors.... The Church was built for the poor alone...the rich, as such,
are suffered merely as a favour...." Later, when the position deteriorated,
especially where children were concerned, other voices rang out denouncing errors, corrupt practices and injustice. The words of Boisguillebert, who
wrote *Le détail de la France*, were all the more convincing because he was an

economist. That illustrious soldier Vauban put forward a complete scheme of reorganization, administrative, financial and social, in his *Dîme royale*; many really moving paragraphs came from his pen. Fénelon too made his voice heard in the *Examen de conscience* and *Remonstrances*, and even in the novel *Télémaque*.

Louis XIV paid no heed to these voices; neither did he appear to take Bossuet's appeal seriously: "Look at these accusers: they are the poor who will bear witness to your unrelenting callousness." In any case, police action was his answer to those who pleaded for a mere humane regime. Pontchartrain and d'Argenson treated such works as *Dîme royale* and *Télémaque* as though they were obscene books or licentious newspapers, or suspected of Quietiest heresy as was the *Maximes des saints*. A few days before old Maréchal Vauban died, the King's Council seized his book and gave instructions that he was to be prosecuted for having published it; Boisguillebert was similarly dealt with. Fénelon was dismissed from the court on suspicion of Quietism. He was not in disgrace, but the circumstances of his dismissal were such that he could not leave his diocese of Cambrai.

We can imagine the hopelessness and indignation experienced by this sincere priest in the face of such obstinacy in what he considered to be injustice and sin. When France stood alone against Europe in 1710, and seemed at the point of collapse, he addressed a daring letter to the Duc de Chevreuse, but intended for the king.[37] He condemned absolutely the king's religious policy, his attitude to war and social evils. "You may reply that God will sustain France," he wrote; "but I ask you what promise you have had. Do you deserve miracles at a time when not even the threat of utter and imminent disaster can reform you, when you persist in remaining hard, haughty, ostentatious, incommunicable, unfeeling and always willing to delude yourself? Will humiliation without humility appease God? Though overwhelmed by your faults you refuse to acknowledge them, and you would certainly begin again if you could survive a year or two. Can you satisfy God with a devotion that consists in decorating a church, saying the Rosary, listening to a

---

37. See above, p. 244, note 4.

piece of music, being easily scandalized, or pursuing some Jansenist? It is
not sufficient to bring to an end a foreign war; you should provide bread
for your starving people at home.... You should remember the true state of
your country, and keep within bounds that despotism which is the cause of
all our ills." A terrible indictment; we may wonder how a man dared to write
such a letter, and, if Louis XIV knew of it, how he could have endured it
without throwing its author into the Bastille.

On the surface these accusations were merited, and the holy anger of
the Archbishop of Cambrai appeared justified. But we are apt to wonder
whether the judgment of God who probes the depths of the heart was so
severe. Bossuet's language was more moderate. He saw clearly the fundamental opposition between Christianity and unlimited absolutism when
he exclaimed: "It is not proper to man to have no superior. The very idea is
bewildering, for man's condition does not lend itself to such independence."

Perhaps the Most Christian King did occasionally forget that he had
Someone over him to whom he would one day have to render an account.
He failed, in any case, to penetrate the meaning of that eternal lesson of the
Gospel which, during his reign, the Sacred Heart repeated to the humble
nun, Margaret Mary—"God is Love."[38]

10. "GOD ALONE IS GREAT"

DESPITE everything the king did not forget that, like all men, he was in
the hands of God. When the hour came to settle his final account he proved
to be the Christian he had always longed to be, even during the wayward
years when sensuality and pride seemed to be in control.

The last years of his reign were a long succession of trials, a painful
apprenticeship of utter renunciation. Within the bosom of the king's family
death struck with such frequency that everyone began to imagine it had

---

38. On the devotion to the Sacred Heart, see below, Chapter V, section 3: "Decline of
Mysticism and Growth of Devotion to the Sacred Heart."

an ally among men. The Dauphin died in 1711; his son the Duc de Bourgogne, Fénelon's pupil, died six months later, preceded by his wife and followed within a month by his eldest son, the Duc de Bretagne. The heir to the throne, the little Duc d'Anjou, was still a baby scarcely out of the cradle.

The general situation was no brighter. Over and over again the war that had been raging since 1701 appeared almost lost: the disasters at Ramillies, Turin and Oudenarde appeared to toll the knell of France once glorious. An extraordinary revival of national spirit produced a counter-thrust at Malplaquet, followed by a victory at Denain. But although the peace signed at Utrecht and Rastadt settled the Spanish dynastic problems it was not advantageous to France, who received nothing in return for her immense sacrifices. The war had left her in a deplorable condition: bled white, drained of money and men, her economy bankrupt, her population had fallen from nineteen to seventeen million inhabitants, and desolation and savagery reigned everywhere.

Confronted with such a painful situation the old king showed his customary strength of mind. He accepted his trials with the dignity which the consideration of his glory demanded, but also with the resignation of a believer—even with a surprising and admirable humility: "Few people have experienced the misfortunes that have befallen me," he said to the Maréchal de Villars. "God punishes me, but I have well deserved it." When he made this admission was he thinking of his former mistresses, of the Protestants who had been the victims of his *Dragonnades*, of the unhappy people of the Palatinate fleeing in the snow, or of the prophetic words of Innocent XI who warned him that God would punish his revolt against the Vicar of Christ? But though repentant he had no intention of covering his head with ashes. He insisted that nothing in his routine should be changed; the requirements of court etiquette were to be strictly adhered to; there was to be no visible sign of the sorrow which everyone, he above all, bore in their hearts. This dignity was also a Christian virtue.

He faced death with the same admirable courage. Towards the end of August 1715 he was stricken with senile gangrene in the legs, and was cared for—if one may use the expression—by his aged and rather incompetent doctor Fagon. He soon became aware that his end was near, and demanded to be told the truth about his condition. When he knew that he could not live beyond the beginning of September he organized his last days with touching determination. Three days before his death he presided over the Council for the last time, dictated some details relating to his will and settled a few court matters. On the eve of his death he commanded that his great-grandson, the future Louis XV, be brought to him, and he gave the child his last words of advice. He said playfully to those whom he caught trying to hide their tears: "Did you then think me immortal?"

This was indeed the attitude of a Christian who had rediscovered himself. All his life he had aspired to dominate events, but now he abandoned himself to God with moving simplicity. Just before the end, an elixir administered to him by an empiricist seemed to give him back his strength, and someone told him he would soon be well. He replied: "Life or death— whatever God wills." Assisted by Mme. de Maintenon, who knew his faults so well, he made his confession to Father Le Tellier. He said that he felt he was at peace with God and had every confidence in His mercy, "but would ever regret having offended Him." On several occasions he asked forgiveness of those present for any scandal he had given them and wrongs that he had done them. During the night of August 31, in a strong and apparently calm voice, he joined the priests in the prayers for the dying. His last words were the recital of the *Nunc in hora mortis* and the well-known verses of the psalm, "O Lord, come to my assistance: O Lord, make haste to help me." The long and painful struggle was over; the struggle of a man in whom the demands of religion had battled with human frailty and the force of circumstances. Louis the "God-given" was then indeed "Most Christian."

A few days later, in the Sainte-Chapelle decked for the royal funeral, a Christian voice pointed to the moral of that amazing and adventurous reign. Massillon, pronouncing the funeral oration of the king who had made Europe tremble, took for his text these words (from the Book of Ecclesiastes[39]): "I am become great, and have gone beyond all in wisdom that

---

39. Eccles. 1:16 (Douay).

298   were before me in Jerusalem: I have perceived that in all that there was only labour and vexation of spirit." At first Massillon remained silent, his eyes cast down. Then he gazed a moment over the congregation, and pointing to the coat of arms—L. L. G., "Louis Le Grand"—he began with these unforgettable words: "God alone is great."

CHAPTER V

Christians of the Classical Period

1. CLASSICAL CHRISTIANITY

CLASSICISM is traditionally linked with the reign of Louis XIV, or rather with his century. It has left its mark in many beautiful works of art and countless literary masterpieces. The plays of Corneille, Molière and Racine, the precepts of Boileau, the funeral orations of Bossuet, the sermons of Bourdaloue and, above all, Versailles itself, the very centre of beauty in its supreme severity—all spring to mind when we speak of the *classical age*. At the same time it evokes an attitude of mind which is reflected in an adherence to rigid rules, constant control of intellect over imagination and passion, a desire to attain an ideal of perfection and stability through order and discipline. The concept was a moral, aesthetic and political one, and not confined to France, though that country led Western nations in their assimilation of its principles. The concept is embodied in the theory of absolute monarchy, the splendour of court etiquette personified in the great King Louis XIV.

As with all traditional concepts we cannot accept classicism without certain reservations. Though it is quite correct to regard the seventeenth century, especially the second half, as the classical age, it is true only in a superficial sense, however splendid that superstratum may be. The more we study the Great Century the more we appreciate that beneath the surface of magnificence a crisis was developing "which touched the whole man in the whole range of his activities, economic, social, political, religious, scientific, artistic; in his entire being, to the very depths of his will and his emotions....

300 The State, the public, the upper classes and the individual strove ceaselessly to re-establish order and unity within themselves and within their own
spheres."[1] From a political standpoint the monarchical structure that had
been built up at the beginning of the century in the face of obstacles had
stood wonderfully firm for fifty years, maintained by the genius of a great
king, though towards the end of the reign it began to show real signs of
decay. Thus the whole classical system is shown to be the result of a struggle
to maintain an equilibrium painfully achieved and under a continual threat
of destruction.

From the point of view of religion the position was the same. What
has been described as *Christian Classicism* was indeed a reality: it had its
own definite characteristics. Linked with the established order, it sustained
absolutism and was its trustee, sharing with it the splendour of the regime.
Sainte-Beuve aptly summed up the relationship when he said that "the
Throne and the Pulpit stood back to back." Classical Christianity is displayed in the pomp and magnificence of its ceremonial on the occasion of
princely weddings and funerals. It was strikingly represented by its lordly,
but sterling, bishops with their imposing *entourages*, their large retinues of
servants and their six-horse carriages. It is recognizable in its masterpieces: the splendid works of Bossuet, such as the *Politique tirée de l'Écriture
sainte* and the *Discours sur l'histoire universelle*, the beautiful chapels of Val
de Grâce and the splendour of the Invalides. That was an austere and stately form of Christianity. It aspired, though often unsuccessfully, to control
morals. It was more submissive than spontaneous, and founded on fear rather than on love; but its faith was exact, solid and unshakable. One would no
more have dreamed of questioning it than one would have questioned the
authority of the king. Such was the faith of Jacques-Bénigne Bossuet.

These outward appearances are not exactly misleading, but do they
reveal the whole truth? In the sense in which classical Catholicism reveals a
kind of conformity with rules it is not truly representative of the profoundly

---

1. Roland Mousnier, *Les XVI et XVII siècles* (*Histoire générale des civilisations*) (Paris, 1954), pp. 276ff.

religious life of a vast number of people. No pause occurred in the upsurge of spiritual ardour noticeable at the beginning of the century. The followers of such men as Bérulle, St. Vincent de Paul and Olier still toiled on, and the leaven of reform was still working. Although there were Christians who, broadly speaking, resigned themselves to the established order and a conception of the world which, after so many years of torment and chaos, they had come to appreciate, there were still a great many who remained quite untouched by "classicism." Just as there were bishops who refused to live a life of ostentation, so did many a simple soul lead an unfettered spiritual life under the gaze of God, even within the recognized framework of classical Catholicism.

The facts prove that in the religious field itself order, discipline and stability—splendid "classical" qualities—were not achieved without continued effort, and sometimes only after a spectacular struggle. Within the Church the classical age was an age of violent crises brought about by Jansenism, Quietism and Gallicanism, and of an altogether more insidious crisis which tormented minds and consciences. Side by side with official orthodoxy profound spiritual aspirations asserted themselves, and it would be difficult to fit them into the framework of the system. The century of classicism was not merely an era of royal pomp and ceremonial in which the apparent function of the Church was to buttress and bestow its blessing upon absolutism. It was also an era of contention in the name of sanctifying grace and pure love, and the very violence of the conflict demonstrated that despite hidden cracks the vital structure of spiritual liberty survived.

We may even wonder whether "classical Christianity" did not conceal an inner contradiction which might have caused the system to fall to pieces. Was not Christianity superimposed upon the classical ideal, to which it was diametrically opposed? Pierre Gaxotte was right when he said: "The seventeenth century was the human century *par excellence*, the century of man's glory." Was not the pompous cult of royalty simply a man-made religion? God occupied a very unimportant position in the immensity of Versailles; even in the chapel, if the king's eyes turned to the altar the courtiers turned their eyes to the king. The purpose behind all that magnificent

302 literature—the works of Corneille, Racine, Molière, La Bruyère and La
Rochefoucauld—was man, and man only. During the preceding period the
"devout humanists" and the masters of the French School surrendered man
utterly to God, although they held him in high esteem. This is also true of
the succeeding period so far as formal expression is concerned, but much
less so in fact; and to a certain extent this attitude explains the definite slowing down of the spiritual upsurge and creative power of the period. It also
explains the development of libertinism or disbelief which predominated
in the eighteenth century. Classical Christianity was therefore destined to
succumb to its own inconsistency.

But it did not yield without a struggle. Religion continued to remain
firmly rooted in institutions and in men's souls. Disintegrating ideas cannot
seriously and suddenly attack the admirable order that binds faith and the
political and social sinews into an entity. Saints, doctors and great preachers
would fight with all their strength to prevent the dissolution of legitimate
hierarchies—the real causes of which no one, except perhaps Fénelon, really
understood, although the signs were easily recognizable. Christians of the
classical age have written the passionate and grandiose story of that struggle
waged on the world's stage and in the depths of souls. Our impression of
the Church during that half-century is something more than an exhibition
of solemnity and stilted majesty; it offers us a picture of pathetic tenacity.

2. AN ERA OF FAITH

THE outstanding fact of Western society in the Great Century was its sense
of religion, deeply rooted in the life of the community, controlling and
dominating its principles; decidedly a fortunate counter-part to the unwar-
rantable interference of officialdom in religious matters, an occurrence of
which the reign of Louis XIV was a remarkable example, though all the
sovereigns of his day vied with each other in the same direction. "In the
Catholic world the close union of and the mutual relationship between the
two powers established by God, their intimate association in the common

field of public life," to use the words of Pius XII,[2] strove to keep alive the   303
spirit of Christianity with which institutions were imbued. The least a viceroy of God can do is to defend God's rights among His people. That the
Church was the trustee of the deposit of faith and the guarantor of stability
and harmony in the life of the community was a fact recognized by everyone. Domat, the king's counsellor in the presidial Chamber of Clermont, in
Auvergne, based his *Traité de droit public* (1697) on the axiom that "Religion is the foundation on which social order is built."

The efficacy of religion was everywhere manifest: in the family circle,
within the framework of society, and especially in marriage, which is the
basis of society. Henri Bremond was right when he observed that Christian
marriage, which experienced a grave crisis at the time of the Renaissance
and the Reformation, recovered its dignity during the seventeenth century
when there developed "a mysticism in marriage which was as far removed
from animal coarseness as it was from the artificial modesty of the pseu-
do-spirituals." St. Francis de Sales's bold and emancipating passage on the
sanctity of matrimony went a long way towards restoring its dignity. Bossuet wrote to Sister Cornuau, whose spiritual notions were rather muddled:
"I have often told you, my child, that the married state is holy. Those virgins
who despise it are not wise virgins." Le Maître de Sacy praised the goodness
and the wisdom of God, who raised the physical union of man and woman
to the dignity of a sacrament. Admittedly these are commonplace and time-
worn notions today, but in the seventeenth century they had the force and
freshness of a rediscovered truth.

The family therefore retained a definitely spiritual character because it
was founded upon a sacrament. "Any man who fears God will be a good
husband, a good father, a good son, a good brother, a good master, a good
servant..." wrote Fortin in his *Conseils fidèles d'un père à ses enfants.* There
existed at that period a widespread custom of recording family events, great
or small, in books popularly known as *livres de raison.* The opening pages of
the books usually contained a few basic principles of faith and some really

---

2.   Speech to the World Congress of the Lay Apostolate, October 14, 1951.

beautiful prayers. The father of the family, as the responsible head of a small social cell, exercised an authority over the family comparable with that of a monarch over his realm; and, like the king's authority, it was essentially spiritual. With our modern ideas of equality we can scarcely imagine today the extent of the father's jurisdiction and the respect accorded to him. The scope of his testamentary rights was much wider than it is today, so that a father's authority endured even after death—a fact which, as Leibniz so profoundly observes, "would be meaningless without belief in an immortal soul."

The fact of religion also entered into a man's work, which is another aspect of social life. As in the Middle Ages, the Christian calendar of feasts prescribed the days on which men refrained from work, and there were too many of them if we are to believe the cobbler in La Fontaine's fable. Linked with the system of trade guilds, which were specifically economic in character and are still just as strong today, there were confraternities of arts and crafts. These associations afforded mutual assistance where necessary and were based on religious principles, though quite distinct from the pious confraternities, whose purposes were spiritual. The election of the executives of a guild was conducted in the presence of the priest in charge of the church to which it was affiliated, and the men elected promised "to do their duty well." The rules of these trade guilds included penalties for those who infringed them: the penalty almost always consisted of some act of devotion, the giving of alms or payment of a fine, and the proceeds went into a collecting-box to honour some patron saint.

The parish was yet another sphere in which religion united men. It experienced a definite recovery under the influence of the reforming ideas of the early part of the century. We remember how Monsieur Vincent changed Châtillon des Dombes from a centre of disorder, selfishness and corruption into a living parish. Until 1667 the parish priest alone was responsible for the maintenance of registers of births, marriages and deaths,[3] and he read

---

3. Under a Statute of Villers-Cotteret (1539) the parish priest registered baptisms and burials and, after the Statute of Blois (1579), marriages. He was therefore responsible

government statutes from the pulpit. A spirited atmosphere therefore existed in parish life, and under a good priest it could be a really Christian atmosphere. The bell-tower was the voice of the village; its measured peals set
the rhythm of daily life. The bell called the people to prayer, sounded the
alarm and celebrated important events within the community. The registers
of that period provide evidence of countless examples of devotion to parish
work by Catholics of all classes.

There is therefore no doubt whatever that, just as in the Middle Ages, the
religion of that period was conjoined with a living faith, directing customs
and laying down rules to impose on everyone respect for the Commandments of God and of the Church. Because men lived within the framework
of Christianity it was naturally very difficult for them not to lead Christian
lives. Bossuet was thinking along the same lines when he wrote in his *Con-
férence avec Monsieur Claude*, "I admit that individuals may be ignorant of
some articles of faith...but they profess them in general when they declare
their belief in the universal Church."

And indeed belief in God was general. To people of the Great Century
faith was natural. "Free-thinkers" existed, but they were still rare; they could
be found only in those small groups of intellectuals and men-about-town
of whom Saint-Évremond (who was compelled to seek refuge in London
in 1661) was a typical example. Their number grew towards the end of the
reign of Louis XIV, and not only in France; none the less they were not very
numerous. Father Mersenne estimated that about the year 1660 there were
fifty thousand atheists in Paris, a figure we can no more accept as reliable
than we can the lament of Mme. de Maintenon that "there are no longer
any Christians in the provinces," or the Princess Palatine's statement that
"the faith is extinct." The wise Father Garasse said that he knew of only five
atheists in Paris, three of whom were Italians.

---

for the complete record of a person's civil status until the time of the Revolution, with
the single exception that from 1667 (under the Code Louis) he had to maintain the
parish registers in duplicate: the original was sent to the bailiff's office and the copy
retained at the presbytery.

It is important to understand that a Christian is one who lives within the structure of a Christian society, and not one who merely conforms. We have only to pick at random any personality of the classical epoch, and we find a soul deeply penetrated with Christian sentiments. Neither is it necessary to select a champion of the Catholic cause, of whom there were many. A woman of the world such as Mme. de Sévigné (who, as appears from her famous letters, enjoyed her fair share of lawful pleasures), read spiritual books and religious history, delighted in discussing problems of faith with her friends Nicole and Abadie, and recognized the hand of Providence in every occurrence. She thought, spoke, acted and reacted quite spontaneously and naturally as a Christian. In this she was not alone. The scoffing La Fontaine prayed like a child; so did Colbert, Turenne and many others. Even many less respectable personalities showed signs of possessing a deep faith: Mme. de Montespan weighed her bread during Lent to avoid breaking her fast. The rugged Cardinal de Retz experienced moments of repentance, and acted like a true Christian when he made amends to all those whom he had treated badly.

Moreover, this great but worldly minded century was also the century of outstanding conversions, including that of Retz. Mme. de Montespan dabbled in witchcraft before coming back to the Church, after which, as Saint-Simon tells us, she distributed her enormous wealth in alms, worked for the poor, wore nails in her belt, garters and bracelets, and, the mischievous memorialist adds, as a supreme act of penance she imposed silence upon her tongue! At Port-Royal there were at least a score of conversions, among whom Antoine Le Maistre, Hamon, Pascal and Racine. In such places as Mont-Valérien, near Paris, Mont-Voiron, in Faucigny, and the forest of Orleans, members of the nobility, the middle classes and former worldly minded priests lived a completely eremitical life. It would be impossible to compile a list of all the converts, even French ones. Rancé, the Duchesse de Longueville, the noble house of the Contis, the shadowy figure of Mlle. de la Vallière—all these are well-known personages. Eustache de Beaufort, Antoine de Chanteau, Gaston de Fieubet, chancellor to Queen Marie-Thérèse, Louis de Bailleul, a president of the High Court, the Chevalier de

Reynel, one of Turenne's lieutenants, and many others besides left everything to spend their lives in a cloister. Though the breach between God and
the world may sometimes be flagrant, it is very often mended in this way.

There are others to whom the word "conversion" may hardly be appropriate, but whose death was utterly and magnificently Christian. We have
already described the exemplary death of Louis XIV himself. The last hours
of Michel Le Tellier, the great Condé, the Comte de Bussy, Montausier and
many others were no less splendid. Two weeks before La Fontaine died he
wrote to a friend: "Dying is nothing, my friend, but do you realize that I
must appear before God?" When Colbert was almost at his last gasp he
received a letter from the king, and upon his wife asking him if he wished
to reply to it he answered calmly: "There is plenty of time for that; I am
thinking of my answer to the King of Kings." The vicar of the church of
Saint-Eustache told Colbert that the parishioners were praying for his
recovery. Colbert interrupted him: "No, Father, not that. Let them beg of
God to have mercy upon me." A society which thus practised "the art of
dying" must be a profoundly Christian society. How wrong was Vauvenar-
gues when he said: "Nothing can be more misleading than to judge a man's
life by the way he dies." The contrary is true: the Christian life is best judged
at the moment of death.

Thus the facts contradict the gloomy assertions of Father Mersenne and
the two great ladies of the "Devout" circle. If we examine further we shall
see evidence of the existence of faith. The frequent reception of the Sacraments, resumed during the preceding period, became more or less general.
After a very careful investigation G. Le Bras[4] concluded that the practice of
frequent Communion was universal at the beginning of the eighteenth century, and he was inclined to think that it never had been more general than
during the period between 1660 and the Revolution. There is evidence[5] that
in the diocese of Séez, for instance, the number of those who received Holy

---

4. G. Le Bras: *Introduction à l'histoire de la pratique religieuse* (Paris, 1942), especially I,
    95, and II, 24.
5. The position is examined by Father Flament in *Revue d'histoire de l'Église de France*
    (July–December 1955), p. 235.

308 Communion frequently was considerable. And elsewhere nearly everybody made their Easter duties. In Spain many confessors counselled daily
Communion. Salazar had to protest against "inordinate frequentation of
the Sacraments." In France the Jansenist Arnauld, whose treatise on *Frequent Communion* made such a stir, was not alone in demanding that no
one should approach the Sacraments without serious preparation. The arguments raised by the subject indicate the intense interest it aroused.[6] It is true
that the excessive strictness of the followers of Port-Royal would eventually
end in keeping scrupulous souls from Holy Communion; but abstention
would certainly not result from indifference.

The enormous amount of spiritual literature produced was another sign
of intense devotion. Evidence of this is to be found even today in the attics
of country houses and on the shelves of second-hand bookshops along the
Seine embankments. One out of every three or four of those little calf-bound
books are books of piety published during the Great Century: Lenten sermons by Bourdaloue and Massillon; methods of mental prayer by Father
Pomey, Father Nepveu and Father Nicolas; Letoumeux's *Année Chrétienne*
and his *Histoire de la vie de Jésus-Christ* (1673), Little Offices, *Élévations*—
spiritual works of every description. And their success with the public was
extraordinary. The *Exercice spirituel* which three anonymous authors dedicated to the wife of Chancellor Séguier in 1664 went into innumerable
editions; a hundred thousand copies were printed of the *Heures catholiques*
(1685), by Harlay de Champvallon—for the publication of which God will
forgive him much. *Lives of the Saints* on the model of those compiled by
Bishop Vialart de Herse were to be found everywhere, and the *Bible* by Le
Maître de Sacy was in every good library. How can we doubt the faith of a
public which so nourished the soul?

Included among this spiritual literature was the Catechism, a compact
and very useful manual of Christian instruction which became widely used.

---

6. The following figures from a statistical survey made at the Jesuit college in Molsheim,
   Alsace, are significant: in 1650 there were seven thousand Communions a year; in
   1670, twenty-one thousand six hundred and forty-one, and in 1706, twenty-three
   thousand.

It began to spread throughout the Church immediately after the Council 309
of Trent. At that time an attempt was made to adapt for use by the general public the larger Catechism compiled by the Fathers. Canisius launched
his Catechism throughout all the German-speaking countries. The great
reformers attached enormous importance to the catechetical method of
teaching in book form, intended for the general Catholic public rather than
for the use of parish priests. One after another the bishops caused Cate-
chisms to be produced for the adults and children of their dioceses, notably
Rheims, Luçon, Bordeaux, Toulouse, Rodez, Vabres, Châlons and Agen.
By way of experiment an inter-diocesan Catechism was introduced for the
three Sees of Luçon, La Rochelle and Angers, but unfortunately it had Jansenist tendencies. Generally speaking these little books were a success; the
questions put became more and more precise and the answers were short
and arresting. The catechesis on feast days began to acquire liturgical significance. The best of these works was the one by Bossuet, which d'Astros used
as a model when he composed his *Impérial Catechism* in 1806.

Many earnest people strove to maintain the popularity of these pious
works and to foster the faith which they taught. Pilgrimages were almost as
successful then as they had been in the Middle Ages. Houses for Retreats
continued to increase; they developed under the twofold influence of the
Jesuits and the Recollects,[7] and continued under the Lazarist Fathers. Much
of the initial success of Port-Royal was due to the retreatants who congregat-
ed there. We know for certain that the mission and retreat given at Vannes in
1695 was attended by 2,436 men and 2,519 women. Saintly people desirous
of assisting each other in the attainment of spiritual perfection, succouring
the unfortunate, or uprooting vice, joined the "Associations Apostoliques"
(some of whose members had belonged to the Company of the Blessed Sacrament)[8] or the Congregations of Our Lady. These societies were directed
by the Jesuits and the Lazarists. Ordinary layfolk gave proof of remarkable
piety: in many a church in Paris and Rome men and women watched every

7. See Volume 1 of this work, Chapter II, p. 135.
8. See Volume 1 of this work, Chapter II, p. 122.

night before the Blessed Sacrament which was always exposed for adoration. Many of them, too, wore some scapular, or even a hair shirt. During the day-time the faithful were to be seen spending long hours at prayer in the churches, bowing down five or six times in succession and then going to kiss devoutly the feet of the crucified Christ. Faith was more demonstrative then than it is today. When a number of people came together they would begin to recite the litanies, despite the opposition of a section of the hierarchy who feared that these praises might be recited parrot-fashion. New litanies were always being composed; among them the Litany of the Holy Angels, the litanies of Providence so much admired by Jean-Jacques Rousseau, and others taken from the Holy Scriptures.

The number of devotions multiplied. The traditional cult of the Blessed Sacrament never ceased to grow. In some ways it was comparable with royal ceremonial; the beautiful monstrance glittering with gold and precious stones was perfectly in keeping with the ostentation of official ceremonies in the "salutations to the Blessed Sacrament," a practice which was spreading. The Benedictine nuns of the Blessed Sacrament, approved by the Pope in 1661, passed their lives in adoration before the Sacred Host with remarkable fervour. There is even a record of a "clock of the Blessed Sacrament" having been invented by a Carmelite friar; it automatically summoned the people to prayer at certain hours in order that they might atone for offences committed against the Sacrament of the Altar. The Oratory recommended devotion to the Child Jesus as perfectly representing that childlike spirit to which the Kingdom of Heaven has been promised. Devotion to the Sacred Heart, the importance of which will be seen shortly, arose from several quarters. Devotion to Our Lady continued to grow. In 1683 Innocent XI instituted the feast of the Holy Name of Mary; and in 1716 the feast of Our Lady of the Rosary was extended to the whole Church. In Germany a few pious women in attendance upon the Empress Eleanora of Neuburg, third wife of the Emperor Leopold, began to dedicate to Mary the month of May, the loveliest of the year, and at Naples a number of ladies in the parish of Santa Chiara pressed the clergy to establish the practice. It soon spread to the whole Church. Some writers are of opinion that there is a danger

of affectation in certain forms of Marian cult. Among these were Father
Crasset, and especially Father Windenfeld, whose good intentions carried
him so far that his writings were placed on the Index; but there is no doubt
that devotion to Mary is a great help to piety, and assists countless souls to
remain pure and humble. St. Louis-Marie Grignion de Montfort was fully
alive to the fact, and became the staunch champion of devotion to Mary.

Christians of the classical period could not doubt that the Blessed Virgin had a special interest in their era, for they knew that high in the Alpine
valley of Laus, where numerous miracles occurred, the Mother of God had
deigned to appear to a humble shepherdess, Benoîte Rencurel, and had
repeated her visits over a period of fifty-four years, from 1664 to 1718.

3. DECLINE OF MYSTICISM AND GROWTH
OF DEVOTION TO THE SACRED HEART

A profound and lively faith was apparent therefore throughout the seventeenth century. We cannot, however, help noticing the change that took
place as the great century of spiritual revival merged into the century of
Louis XIV. After what we have seen it would be an exaggeration to talk
of spiritual decline or decay; but there were several definite signs of an
approaching weakening in intensity.

The spiritual tide still flowed vigorously, but it was less lively than
hitherto: it ceased to race. The problem affected France more than any
other country because she had remained the spiritual guide of the entire
West until about 1660. Up to that time a number of mystics who were also
extraordinary men of action had been hard at work, but in the succeeding
period there were scarcely any. They had their followers, but these lacked
creative qualities. The spiritual men of those years profited from the lessons
of their predecessors. Bossuet and Fénelon were writers of genius, but they
were not saints.

The personal rule of Louis XIV had begun in a very different atmosphere from that of his father, and by that time such great spiritual leaders

312   of the preceding period[9] as Bérulle, Vincent de Paul and Olier were either dead or about to disappear from the scene. That wonderful Ursuline nun Marie de l'Incarnation had gone to die in far-off Canada; Father Surin was fighting his last fight against the Devil in the haze of madness; for Maria d'Agreda the day of the great awakening was drawing near. Of all that glorious cohort John Eudes alone remained, having laid the theological foundations of the devotion to the Sacred Heart.

There was no lack of spiritual men, even mystics of some consequence, but they were disciples rather than masters. Along the path traced by Father Chardon came Father Piny, the apostle of pure love, and Father Massoulié, an ascetic rather than a mystic. After Louis Lallemand, whose *Doctrine spirituelle* was published by his followers in 1695, came Fathers Nouet and Crasset of the Society of Jesus, men of no mean spiritual qualities. It was Father Crasset who guided the humble and sensitive soul of Mme. Helyot in the way of holiness. That saintly woman would buy the wares of flower-girls so that she might have the opportunity to speak to them of God; and her radiant holiness changed her commonplace husband into a mystic who wrote some extremely beautiful meditations. Later came Father de Caussade (1675–1751). His admirable *Instructions spirituelles* defended mysticism when it was most bitterly attacked, and upheld the principle of "Surrender to Divine Providence." Among the Carmelites was René de Saint-Albert, who taught the prayer of simplicity; he had two serious competitors in Portugal—Joseph of the Holy Ghost and Anthony of the Holy Ghost, and in Spain another Joseph of the Holy Ghost, who was General of his Order. Father Philippe de la Trinité was a theorist rather than a mystic but all were inspired by the writings of St. John of the Cross. Perhaps the most outstanding fact was the reappearance in Italy of a spiritual school, whereas scarcely anyone of note emerged during the preceding period other than St. Joseph of Copertino. Among those who occupied a leading place in the band of spiritual writers were the stigmatic Franciscan nun St. Veronica Giuliani of Turin, Blessed Sebastiano Valfre, Blessed Gregorio Barbarigo, who deserves

---

9.   See Volume 1 of this work, Chapter II, p. 153.

to be called the Charles Borromeo of Padua, Cardinal Giovanni Bona, and above all St. Leonard of Port Maurice, O.F.M., whose activities belong more especially to the following epoch.[10] In short, the only figures comparable with such leaders as Bérulle, St. Vincent de Paul, J. J. Olier and St. John Eudes, from the point of view of experience and influence on their age, are Louis-Marie Grignion de Montfort (1673–1716) and St. Margaret Mary Alocoque (1647–1690), a sister of the Visitation. The former did magnificent work as a missionary, was a mystic of a high order and had a great devotion to Our Lady. St. Margaret Mary led a wonderful life of prayer in her convent at Paray-le-Monial, and gave the world the devotion to the Sacred Heart of Jesus.

More disturbing than the decrease in the number of great spiritual men and women was a kind of backward pull on spiritual life, occasioned by a violent conflict between two hostile concepts.

From the earliest Christian ages various methods have been devised to help souls in their ascent to God. Some have insisted upon asceticism, on the necessity for man to learn in the agony of his soul to understand his own profound wretchedness, and to subdue his flesh and his mind. Others, relying on the truth that "God is Love," believe that if love is sufficiently strong in a man's heart it will eradicate his sinfulness and enable the soul to soar towards God. Genuinely spiritual-minded writers know that both ways are inseparable; the "purgative way" precedes the "mystic way," and no one can hope to reach the heights until he has conquered himself. This view was natural to such saints as Francis de Sales, Vincent de Paul, Teresa of Avila and John of the Cross. But from about 1660 antagonism between the two tendencies became more marked, possibly because Cartesian rationalism had accustomed men's minds to distrust the irrational or because the austere morals of the Jansenists emphasized the abyss between human and divine virtues. It was certainly due in part to the excesses of the Quietists, disciples of the mysticism of pure love—the allegedly "quick way" to

---

10. See Henri Daniel-Rops, *The Church of the Classical Age: The Era of Great Splintering* (Providence, RI: Cluny, 2024), Volume 2, Chapter V.

314 God.[11] An anti-mystic reaction was unleashed. Maria d'Agreda's *Mystic City of God* was condemned by the Holy Office in 1681, reinstated by Innocent XI, then condemned by the Sorbonne. The attacks became more violent against the "easy methods of prayer" as advocated by Father Pomey, Father Nepveu and others, against the Viennese writer Avancini's *Life of Christ*, and other suspect authors. It required three lively treatises by the Augustinian Father Nicole, a prominent member of Port-Royal, to hammer those whom he described as visionaries. Bossuet and the Jesuit Bourdaloue joined the fight and in turn opposed the "short way." The true mystics were thus compromised by the Quietists and were engulfed in their defeat, with the result that their popularity waned and they eventually suffered a veritable eclipse that lasted until our own era. The fact that between 1687 and 1799 Rome condemned no less than eighty spiritual works demonstrates the extent of the hostility.

On the other hand the ascetic tradition ran the risk of deviating as a result of Jansenism. It was not perhaps the doctrine of the Bishop of Ypres that mattered in this domain so much as the interpretation that the Abbé of Saint-Cyran[12] characteristically drew from it. Under the influence of the "ascetics" Christian experience became austere, severe almost to the point of being unnatural. The sense of sin, which, as we have seen,[13] was so profound at the beginning of the century, may very well be stimulated to the point of exaggeration. Jansenism coloured the faith of countless souls even in those circles in which it failed to score success. There is an undoubted grandeur in the stern demands of Christianity. Of course it was a splendid thing that so many souls in classical times should have been able to say in their distress, as did Mme. de Sévigné: "What is my position in relation to God? What have I to give Him? What can I hope for? Am I worthy of heaven, or have I deserved hell?" But was it right to deny the soul that great upsurge of love that might whisk it away from its uncleanness and cast it

11. See below, Chapter VI, pp. 467ff.
12. See below, Chapter VI, especially p. 430ff.
13. See Volume 1 of this work, Chapter II, p. 132.

at the feet of God? This rigid tendency threatened to harden the Christian experience and render it inaccessible to even a modest awareness, and for that reason the so-called "casuistical" Jesuits fought against it. It also runs the risk, as will be seen in the long dramatic struggle against Jansenism, of restraining the faithful from approaching the Sacraments, on the ground that they are unworthy: a dangerous incline that provides an excuse for all sorts of weaknesses. And what was left to prevent the spiritual life from collapsing when the tragedy of Jansenism had more or less discredited the ascetic approach?

We have a striking example of this profound crisis of the Christian soul in the manner in which devotion to the Sacred Heart, the most providential acquisition of the classical century, asserted itself; it was the greatest mystical fact of the era. The devotion has become so well established today that we are apt to overlook completely that for a long time it stood as a sign of contradiction within the Church. The origins of the cult go far back. St. Augustine had already said that the heart of Jesus, pierced by the soldier's lance, shed its blood for the remission of men's sins. In the Middle Ages St. Bernard, Guillaume de Saint-Thierry, Richard de Saint-Victor, and later St. Mechtilde, St. Gertrude, St. Anthony of Padua, and later still Tauler and Suso, had spoken of the heart of Jesus as a refuge and a shelter offered to the poor heart of man. The more ascetic saints—Lutgard, Angela of Foligno, Catherine of Sienna—stressed the need to study the heart of Jesus in order to live better, rather than the personal relationship of the Christian to Christ, as one heart to another. During the sixteenth century devotion to the Sacred Heart flowed like a subterranean stream through almost the whole of Catholic thought. It came to view in the lives of Blessed Louis de Blois, St. Ignatius of Loyola, St. Peter Canisius, St. Francis Borgia, the Venerable Louis of Granada, St. Teresa and many others. St. Francis de Sales spoke of it to his Sisters of the Visitation in terms which suggested the devotion that would soon come to birth. Already the cult existed among the Carmelites in Liège, in the convent of Unterlinden in Colmar and in the Chartreuse at Cologne, where John Justus Lanspergius was its zealous advocate.

St. John Eudes, who founded an Order,[14] established seminaries, and was a tireless missioner and reformer of the clergy, was also the great apostle of the Sacred Heart in the seventeenth century. As a result of long meditation, a deepening of his faith and the grace of interior light he came to see in the flesh of the Heart of God made man the symbol of the uncreated love of the Almighty for His creature. In the Divine Heart he discovered the great mysteries of Christianity: Creation, the Redemption. Through an understanding of this Heart he approached the Real Presence in the Holy Eucharist. It compelled men to desire to make reparation for the indignities and sufferings which sin has inflicted upon it. Filled with this grandiose idea, which indeed profoundly sums up the whole Christian theology, St. John Eudes composed his beautiful Office of the Sacred Heart in 1670. Two years later he established the Feast of the Sacred Heart in the houses of his Society. Thirty years previously he had already instituted a feast of the Heart of Mary.

This devotion was theological in character; it could never have emerged from any organization of limited scope, or from any "Third Order" of the Sacred Heart, had not Margaret Mary Alocoque, the humble nun of Paray-le-Monial, been favoured with extraordinary graces. Christ appeared to her, spoke with her, commanded her—an "abyss of unworthiness and ignorance"—to "spread the flames of His burning charity." The Heart of Christ, "encircled by a Crown of Thorns and surmounted by a Cross," would be exposed for the veneration of Christians "as the supreme effort of His love on behalf of the ransomed world." These revelations were repeated three times between 1673 and 1675.

Devotion to the Sacred Heart was suddenly to assume extraordinary proportions. Millions of Catholics would repeat throughout the centuries the tremendous words of Christ to Margaret Mary: "Behold this Heart which has so loved men." But it did not happen immediately.

The epoch proved to be stubbornly opposed to revelations of this kind. At first her superiors treated St. Margaret Mary as though she were mad. Father de la Colombière was replaced; as Superior of the Jesuit house at

---

14. See Volume 1 of this work, Chapter II, p. 91.

Paray he had directed her soul, and declared his belief in the truth of the revelations. Father Croiset, a teacher at Lyons who took over the nun's instruction, was also transferred elsewhere; and such was the universal distrust of
mystics and everything connected with the theory of "pure love" that his
book was placed on the Index. An attempt made in 1697 to induce Rome to
recognize the feast of the Sacred Heart failed. Margaret Mary died in 1690;
she had never ceased to repeat that God had charged her with a mission, and
that the "adorable Heart" would reign over the world. But she did not live
to see the triumph of that devotion to which she had dedicated her life. She
only just managed to see the devotion adopted in a few convents of the Visitation, and a few confraternities of the Sacred Heart approved and enriched
with indulgences. Wherever rigorists were to be found they put obstacles in
the way of this mystical devotion. We are surprised to find that even Bossuet, whose voice might have trumpeted the good news abroad, did not press
this intensely theological and profoundly moving devotion upon his age.
Such a lack of appreciation clearly points to the anguish of the Christian
conscience. Yet the ascetic and the mystic meet in two prayers which sum
up the whole devotion to the Sacred Heart of Christ: "O God, who joinest
together in one will the hearts of Thy faithful, grant that nations may love
Thy commandments"; and "Jesus, meek and humble of Heart, make our
hearts like unto Thine."[15]

---

15. Opposition to the devotion to the Sacred Heart continued well beyond the seventeenth century. In 1720, at the time of the great plague in Marseilles, the Bishop
of Belzunce consecrated his diocese to the Sacred Heart and introduced the feast.
Despite his earnest and repeated entreaties Rome, suspicious of anything resembling
inordinate mysticism, refused to approve the devotion. It was not until 1765 that
Clement XIII approved it at the request of the Polish bishops. Maria Leczinska, a
Pole who became Queen of France, was then able to spread the devotion throughout the country. But even then it was permitted, not prescribed. Moreover, when
an attempt was made to establish the devotion in Paris, incidents were provoked by
Jansenists who, at their "synod" held at Pistoie in 1786, described the devotion as
idolatrous. It was not until 1856 that Pius IX extended the Feast of the Sacred Heart
to the Universal Church. The process of beatification of Margaret Mary was opened
in 1714, interrupted, and then reopened in 1819. She was not beatified until 1864,
and not canonized until 1920. It remained to our epoch to interpret the true meaning
of this devotion. This Pius XII expressed in glowing terms in his Encyclical *Haurietis
Aquas* on the occasion of the centenary of the feast in 1956.

4. FAITH AND THE WORLD: THE THEATRE

SOCIETY may be undivided in its belief in Christianity, but the extent to which that belief reacts on morals remains an eternal problem; so prone is man's sinful nature never to live fully in accordance with the demands of faith and conscience that no era has yet been able to solve the problem. Racine's famous lines, inspired by St. Paul and St. Augustine, remain true in any century:

> *"Mon Dieu, quelle guerre cruelle,*
> *Je trouve deux hommes en moi,*
> *Je ne fais pas le bien que j'aime,*
> *Et je fais le mal que je hais."*[16]

In considering that profoundly Christian society we must not be surprised to encounter some very dark background shadows in the picture. The progress made during the preceding period was undoubtedly maintained, and the savage cruelty of the upper classes no longer existed. Though the practice of duelling had not altogether disappeared it was at least less common; and moral behaviour had improved. But there still remained much to be done. The scandal consequent upon the conduct of Louis XIV and other European sovereigns did not tend to encourage virtue. Passions were violent and instincts wild. The criminal use of poisons was evidence enough.

Among the mass of the people ordinary faults were widespread. If we are to accept the verdict of many bishops of the period we must believe that debauchery and drunkenness were common among Christian people. Every occasion provided an opportunity for merrymaking: Sundays, fairs, even pilgrimages and the feasts of patron saints. The events at Séez, described by Daquin, were exactly similar to those which Cardinal Le Camus mentions as having taken place in Grenoble, and to those at Autun which caused such

---

16. "What a cruel war, my God, is waged between the two men within me; I do not the good that I love, but the evil that I hate."

pain to Roquette. In Bavaria a pastoral letter criticized the conduct of some who took part in a pilgrimage to the shrine of Our Lady at Altötting. In Italy the brawls and free fights which broke out at every opportunity caused great indignation. Superstition was rampant; there was no country in which people did not believe in witches and sorcerers. "To get a true picture of the ridiculous superstitions prevailing and foolish practices of every description resulting from ignorance and simplicity," writes a contemporary, "one has to know something of our country people and above all the peasants in our most outlying provinces." Superstition permeated the whole of Christendom, and many bishops had to take steps to check the stupid worship of relics and images. Bayle, author of the famous *Dictionnaire*, was obviously exaggerating when he wrote that "the devil indeed put his shoulder to the wheel to turn religion, which is the finest thing in the world, into a mixture of foolishness, eccentricity, nonsense and appalling crimes." But perhaps he was not altogether wrong.

Such dark shadows, however, were not the worst of the evils. They have always existed, and those who see irregularities in everything, as a few pious bishops were apt to do, might have had an almost professional tendency to exaggerate them. St. Augustine says that the work of the Holy Spirit in the Church is accomplished slowly, almost unconsciously, but without interruption. It must be allowed time in which to become effective. Here we must draw attention to a tendency characteristic of the age, but one which in a sense was more disturbing than the drunken squabbles and sexual indulgence of the peasants.

We might describe this tendency as a growing distinction—at least in certain circles—between religion and life. The real conflict, denounced by so many preachers from the pulpit, lay between "the world" and faith. Such was indeed the essence of the struggle between Christianity, which strove to remain one in its teaching and universal in its scope, and those who in different ways aspired to limit its activities to a restricted field. It consisted in allowing preachers and spiritual directors to intervene in some spheres of life (even though their advice was rarely followed) and excluding a great part of man's life from ecclesiastical jurisdiction.

This was diametrically opposed to the teaching of St. Francis de Sales, whose whole purpose was to combine Christian faith and life into a single entity, even in its lesser aspects and activities, and thus enable the soul to weave the thread of small virtues in the factory or the kitchen, in the court or in the shop. That conception of Christianity was now threatened: one might be a Christian without having to live entirely as a Christian. The people had before them the example of the Great King himself, a convinced believer whose behaviour was questionable from many points of view. There was a definite tendency even among the best people to confine religion to the seclusion of the inner man, a propensity fostered by the spiritual atmosphere of the early part of the century, and resulting in a kind of deep-seated cleavage. It is thus possible for a very lively faith to go hand in hand with an attitude of mind that is substantially non-Christian. Many chronicles of the period bear witness to the danger of formalism. "All people know of religion is based on confraternities, indulgences and congregations," wrote Cardinal Le Camus in a letter in which he condemned "the love of pleasure and luxury among all classes." There existed a type of casuistry which allowed men to think they could save their souls by making some sort of compromise with human frailty. At court excellent Christians (Mme. de Sévigné, for example) were proud to be seen frequenting the *salon* of Ninon de Lenclos, who was notorious for his intrigues and his atheism. Among the middle class, who were becoming increasingly important, there existed an economic and business morality that deviated more and more from the Christian moral code. The Jansenists failed completely in their attempt to secure the condemnation of loans against interest. A type of social morality with which medieval Christianity was imbued began to part company with religion, and the time had not yet come when great popes would raise their voices against this state of affairs. Class selfishness was growing; it would become manifest in the eighteenth century, which was to fall a victim to the evil. Society was hardening, becoming more segmented and less inclined to charity. Massillon was right when he wrote: "Without exactly losing our faith we allow it to weaken within us, and make no use of it." Such was the advent of the modern world with its dechristianized élites and its great evils—"Money has appropriated the Kingship of God."

We shall see that the cleavage between faith and life was perceptible in literature and art. To be a Cornelian hero it was not essential to be a Christian; with the exception of Polyeucte the characters of Corneille's plays, so jealous of honour, so prone to vengeance, possess none of the evangelical virtues. Neither is Christianity to be found in the passion of Racine's heroes and heroines. The author of *Phèdre* resorted to some extremely skillful arguments to persuade his old masters of Port-Royal that his tragedy really illustrated their own moral theories! Too many classical writers convey the impression that they have raised a barrier between their faith and their art, so that the former may not intrude upon the latter. La Fontaine is an example: the "moral" in most of his fables runs counter to the precepts of the Gospel. Among others, La Rochefoucauld and Mme. de La Fayette tacitly advance the theory that reason is sufficient to make a lady; Christian morality is not rejected outright, but its repudiation is implied by omission.

Nothing emphasizes this separation more than the famous dispute that arose over the theatre and was debated so passionately, especially in France. The Fathers of the Church condemned the theatre during the era of the decadent Roman Empire, when the stage served to parade scurrility. By the Middle Ages the theatre had so successfully made its peace with the Church that it took its subjects from religious themes, and was able to stage its plays in the porches of cathedrals. But the "mystery plays" gradually deteriorated. They declined from the comic to clownery; they parodied the creed and made fun of the hierarchy. Some restrictive action was necessary, and the Paris Parliament forbade them in 1548. Official censure embraced the whole theatre despite really serious attempts by several responsible people, including Richelieu, to narrow it down. In other Catholic countries, such as Spain, there was no censure whatever. The tradition of the Spanish mystery play was maintained by Calderon de la Barca (1600–1681) with his *Auto di Nascimiento* and *Farsa del Sacramento*, rich in symbolism in which his dramatic genius was placed at the service of the Catholic faith. "Devout comedies" combined sermons with biblical plots or with themes taken from the lives of the saints, and they met with enormous success.

322   In France, where the craze for the theatre was unbelievable, the position was extremely odd. The halls were packed, the actors were earning money, leading actors and actresses became celebrities, and tragedies and comedies were given at court. At the same time the official attitude of Christianity was such that all plays and players were absolutely condemned. The combined influence of the Company of the Blessed Sacrament and Port-Royal undoubtedly explains the rigid attitude adopted. In 1666 Nicole described "poets of the theatre" as poisoners of the public, and likewise condemned writers of novels. A similar attitude was evinced by the Protestant synods. The production of Molière's plays *Tartuffe*, *École des Femmes* and *Don Juan* let loose a storm of protest. In 1693 the Theatine Father Caflaro published a letter in which he discussed the question whether plays should be allowed or absolutely forbidden. Bossuet replied with his *Maximes et réflexions sur la comédie*, and the least one can say is that his language was not temperate. Bossuet regarded all plays as depraved: Molière was soundly trounced. The *Rituel parisien* excommunicated actors by name,[17] and, as we know, Molière's remains were refused the right of Christian burial. The parish priest of Saint-Barthélemy, referring to Molière, said publicly: "He is a devil in man's clothing, and should be burned." The King of France, however, discountenanced these outbursts; he was godfather to one of Molière's sons, and publicly encouraged plays. Meanwhile Rome, where comedy flourished, declined to join in this hostility. The result was that all the Italian comedians in Paris professed to be the Pope's subjects in order to escape excommunication!

This vigorous condemnation achieved no result after all; perhaps because it was too severe, in which case the responsibility for the rupture between religion and life lies with the authorities rather than with the Christian people. "What a strange situation," exclaimed La Bruyère, "when a crowd

---

17. Excommunication was not a mere matter of form. "In order to receive the Last Sacraments actors had to read a statement renouncing their profession. Some had not the courage to do so. The case of Mlle. Champmeslé is touching. She refused to repudiate her past, and declared that it was noble to remain true to one's art to the last. 'If I get well I wish to return to the theatre.' It was only a few hours before her death, and probably because there was no hope of recovery, that she yielded." A. M. Carré's *L'Église s'est-elle réconciliée avec le théâtre?* (Paris, 1956).

of Christians of both sexes gather together in a hall to applaud a crowd of   323
actors under sentence of excommunication!" Chalucet, Archbishop of Toulouse, acted more logically when in 1702 he excommunicated the audience.
Fortunately the Nuncio, who enjoyed the theatre, was then resident in Paris.

5. THE VOICE OF THE PULPIT

SOCIETY did not, however, lack advice and warnings during the Great
Century. In fact, one of the most striking features of the epoch is the
important part played by preaching. If it were not impertinent one might
say that the success of the pulpit competed with that of the stage. As great
an audience listened to those who "made man tremble under the judgments
of God" as there were spectators who laughed at the pranks of Scapin and
the cryptic profanity of Don Juan. The writers of great sermons were as
famous as the comedians and the tenors; some of their names are legendary.
The miracle of their eloquence was discussed in the streets and in the news-
sheets. At the end of a sermon by Massillon on the Last Judgment the whole
congregation rose as though he, the supreme judge, were about to place the
elect on his right and the damned on his left. It is impossible to exaggerate
the importance of pulpit oratory during the classical period. If it reflects the
spiritual maladies which still remained to be cured it was without doubt one
of the chief instruments, perhaps *the* chief, in the transformation of morals.

The phenomenon was general, for all the great Catholic countries had
illustrious preachers at that time. In Italy the Jesuit Paolo Segneri (1624–
1694) joined the conflicts against Quietism and Probabilism. His limpid
and tasteful eloquence nearly always avoided the comical buffoonery then
fashionable. The Capuchin Giovanni Francesco d'Arezzo, who later became
Cardinal Casini, lashed his audiences so vigorously that we are inclined to
wonder whether his words can have been really effective. In Portugal Father
Antonio Vieira (1608–1697), another Jesuit, was for a long time a great
missionary in Brazil; he returned to his own country, where he stirred vast
crowds. In Spain Father Tirso Gonzalez, who became General of the Society

of Jesus, and Don Jaime y Cordoba, nicknamed "Father of the Poor," both reacted against the bombastic and pompous style of eloquence; while the Augustinian de Carayon went so far as to say during the funeral oration of a queen that "the very moon has gone into mourning so that human beings may don their black"! The fashion in Germany contrasted with the French classical taste; sermons were sentimental, little concerned about logic and enriched with legend and symbolism. A very successful exponent of this *genre* was the Augustinian Ulrich Megerle (1642–1709), who in religion bore the name Abraham of Saint Clare; he was the official preacher at the court of Vienna, and his collected sermons on "Judas, the Master Rogue" are still read today. More popular orators were Rauscher, Pursel and Knelling, who added a pleasant touch of humour to the sentimental.

But it was in France that pulpit oratory reached its zenith. Preachers had the advantage of an almost universal language that had reached an unprecedented state of perfection to which they themselves had contributed; and their audiences were growing more and more appreciative of lucidity and finesse in sacred eloquence, which had attained a level never before known. The king himself set a high value on the art, and encouraged it as much as possible by showing marks of favour to the most eloquent among the preachers. He recognized that they held a special place among the great men who contributed to the glory of his reign.

Pulpit oratory had been completely transformed in a short time. The first half of the century was a period of development during which the burlesque type of sermon gradually disappeared. The famous "Little Father André," who died in 1657, used to compare the four evangelists with the four kings in a pack of cards. On one occasion, seeing a few members of the congregation so near the altar that they touched it, he said the biblical prophecy that calves would be seen on the altar was about to be fulfilled!

St. Vincent de Paul taught his Lazarist priests that true eloquence should be direct; that it should strike the heart and the mind and avoid "monumental periods" and booming effects. Fathers Le Jeune and Senault, both Oratorians and later masters at Port-Royal, Saint-Cyran and Singlin, instilled into preachers a sense of gravity and dignity which had so often

been disregarded in the past. The Jesuit Lingendes and Bishop Godeau followed precisely the same idea. It is surprising to find that Cardinal de Retz
did likewise; his Lent and Advent sermons from 1640 to 1648 brought all
Paris to the church of Notre Dame.

By about 1660 pulpit oratory in France was at the height of its success,
though it was not entirely free from serious and obvious defects such as affectation, bad taste and a superficial gloss of erudition. Even the best preachers
did not escape these faults. Bossuet, for example, referring to the fall of great
empires, which he regarded as proof of the intervention of Providence, mentioned those of "Bacchus and Hercules, renowned conquerors of the Indies
and the East." He compared the Blood of Christ with the blood that Catiline
forced his fellow conspirators to drink. On another occasion, when recalling
to mind the tortures suffered by St. Gorgonius, he spoke of the "foul efflu-
via emanating from the fat from his roasting body." But apart from all such
extravagances there were great qualities in those sermons produced in such
profusion. The richness of their style and the soundness of their doctrine were
amazing. Great skill went into the composition, the general arrangement, the
setting out of facts, the realism of the imagery and, among the greatest preachers, the melodious arrangement of words. Bossuet was renowned for the harmony and rhythm of his periods, Bourdaloue for his impact and Fénelon for
the music of his words. And what courage these men had! They denounced
the folly of splendour, sensual pleasures, pride and hardness of heart; they
handled invective and innuendo with a precision that would never be tolerated in our day, despite our professed broadmindedness. Massillon preached
against the thoughtless cruelty of men in high places, who imagined they were
in the world entirely for their own benefit. There is Bourdaloue's famous sermon on impurity, preached before the young Louis XIV, the lover of Mlle. de
la Vallière and Mme. de Montespan. These two sermons were not far removed
from the great biblical reproaches of the Jewish prophets to the guilty kings of
Israel. When the nobles complained to Louis XIV of the acrimony of Mascaron, he replied: "He did his duty; now we should do ours." It is to the credit
of the king, his court and society generally that they actually listened to those
great voices reminding them from the pulpit of their duties towards God.

326   Not all the preachers of the classical age won a lasting reputation. Many who drew the crowds are quite forgotten today; some are mentioned, but not on account of their eloquence. Soanen made a great impression at court before becoming Bishop of Sénez and subsequently involved in the Jansenist affair. Another, the Abbé Charles Boileau (unrelated to "the lawgiver of Parnassus") was so much appreciated by Louis XIV that the king had him elected to the Academy. But who now remembers the Capuchin Father Séraphin, whose improvised sermons, before Massillon's time, electrified the court? Or Father Nicolas of Dijon, another Capuchin, who had the rare gift of making apt quotations from the Scriptures and the Fathers of the Church? There was the Abbé Anselme, who was the fashionable orator at Versailles about the year 1686; Cassagnes and Cotin, whose eloquence took them to the French Academy; and Dom Cosme, who preached as many Lenten sermons at the court as Bossuet did, but whose name was none the less omitted from Cardinal Grente's exhaustive *Dictionnaire des Lettres*. Some there were who did not deserve such unaccountable indifference; the Oratorian Fromentières, for instance, who preached the funeral oration of Anne of Austria and the sermon on the occasion of the taking of the veil by Mlle. de la Vallière; and Father de la Rue, a Jesuit who became an important figure at court from 1687, where he preached the Advent and Lenten sermons for four years running, and pronounced the panegyric upon Bossuet at Meaux. Father Gaillard, another Jesuit, was the last preacher whose sermons the king enjoyed in his old age. The number of preachers of the classical century is inexhaustible. When Father Houdry, himself a prolific preacher, produced a collection of the masterpieces of sacred oratory, the work ran to twenty-three volumes, and even then he had to omit three-quarters of the material.

Of these great men six emerge as having withstood the test of time with varying degrees of success. It is interesting to note, however, that although their contemporaries recognized the greatness of them all, they did not classify them in the order we follow. When the Abbé de Clérambault spoke in praise of Bossuet before the Academy, he said that Bossuet had "allowed his rivals to attain the highest level of eloquence." It was not until the advent of Nisard and the nineteenth-century critics that the Bishop of Meaux was

given his rightful place in literature.[18] The keenest minds, among them La 327
Bruyère, were struck by the "power and magnetism" of Fénelon's oratory
though he was not immediately successful in drawing the crowds.

Whom then did the classical century deem to be the principal representatives of pulpit oratory? One was Fléchier (1632–1710), whose funeral oration for Turenne we so much admire, together with his elegant and polished
style and his "noble church music," those little ornaments which he claimed
would create "a taste for virtue." But he is so often solemn and pompous
that we are inclined to endorse all the criticisms hurled at academic sermons.
Another was Mascaron (1634–1703); the court doted upon him, and Mme.
de Sévigné praised him to the skies. Though his oratory does not leave us
untouched we find him uneven, and he is apt to mistake metaphors for ideas.
Later, towards the end of the reign, we have Massillon (1663–1742). He it
was who preached the funeral oration of Louis XIV, with its famous dramatic exordium, and who continued into the first half of the eighteenth century the great tradition of classical sermons. Voltaire and the Encyclopédistes
would set him in the forefront of pulpit orators. Though Massillon's similes,
hyperboles, paraphrases and antitheses appear to depend upon an extremely
questionable form of rhetoric, he was certainly not lacking in psychological
precision, in critical acumen, and even in lyricism and warmth.

6. THE SEVERITY OF BOURDALOUE

BOURDALOUE was the typical preacher, "the attorney-general of moral
law," as Bishop Calvet remarked. It seemed that his sole vocation, the one
purpose of his life, was to remind his contemporaries of the Commandments

---

18. In ten years (1659–1669) Bossuet preached four "Stations" at the court, that is, no
more than Dom Cosme and one-third of those preached by Massillon. His funeral oration for Henrietta of England was given in a little chapel at Chaillot, while
François Favre preached his at the church of Saint-Denis, and Father Senault the most
important one at Notre Dame. Mme. de Sévigné wrote that she found the sermon
preached by Bossuet for the Profession of Louise de la Vallière "less divine" than that
preached by Fromentières at the clothing of the king's former favourite.

THE CHURCH IN THE CLASSICAL AGE

of God and the demands they make on man. He never relaxed in his determination to point out to man the narrow way, clearly determined by reason and experience, that leads to heaven through the light of faith. For thirty-five years, tirelessly and unflinchingly, he shouldered this responsibility; and indeed without regard for people's feelings. "He strikes out unmercifully," wrote Mme. de Sévigné, "uttering truths right and left.... It is every man for himself! But he goes straight ahead." Indeed nothing could stop him. He denounced the court as "the seat of pride, the centre of corruption, the school of godlessness," a treacherous sea "where the noblest virtues are shipwrecked." He spoke with accents worthy of Amos and Hosea. When the poisoning scandal burst he did not hesitate to refer to it, pointing at Mme. de Montespan, who was still the king's mistress. Those whom he assailed showed their disgust secretly, or at least discreetly. One day when he was ascending the pulpit at Saint-Sulpice, the great Condé sneered: "Look out, gentlemen; there goes our enemy." On another occasion, when Bourdaloue successfully launched one of his "furious attacks against the conscience of his audience," and the congregation had evinced some measure of annoyance, Maréchal de Grammont exclaimed loudly: "*Morbleu!* He's right!"

To say that people ran to hear him speak would be an understatement; they literally fought to get in. They arrived long before the sermon was due to start, and the wealthy had their places kept for them by their lackeys. The atmosphere was rather like that of a theatre before the curtain rises, everybody chatting and calling across to one another. Suddenly the preacher arrived, elbowed his way through the crowd, ascended the steps and appeared high up in the pulpit. There he stood until there was perfect silence, motionless and with eyes closed, praying.[19] At length he opened his eyes and began to speak, softly at first, as if to clear the way. Then he gradually increased his speed, rising to that "thundering and dreadful pitch" described by the journalist Robinet, reaching such a pitch of menace and holy violence that he frequently had to stop and sit for a moment to recover himself.

---

19. This was the pose depicted in Jouvenel's engraving; hence the legend that Bourdaloue learned his subject by heart and spoke with his eyes closed.

"I felt so powerfully attracted by the force and correctness of his arguments," wrote Mme. de Sévigné, "that he staggered me. I could not regain
my composure until he decided to pause." It is impossible not to think of
Bourdaloue when we try to imagine the great esteem in which preachers
were held in classical times. He was born in 1632, at Bourges, where his
father was a counsellor of the présidial court. Bourdaloue was above all else
a Jesuit. Nothing else was of importance. As a student, novice and teacher he received the long and sturdy training that St. Ignatius had planned
for his sons. He represented the Society at its best, in such a way that his
every word and gesture refuted the criticisms of Pascal's *Provinciales*. In him
there was nothing secretive, nothing underhand, no element of guile; still
less did he tend towards the lax or easy-going. He spent most of his time in
the loneliness of a cell devoid of ornament except for a portrait of the king
given him by Louis, which his superiors allowed him to retain. Beneath a
shy exterior he concealed a profoundly intimate spiritual life, as far removed
from the disturbing fantasies of the Quietists as it was from exaggerated Jansenist austerity. He did not confine himself to the preparation and delivering of sermons. "His sublime eloquence," as Lamoignon said, "sprang above
all from his thorough knowledge of the world." A confessor and spiritual
director, he exercised a considerable influence apart from his preaching,
because his life, as Mlle. de la Vallière so wisely said, was "penetrated with
the truths he preached." When he felt the approach of death he expressed a
wish to retire into some secluded house of the Society; but on being told by
his superiors that he was irreplaceable, he yielded and remained at court. He
died, still active, in 1704.

Bourdaloue's art—if art it may be called—was based above all on logic,
fact and absolutely methodical argument. Others might take wing and soar
to such heights of eloquence that they lost contact with the earth; he based
his pathos on pure reason. Bourdaloue usually divided his sermon into three
or four parts, each being subdivided into sections. This arrangement tended
to deprive it of dramatic swing and forceful impact, but it gave the discourse
an admirable orderliness that appealed to his contemporaries—despite
Fénelon, who scoffed at the method. Moreover, Bourdaloue was a moralist

rather than a theologian; too often he neglected to support his arguments with dogmatic facts, but he had a profound knowledge of souls. He was another La Rochefoucauld, lacking the bitterness of the author of the *Maximes*, but possessing his sense of truth. His ability to analyse the human heart, to lay bare its secrets and its frailties great and small, has rarely been equalled. So precise was he in his descriptions that shrewd minds thought they could name the sinners, male or female, whom his pictures conjured up. He might have been really great had he possessed the breadth of view and the abundant intellectual qualities of Bossuet, the sensitiveness and the unflagging curiosity of Fénelon, without mentioning their other gifts of genius. Bourdaloue was a preacher, the greatest of his time, but he was nothing more. Bossuet called him "our master." As far as technique went he was the master of French preaching, and for that reason has survived to the present day. But order and method can be learned; genius cannot.

7. BOSSUET

WHEN we think of Bossuet, the great Bishop of Meaux, whose name stands for all that was Catholic in the classical age, we imagine him first as a preacher, a religious orator. His activities were indeed devoted to these necessary tasks: expounding Christian doctrine, exhorting his fellow men to a better way of life, exalting the truths of religion on great occasions in order to redeem through them the nation's soul.

So too he appears in the full-length statue of him that stands beneath the dome of the French Academy. Such was the pose in which his contemporaries often saw him—grave and reserved, looking straight ahead, his hand extended to emphasise his exordium or his reproach, so obviously engrossed in his sacred task that it would be difficult to imagine him in any role but that of the mouthpiece of God. When we utter his name and remember what he left to posterity we cannot but think first of his oratorical writings. He delivered eleven funeral orations, of which the most famous were those of Henrietta of England and Condé, with their gripping exordia flowing majestically into the body of the subject, like folds of the funereal tapestry that adorned the church; remarkable too were such descriptive passages as the death of the queen and the battle of Rocroi. His innumerable sermons, almost all written up from short notes, still have the power to move us, even though they lack the glamour of his eloquence and the warmth of his presence. Among these were his sermons on the unity of the Church, the "eminent dignity of the poor," and death.

With Bossuet pulpit oratory attained its zenith. Though solidly buttressed by dogma and by his voluminous reading, his words never lost that spontaneity and easy flow which are the hallmarks of great oratory. He developed his thoughts relentlessly and coherently, but without any of the deliberate rigidity that limited the powers of Bourdaloue. Bossuet thus succeeded in contriving a blend of opposite qualities: strength allied with flexibility, conciseness with richness of vocabulary, logic with persuasive warmth. His mood varied; in turn he could be solemn, realistic, lyrical, logical, poetic, didactic and occasionally familiar. His psychological analysis probed to the very depths of the being; his historical references gripped the attention by the force of their relevancy. What consummate art lay in the series of periods, the balanced development of his argument and that "domelike sentence" of which Valéry speaks, rising by stages, each one awakening more deep-toned reverberations, then descending in flowing accents until it reaches the deliberately sought words that bring it to a close in perfect harmony—a powerfully abrupt closure or the whispering echo of a lingering lament.

Bossuet was all that, but he was much more besides. Belonging to those few "who have most superbly made use of the power of speech," he could not confine himself within the limitations of oratory. He was also a writer who possessed the qualities of sensitiveness, imagination, rhythm and precision; he was the greatest historian of his day, a moralist who rivalled La Rochefoucauld and La Bruyère, and a spiritual director comparable with St. Francis de Sales. As a polemist he was the equal of Pascal, and so brilliant that his contemporaries admired him above all as a controversialist. In a way he was also a politician; but at the same time his *Lettres sur l'Amour de Dieu* and his *Methode pour faire oraison de simplicité* show that he was a remarkable spiritual writer. More than anything else he was a doctor, a direct descendant of the Fathers of the Church, among whom he would certainly have been numbered had he lived in their time, for he was a capacious religious thinker, the most solid of his century. He achieved all these things with regal facility; his manifold flexible qualities enabled him to engage in every kind of activity at once, any single one of which would have been sufficient to absorb one mind and fill a lifetime. Behind everything he was and did lay an intensely rich experience of humanity; in consequence he was the guiding light of his era, its witness and its most typical representative. If his intellectual stature is to be measured by the extent of ground he covered, that is to say by the range of his interests rather than by the results he achieved, we may rightly describe Bossuet as a genius. One might hardly have expected genius to spring from a family of provincial magistrates whose ancestors had been vine-growers and cloth merchants; but such indeed were the Bossuets—honest, headstrong, of good reputation and above average intelligence. Jacques Bénigne, the seventh child, revealed great gifts from an early age. He was born on September 27, 1627; his godfather read his horoscope and discovered that a great career awaited him. The child soon confirmed that prophecy. At the Jesuit college in Dijon he proved a serious student, a stickler for Latin and of a piety which his teachers admired. He clearly deserved to bear the family motto "Good Wood Bossuet" inscribed around a twisted vine-plant. He received the tonsure at nine years of age, though not on account of his piety; it qualified him to receive the revenues of a canonry at Metz and involved no religious obligations. His resourceful father, who had settled in that city, managed to secure the dignity for him when he was fifteen years of age. His intellectual qualities were so evident that his parents sent him to the Collège de Navarre at Paris, the teachers' training college of the day, where he made a great impression and became the favourite pupil of Nicolas Cornet, who occupied the chair of theology. At twenty-five Jacques Bénigne became a doctor of the Sorbonne. On the day of his ordination, the same day upon which he presented his thesis, the great Condé himself was present, and he caused general astonishment by a

sermon delivered extempore, as though for fun, during a social evening at
the Hôtel de Rambouillet.

But his new state was no mere game; to him the priesthood was something more than a career. By the time he was fourteen he had read the
Scriptures through, and declared he received from them "a sense of joy and
enlightenment." Later, under the austere Cornet, he acquired a taste for
theology, which he never lost. The turning point was reached at the age of
twenty-one. He was making a retreat in preparation for the subdiaconate
when he experienced a spiritual crisis very much like Pascal's "night of fire."
He came to appreciate the instability of human affairs, and in a sublime
piece of writing set down his anguish and his resolutions. That date was a
milestone in his life; it showed clearly that the greatest conflict of his life was
the one that took place within himself. His reading of the works of Bérulle, and above all his meeting with St. Vincent de Paul, added the finishing
touches. From that eager, ardent lad, as Bossuet described himself, Vincent
formed a man of the Church, a man of God. Bossuet was acquainted with
the atmosphere of Saint-Lazare, having taken part in the Tuesday Conferences[20] at which he later preached; he therefore understood the meaning of
a lived religion and a true priestly vocation. His mind was made up. When
the young doctor learned that his master Cornet was about to offer him
the chair of theology he declined this "open sesame" to an exceptionally
brilliant career. As a zealous priest he assumed the responsibilities of his canonry at Metz, of which he already held the title and revenues.

That was the kind of man he would remain throughout his life. The cast
of his character was clearly outlined in his youth, and though it matured it
never really changed. The artists Mignard, Nanteuil, and later Largillière
and Rigaud, have portrayed him at different ages; but the several paintings
reveal very little change. They all show a healthy balance, self-control, a
robust pride, a kindly disposition with a touch of condescension and a great
deal of confidence in life and in himself. The thick lips and the broad nos-
trils suggest perhaps fulsome appetites, and that his apparent serenity was

20. See Volume 1 of this work, Chapter I, p. 32.

not acquired without a great struggle. But this Burgundian was a healthy fellow, a tireless worker; after a day of priestly duties he could spend half the night wrapped in a bearskin rug, writing letters, sermons and treatises. And he had a healthy mind: logical, precise, with an instinctive dislike of the vague, the doubtful and the morbid; more brilliant than intelligent, but not unduly precocious. He was sensitive, however, and capable of exquisite tact, to which his penitents bore witness; so fundamentally good that his occasional simplicity allowed him to be taken in by the wiles of the wicked—of whom his nephew was one. He was generous at all times except when carried away by the excitement of battle; then, as in his clash with Fénelon, he would lose his sense of proportion and even of charity. He had few other faults apart from his passion for a fight, an inordinate liking for court life, its pomp, its honours and the desire to wield power and influence.[21] Had he been more humble, more meek and more detached from the world, he might have been a saint. He was but a man, yet a man whose greatest merit was to desire to put into God's hands all he did, said and hoped. He was a man of faith.

Faith was the central fact of his character and of his life. He staked his all upon eternity. His faith was simple and direct, rejecting doubt and ambiguity whenever essentials were at issue. Yet it was a lucid faith, sure of its foundations, aspiring to dominate every facet of life and possessing a natural horror of sin. Such a faith was absolutely and wholly Catholic; in other words it was not born of personal cogitation and the arguments of conscience, but of profound adherence to authority and tradition, and of the felicitous sensation of "feeling with the Church." Nothing could be further from Bossuet than the heretical mind. He described a heretic

---

21. He also had a liking for material wealth, money and good living. He owned real estate in Paris, and charged his tenants a high rent. But the famous story, spread by Voltaire, that he was secretly married to Mlle. de Mauléon has been absolutely refuted, especially by Amable Floquet in his *Études sur la vie de Bossuet*, and by Canon Urbain. The truth is that out of sympathy for the lady Bossuet stood surety for her in connection with a loan she raised when buying some shares. The contract was seen by one Jean-Baptiste Denis, a priest who had been driven from Meaux for misconduct, and he confused it—perhaps deliberately—with a marriage contract. See the details of this affair by A. Augustin-Thierry in *Ecclesia* (December 1952).

as "one who has an opinion," and it would have been impossible for him
to hold any opinion that was not within the framework of revealed truth
and dogma. He has often been unjustly described as a Jansenist because
he condemned those who "make the gate of heaven too wide," just as he
condemned those "whose hardness makes piety dry and odious"; but he
tended to be Augustinian and was certainly more inclined to a religion of
fear than to a religion of tenderness. That did not, however, prevent those
quasi-mystical elevations (apparent in his *Méditations sur l'Évangile* and his
Élévations sur les mystères) that led him to "consume his heart in the infinite
depths of love" and enliven his devotion to Christ, Our Lady and the saints.
In short, he was the most solid, the most well balanced of the Christian
thinkers of his day.

Such a man seemed so clearly predestined to wage war on God's behalf
that it appeared quite natural for him to have chosen the career he followed.
He spent seven years at Metz as archdeacon of the Chapter, and was an
enthusiastic propagandist among Protestants and Jews, but he continued to
cultivate his mind in the privacy of recollection. Then he was called upon
to preach in Paris, where six "Stations" (four of them at court) and as many
funeral orations enhanced his renown, and he soon became an outstanding
success. In 1670 he was made Bishop of Condom, though he never resided there; and in the same year he staggered the court with his magnificent
funeral oration on Henrietta of England. A few months later Louis XIV
chose him from a list of a hundred candidates to be tutor to the Dauphin.
It was a difficult task which lasted twelve years, and he performed it with
more zeal than pleasure, more credit than personal satisfaction. In 1681, as
first chaplain to the Dauphin's wife, he was given the bishopric of Meaux;
it was an unassuming see, but near Versailles. Henceforward until his death
he devoted himself to his episcopal duties with the earnestness he applied to
everything he undertook. He supervised the administration of his diocese,
controlled the seminary, presided over meetings of the trustees, prepared a
draft catechism and busied himself with the poor. Meanwhile he remained
the great official orator, always at the service of the court on ceremonial
occasions or when some responsible person was needed to solve a difficulty

or settle a dispute. He was the guide, philosopher and friend of the Church of France and, in a way, of the Great King.

It is difficult to say whether Louis really liked him; but he certainly respected him. As Sainte-Beuve so aptly put it: "They understood each other." Bossuet's character and even the quality of his faith led him to identify himself naturally with the accepted order of things, which seemed to justify his own way of life; and he strove not merely to adhere to that concept of the world which pertained to the principle of monarchy by divine right, but even defended and consolidated it. His *Politique tirée de l'Ecriture sainte* was written with this purpose in view; so was his *Discours sur l'histoire universelle*, in which, by showing God's work through human acts and events, he vindicated a system in which everything was stable, well ordered and based upon obedience and faith. He knew the dangers and limitations of the system, and when royal absolutism ran the risk of compromising through pride the established order of God, Bossuet intervened with the object of preventing a rift and fostering harmony between the two authorities whose responsibility it was under heaven to rule the world. He acted thus in the Gallican crisis.[22] It was through this attitude rather than through his language and style that he showed himself to be the classicist *par excellence*—if it is really true that classicism is the result of a conflict with, or perhaps a victory over, the forces of destruction and disintegration.

Thus the life of Bossuet was a contest; especially after he had shaken off the shackles of his official duties as tutor to the Dauphin and felt free to do battle with anything that threatened the Catholic order, to which he was passionately devoted. He did not lack adversaries; indeed, they were innumerable and powerful. First there was "the world," that looseness of morals which extended even to those circles where one would expect an example of virtue and loyalty. He knew the danger better than anyone, and against the world he "followed his profession conscientiously," as Lanson said, "without brutishness or flattery, without complacency or insolence."

---

22. See above, Chapter IV, p. 282.

The world had its accomplices: casuists, probabilists, laxists and all those 337
impudent theorists who imagined and taught that it was easy to lead a
Christian life. There were also the free-thinkers, whose ideas absolutely
horrified him. Their influence appeared to be spreading; Fontenelle had
just been elected to the Academy. The absurd intellectual pride of incredulity, the irony of the sceptics, the animal-like indifference—all those factors seemed to him as "seditious" as they were shameful. Again, there were
heretics who strove to shatter that unity of the Church which he extolled
in his writings. Finally there were the Protestants, whom he did not hate
but regarded as brothers. For them he had written in his youth his *Exposition de la doctrine catholique*, a small but brilliant book which had stirred
many consciences; it was against the Protestants too that he later wrote his
Histoire des variations des églises protestantes in order to convince them of
their errors.

Up to about 1690 it seemed to Bossuet that he had won all his battles, and that his enemies acknowledged defeat; the king had been won
over, the errors of Probabilism had been condemned, and the Huguenots
were clearly nonplussed by his *Histoire des variations*. Later, however, the
beautiful harmony which seemed to reign as a result of his endeavours
appeared to disintegrate. New perils rose up before him. Suddenly he perceived a danger in the philosophy of Descartes, whom he had approved as
a sound thinker and to whose philosophy he had introduced the Dauphin.
Now he saw the conclusions which unscrupulous men might draw from
it. He exclaimed prophetically: "I see a great combat preparing within the
Church. More than one heresy will spring from the misunderstood principles of Cartesian philosophy." He was also disturbed by Malebranche, the
Oratorian metaphysician, whom he suspected of wishing to reduce ethics
to a mere question of order, eliminating the supernatural and the spirit of
penance, and glorifying a form of liberty which made nonsense of authority and tradition. He considered that, even if the aims of Malebranche
himself were honest, his disciples were plunging headlong into heresy. And
Richard Simon, another Oratorian even more suspect, ventured to apply
the critical method to the Bible, thus "substituting grammar for theology."

On one occasion Bossuet managed to persuade Chancellor Michel Le Tellier to forbid the publication of one of Simon's works, but the adversary repeated his offence and the attack had to be renewed.[23]

Continual strife and his uneasiness at seeing God's order gradually threatened made Bossuet obstinate, almost unfeeling, and his clear-sightedness began to diminish. He failed to perceive that once the vocabulary of Richard Simon's theories was explained, those theories could serve as weapons of Christian apologetic against atheistic criticism. When, under the influence of a book by Father Caffaro, he raged and fumed against the theatre, insulted Molière and included the plays of Corneille and Molière in his condemnation of the Byzantine spectacles, he was unable to recognize that his excessive severity was crippling his own constant endeavour to permeate life with the spirit of Christianity; he was almost forcing Christians to secede. When he published his letter to the Pope on the subject of Chinese idolatries and superstitions, he was unaware that the attitude he adopted against "Chinese rites" and the possibility of establishing a Chinese Church was diametrically opposed to the attitude of St. Paul, who, in order to convert the Gentiles, became "a Greek among Greeks."[24] Finally, when he lent the whole weight of his authority to crush not only Father Lacombe and Mme. Guyon, but even Fénelon, his own disciple, friend and colleague,[25] and when he took up cudgels against the mystics and all the Maria d'Agredas of this world, he failed to see that in condemning mysticism outright he was depriving Christian experience of the precious stones in its crown, and reducing it to a kind of emaciated moralism and dogmatism. It was this lack of understanding, as well as his taste for austerity in religion, that caused him to be too lenient, if not too complacent, towards Jansenism, which was really more dangerous than Quietism. This was noticeable in the Quesnel affair.[26] Undoubtedly these were errors of judgment; they reveal

23. Descartes, Malebranche and Richard Simon are dealt with in *The Church of the Classical Age: The Era of Great Splintering*, Volume 1, Chapter I.
24. See ibid., Chapter II.
25. See below, Chapter VI, p. 490.
26. See below, Chapter VI, p. 503ff.

the limitations of his genius and intellect, but they also suggest that his normal approach to problems was that of one who struggles to hold his ground
rather than to extend his conquests, and that he was a prophet of the past
rather than a creator of the future.[27]

He died eleven years before his king, on April 11, 1704, and thus did
not witness the sudden decay that marked the end of the reign. He died,
not like a saint, but like an upright man in an age when men knew how to
die. Almost his last words were addressed to his secretary, who spoke to
him of his glory: "Enough of this talk. Let us ask pardon of God." Yet he
achieved a renown that has increased with time; for time has eliminated
accidentals from his work and emphasized only the essentials. His glory is
perhaps somewhat cold and pompous—"one of the religions of France," as
Sainte-Beuve said; a glory that failed to recognize the humanity concealed
beneath the solemn exterior, and in which much injustice is blended with
admiration. The noble title given him by Fénelon[28]—the Eagle of Meaux—
describes him perfectly in his steadfastness and courage, in the manner in
which he soars to the heights, or in which he strikes down an adversary. In
short, what we admire in Bossuet is not so much the outstanding figure of
that great court, or even his mastery of the French language, but the man
who fought so hard to promote loyalty to Christian principles, the champion of Christ's cause.

8. THE ANGUISH OF FÉNELON

IT might appear unnatural to rank Fénelon among the great preachers of the
seventeenth century, as though we were approaching him through one of
the lesser aspects of his rich personality. Although he did preach a great deal,
at the *Nouvelles catholiques* at Saint-Cyr, during missions for the conversion

---

27. Joseph de Maistre's criticism is none the less excessively severe: "He flattered the powerful, while the wretchedness of the people never drew a protest from him."
28. "I picture you," he wrote to Bossuet, "in your skull-cap, holding M. du Pin as an eagle
holds a frail sparrow-hawk in its talons."

of Protestants and especially in his own diocese, he could not be included among the leaders of religious oratory of his day. In fact, we have only six of his sermons, firstly because he was in the habit of improvising, and secondly because most of his notes were destroyed in a fire at his palace at Cambrai. His contemporaries, however, admired him as a pulpit orator. "One feels the power and ascendancy of this rare mind," wrote La Bruyère, "whether he preaches spontaneously or whether his sermon has been well prepared." Reading his *Dialogues* on the subject of eloquence generally and pulpit oratory in particular, we are able to appraise the soundness and relevance of his views upon this difficult medium. He makes great fun of those preachers "who speak Latin in French," who are for ever dividing, subdividing and paragraphing (so much for Bourdaluouel), and those who, to avoid appearing second rate, try to be lofty (so much for Fléchier, and perhaps also for Bossuet!). He recommends simplicity, no shoddy brilliance or affectation which is afraid to appeal to the emotions; let the sermon even be passionate, but let it preserve grace, gentleness and harmony, seeking to convince rather than to terrify. His own sermons followed precisely these principles; the flow of the sentence and the persuasive force of the sentiments are in perfect accord, and a touch of lyricism gives life to the argument and softens down the erudition. Such a style of eloquence was rare in his time; it was the forerunner of the form popular today, and it earned for Fénelon the famous title Swan of Cambrai.

Fénelon's dominant position among the preachers of the Great Century was not, however, entirely due to his brilliant gifts. If it is true that the role of those who speak in God's name is to convey His judgment to men and to remind them of their baptismal vows, Fénelon above all others stands out as the living conscience of his era. Bourdaloue, Mascaron, Massillon, and Bossuet in a lesser degree, courageously denounced social evils and the positive failure of society to follow the precepts and spirit of the Gospel; but no one asked himself the question whether from the point of view of Christ's teaching the system of classical Christianity did not contain deficiencies and errors. Fénelon alone, at least among the higher clergy, dared to pass a Christian judgment upon the established order; and though he did

not condemn it outright, he proposed measures which might have made it   341
more Christian. He was affected by the profound crisis of his epoch, probably to a greater extent than Bossuet, because he was more prone to anguish
of the spirit; he appreciated the necessity to overcome the disintegrating
forces which threatened the structure of Christianity. But instead of fighting simply to defend and resist he struggled to build anew and to create. He
looked as passionately to the future as his rival did to the past, and he asked
himself what he should do to keep faith alive in a new kind of world. To
achieve his purpose he looked to a young, daring and conquering form of
Christianity such as he had acclaimed in that splendidly impetuous sermon
on the Calling of the Gentiles—the religion of the Revolution of the Cross,
which addresses itself to the heart.

There is something fascinating about Fénelon as a man. In Bossuet we
admire his genius, his power, the unrivalled balance in his life and thought.
Fénelon is nearer to ourselves. He is more prone to human frailty, is more
apprehensive, more anxious and more delicate. At twenty-one years of age
the young Bossuet solved his spiritual crisis by binding himself so completely to the demands of Christianity that he never again appeared to experience any painful spiritual conflict. Fénelon, on the other hand, spent his
whole life searching for interior peace. He suffered in consequence of his
contradictions. Psychologically he lacked balance: he vacillated between
self-assurance and disgust of self, optimism and despair. This lordly archi-
episcopal duke, owning a wealthy and beautiful diocese, was none the less
unhappy within himself. If he appeared agreeable, kindly and charitable in
the eyes of men, he knew that before God he was full of pride, hardness and
selfishness, "an abyss of subtle defects," and this knowledge overwhelmed
him. He admitted moreover that he did not understand himself: "I cannot
explain my inner self. It escapes me, and appears to be for ever changing. I
have no idea what I am." It was a tragedy, and shows how vain and inadequate were the epithets "tender, charming, refined, changeable, romantic"
with which too many contemporaries have labelled him. It is sufficient, in
any case, to study his portraits, especially those that show the pained and
reticent expression of his old age, to appreciate that he was something more

342 than the charmer who, as Saint-Simon said, "was as careful to win over servants as he was their masters," a handsome man of such noble bearing "that one had to make an effort to avoid looking at him." He possessed gifts quite different from the "finesse, grace, decorum and above all nobility" with which the curt memorialist credited him. His sensitiveness caused him suffering, his ardour provoked anguish of mind and his generosity made him imprudent. He was one of those rare and lofty souls who remain untouched by the temptation to act shabbily or to do anything for personal gain.

With these fascinating qualities went true genius, a profound and brilliant intellect that immediately and instinctively transformed everything it touched. Even in matters that did not necessarily concern an archbishop or even a preacher the attitude he adopted was always the right one, and yet original. For example, the ideas contained in his well-known treatise on the education of girls were so obviously sensible that we might be tempted to regard them as truisms were we to overlook the fact that they now form the basis of our modern teaching practice. He dealt similarly with the French language in his celebrated *Lettre à l'Académie*; he was far ahead of his time when he claimed that historical works should be critical, impartially written and supported by evidence. Unlike Bossuet, who condemned the theatre, he did not altogether disapprove of it; he discriminated between the good and the bad, and the future confirmed the justice of his attitude.

He excelled in almost every field. As a moralist he equalled Bourdaloue; in vision and the niceties of analysis he excelled Bossuet. As evidence of this we have his letters on indolence, on pride and the vanities of the world—all masterpieces of style, fluency and precision. He was an artist and a poet with a lively imagination, but above all he was impressed by the world's beauty—a rare quality in his day, especially among preachers—and very conscious of man's place within that world of beauty. He was much more of a philosopher and metaphysician than Bossuet: in his *Traité de l'existence de Dieu* he set forth brilliantly the traditional arguments and, as a good dialectician, criticized Malebranche forcefully though a little unjustly. A parish priest at Saint-Sulpice accused him of "lacking theology," and others have repeated the charge; and the fact that his *Maximes des Saints* was condemned (in

rather strange circumstances[29]) has caused some writers to pass a hasty judgment. They overlook the twenty or so works produced prior to the Quietist
crisis, and which were never suspect. Those writings "constitute a mass of
mystic theology without precedent"[30]; and his *Dialogues sur le système de
Jansenius* is perhaps the most lucid account ever produced of Jansenist doctrine, and contains its most convincing refutation. These works of Fénelon
may not cover such a vast field as those of Bossuet, but in many respects they
equal Bossuet's in quality. Fénelon lacked the capacity to give his thought
that rigid, unbroken front which his rival achieved naturally; neither did he
succeed in attaining internal unity and intellectual synthesis.

Under such conditions and with his temperament, his deficiencies
and his reverses, how could his life be anything but exceptional, beautiful
and sad, brilliant and, in a way, a failure? Cardinal Grente, one of his most
impartial admirers, has pictured Fénelon "attaining high honours at a single
bound, where he shone and exerted an influence...then, at the summit of his
hopes, his hand outstretched to seize the object of his ambitions, embark-
ing upon a venture...encountering the Church's condemnation and the
king's disfavour...meeting with disappointment...and finding consolation
in magnificent self-sacrifice." The human destiny of François de Salignac de
la Mothe Fénelon was such that he rocketed to great heights, at great speed,
and then crashed cruelly back to earth; but what complexity, what emotional and intellectual adventures, and what interior violence within the space
of that unusual life!

Fénelon was born on August 6, 1651, at the Château de Fénelon. The
earnest zeal with which the thirteen-year-old lad from Périgord attacked
his classical studies at the college in Cahors, the zeal that developed and
moulded the young seminarist at Saint-Sulpice under the direction of the
ascetic M. Tronson, also bound the adult to the duties of chaplain to the
Nouvelles catholiques to the Protestant converts and potential converts and
to the missions undertaken at the king's command in Aunis and Saintonge

---

29. See below, Chapter VI, p. 495.
30. François Varillon, whose book is quoted in the bibliographical notes.

after the revocation of the Edict of Nantes. He never did anything by halves. Appointed tutor to the Dauphin's three sons he did not confine himself, as Bossuet had done in the case of their father, merely to giving them a correct education; he strove to make them (and especially the eldest, the difficult Duc de Bourgogne) princes after the heart of God. Better still, he dreamed of making France, through the eldest, who would one day be king, a realm worthy of St. Louis. It was the same urge that influenced his relations—imprudent though they were—with the Quietists; and he thought he recognized in the dubious Mme. Guyon the messenger of the truth for which his soul thirsted. With the grace of a great nobleman he still remained absolutely loyal to her in her sorrow, even after his eyes had been opened. Then came the test. When he saw that the king was determined to destroy him[31] he most certainly knew that it was not solely on account of his religious theories; perhaps the great despot could not endure that Fénelon should see him with the eyes of a priest, and resented the archbishop's attempt to educate the heir to the throne in principles that refuted the errors of the regime. But Fénelon did nothing to soften the king's anger; he did not descend to flattery and grovelling. His heart was torn, but he reacted vigorously. Exiled to his diocese, he devoted himself with the same enthusiasm to his episcopal duties, dedicating himself to the best of his ability to the tasks God had entrusted to him. He proved himself capable of sublime charity in dealing with the miseries resulting from the War of the Spanish Succession, though something in his complex and inconsistent nature continued to draw him towards Versailles, to which he hoped to be recalled and restored. When the death of his pupil the Duc de Bourgogne destroyed his last illusions he buried himself in solitude, endless work and sadness. At the approach of death he at once abandoned grief and anguish, and his soul rose up sublime to face God's Providence. In his agony, on January 7, 1715, he murmured: "I love Him more than I fear Him."

Faith was the one stable factor, the very pivot of this eventful destiny and complex personality. Fénelon's faith was admirable; he was just as

---

31. See below, Chapter VI, p. 492.

typical as Bossuet of the religion of an age when God was not "dead." His   345
whole being teemed with faith: "His very arguments were instinct with the
spirit of adoration." Faguet remarks that nothing could be more absurd than
to see in Fénelon "a sensitive and humanitarian philosopher, an apostle of
tolerance, a friend of the people and a fore-runner of intellectual emanci-
pation." The proof of his faith can be seen in the austerity of his episcopal
life, his unquenchable charity, the continual reference to the will of God
which marks his thought and his uninterrupted devotion to God's cause.
He certainly did not fight for that cause in the manner of Bossuet, but their
goals were identical. His faith had not the monolithic character of his rival's;
though it was not assailed by doubt it experienced the effects of his complex
temperament. We must not imagine that these two men did not agree on the
essential loyalty to tradition and submission to the Church, merely because
they opposed each other on one point. They both professed adherence to
fundamentals and to the exacting demands of Christian morality. "Acts of
magnanimity and all natural tenderness are simply a more refined, more
alluring, more flattering, more pleasant, more diabolical form of self-in-
terest. We must die unreservedly to all friendship." Those were not Bossuet's words; neither were they written by Saint-Cyran or the great Arnauld.
Fénelon addressed them to Mme. de Maintenon, who was then his penitent.
In so far as Quietism might be deemed synonymous with a sort of easy-going
attitude, Fénelon was certainly no Quietist, despite serious errors in his use
of words and a certain rashness of approach. But he saw his religion—whose
demands he accepted—in the light of his own personal temperament; that is
to say, with passion, gentleness and tenderness, with that utter confidence in
God so well expressed in his last words. He was a true mystic; his was a soul
for whom Christianity was not discipline, order and a system of precepts
and institutions, but primarily adhesion, love, the offering of one's whole
being to supreme love, an abandonment to the promises of the Redeemer,
even to the harrowing consciousness of our own spiritual destitution. When
so many saints and outstanding figures throughout the whole history of the
Church have experienced this spiritual approach no one can reject the message of that great seventeenth-century trustee of the doctrine of "Pure Love."

Ultimately that is what gives Fénelon's genius its originality. Because this semi-invalid and zealot was able in his best moments to see everything from God's point of view, he discovered things which he was almost the only one to perceive. He towers over his era like a wild swan in flight. To so many problems that soon brought anguish to men's souls he put forward Christian solutions destined to prevent catastrophe. Fénelon the "politician," a picture that delighted the eighteenth century, cannot be understood without Fénelon the mystic. When he wrote his *Télémaque*, a poetic tale in which he subtly sat in judgment on the world of his day; when he addressed his famous letter to the Duc de Chevreuse[32]; when, even more rashly, he composed the *Tables de Chaulnes*, he was denouncing the evils of the regime itself, the very evils that right-minded Christians condemned and which would eventually compass his own destruction. Louis XIV might well treat him as a "visionary wit"; history has not proved Louis right. Fénelon was ahead of his time, a fact which after all explains his failure. His lucid genius enabled him not only to see the monstrosity of violence, the social injustice of his age, and the folly in the pomp of the Great Reign's ostentation, but also to discern what was unacceptable to a Christian in unlimited absolutism. From certain points of view he may have erred; to some extent he may have laid himself open to criticism by those who recognized in him a harbinger of the intellectual crisis which would shatter the traditional order of things.[33] None the less his is the most moving voice of that age.

9. THE REFORM IN JEOPARDY: RANCÉ

IT is sufficient to mention such names as Bossuet, Fénelon, Bourdaloue and Massillon to show that the great tide that had its source in the Council of Trent a hundred years earlier was of a lasting nature despite the preponderant

---

32. See above, Chapter IV, p. 244, note 4.
33. Intellectual posterity has been prejudicial to him, as frequently happens in the case of great thinkers. Rousseau's great admiration for Fénelon, of whom he said, "If he were to return here below I should become his slave," has rendered him suspect.

factor of classicism. In whatever field the Tridentine spirit had asserted itself that trend was to be found, less ebullient perhaps since it had undergone change, but more efficacious. The Church of France continued to furnish examples of the reforming and missionary spirit, but it was also still present in Italy, Spain, Poland and Austria.

Following the Council of Trent the most eminent agents of reform were the bishops, such as St. Charles Borromeo, his disciples and imitators. They were more numerous immediately before and after 1600, giving example of the highest virtues, with St. Francis de Sales at their head.[34] The "Borromeans" too were still active: in Italy there was Blessed Gregorio Barbarigo whom we have mentioned as one of the great spiritual leaders of his time. From 1664 to 1697 he laboured in Padua and Bergamo. He was a remarkable bishop, anxious about the training of priests, continually visiting his flock, preaching, holding conferences and writing a great deal. In France several of the best bishops of the Great Century were still hard at work at the beginning of the personal rule of Louis XIV, such as Étienne de Vilazel at Saint-Brieuc, Pavilion at Alet and Vialart de Herse at Châlons-sur-Marne. The example given by Blessed Alain de Solminihac was continued by other splendid figures. Among them was Louis de Lascaris d'Urfè, Bishop of Limoges from 1676 to 1695, who wore himself out in pastoral visits, hearing confessions, presiding over synods and Church conferences; in short, he was a veritable hero of penance and charity. There was the austere Cardinal Le Camus, Bishop of Grenoble from 1671 to 1707, who turned what has been called "France's sink of iniquity" into a well-ordered and healthy diocese. Le Camus has been referred to as the "Rancé of the episcopate."

Lascaris and Le Camus were nominated by Louis XIV, a fact which shows that the episcopate was not altogether bad during his reign. We have seen[35] that the king was careful in making such appointments.

Not that all of them were as perfect; politics, blood ties, court influences and other less honourable reasons too often led to the appointment

---

34. See Volume 1 of this work, Chapter II, p. 78.
35. See above, Chapter IV, p. 252.

of bishops who should never have been in charge of a diocese. Courtier-bishops, who were more concerned with the intrigues of Versailles and the "Journal of Benefices"[36] than with the needs of their dioceses, were still plentiful. Worse still, some of the bishops were also members of the nobility. They added the revenues of various abbeys to those of their diocese and kept a stately retinue; some had about thirty servants in livery, and they built those beautiful episcopal palaces that have survived to the present day. They were not necessarily bad men. François de Canisy, and Antoine de Charpin de Genétines who succeeded Louis de Lascaris d'Urfè in Limoges, were typical of the bishops who were members of the nobility but were also good administrators and even reformers. Naturally there were politicians among them of doubtful morals, such as Harlay de Champvallon, and some absurdly conceited (e.g., Clermont-Tonnerre and others). Some of them were excellent: Bossuet of Meaux, Fénelon of Cambrai, Massillon who was so popular in Clermont, Fléchier of Lavaur and subsequently of Nîmes, Mascaron of Tulle and later of Agen; all these were beyond criticism. We even have examples of outstanding episcopal virtues: Claude Joly, Bishop of Agen, Louis d'Estaing, Bishop of Clermont-Ferrand, Gabriel de Roquette, Bishop of Autun. At Besançon Antoine-Pierre de Grammont worked valiantly for the restoration of a tumbledown diocese; Jean d'Aranthon d'Alex did better still in Annecy. Tournai, which was then French territory, had the stern Choiseul, while Gap from 1706 onwards had Berger de Malissoles,

36. The "Journal of Benefices" was the object of lively rivalry on account of the financial rewards involved. The incumbents of "dirty" bishoprics were envious of those who were well endowed. We have the evidence of François Hébert, priest of the "royal parish" at Versailles from 1686 to 1704. No one in France had a better opportunity to observe intrigues, and he wrote of them in his *Mémoires*: "It is astonishing to see bishops indulging in the kind of luxury one would condemn in a woman. Their retinue and their furniture were affected by the depravity of the age.... It was this habit of luxury which prompted some of them to secure transfer to sees that offered a greater income than the one they began with; and these changes were continually taking place because everyone desired a better table, a larger number of servants, more of life's amenities.... A number of bishops rarely resided within their dioceses because, in their eagerness to become richer, they would do anything to achieve their aim. Not only were they subservient to the king, but they would woo courtiers whom they knew to be in favour, and worse still they paid attention to ladies whose morals they should have reproved had they been inclined to do their duty."

the "Saint of the Alps," who visited every parish once a year and five times refused to leave his impoverished diocese for a more wealthy one. We cannot overstress the important part played by those sterling bishops, who were wisely allowed to remain a long time in the same Sees and thus maintained the solid structure of the Church. This was true not only of France but of all the great Catholic countries. A body of excellent bishops laboured in Spain; among them Severo Tomas in Gerona, Pascual d'Aragona in Toledo, Estrado de Marroqui in Palencia, and Jaime Cordone, who introduced the devotion to the Sacred Heart into his diocese and whom his flock called "Father of the Poor."

Slowly the clergy improved, thanks to the perseverance of many bishops. But corrupt practices still existed, and we have only to glance at the record of some of the seniors to form a fairly dismal picture of the state of the lower clergy. Claude Joly of Agen had to order his priests under pain of excommunication to wear the tonsure and soutane, to reside in their parishes, to hear confessions and say Mass correctly, to teach the Catechism and refrain from visiting taverns. These facts speak volumes for the obstinate persistence of such evil practices. Many other bishops were obliged to issue similar instructions, among them Roquette of Autun and Le Camus of Grenoble. The same kind of thing was happening in Gratz, Barcelona and Florence, while the Patriarch of Venice was compelled to issue a directive governing the participation of clerics in the carnival celebrations. But the situation was nothing new, and the subject requires no special emphasis.

Despite these obvious defects the mass of the clergy remained a vital force during the Great Century. On the whole it preserved its prestige and authority. The number of priests was still large and there was no shortage of vocations. All rural parishes had a priest in charge and a vicar; in the towns the parish priest had two or three assistants and a whole body of approved auxiliaries, unbeneficed priests and chaplains in charge of confraternities. Not every priest in this motley collection was a happy choice, but the efforts made since Trent—reinforced by Bérulle, St. Vincent de Paul, Olier and others—to train priests and make them true to the "sacerdotal ideal," had unquestionably born fruit. In some respects the classical mind seemed most perfectly reflected in the priests. There emerged, as Bishop Calvet said, "a priestly type, grave, temperate, of exemplary behaviour and good sense, wedded to order and uniformity," a type which Jansenism would eventually confine within the rigidity of its doctrine and practice, and even of dress. No doubt such men were rightly blamed for their lack of originality and for not leaving enough room in religion for "the folly of the Cross"; but the really important fact is that those priests, many of whom were heroically virtuous, reacted against the bad old ways of spiritual laxity.

By degrees the movement to establish seminaries either on the Tridentine or French model gained ground. When Bishop de Choiseul was entrusted with the diocese of Tournai, after the territory became French, his first care was to found a seminary. Cardinal de Fürstenberg did likewise in Strasburg when France took over the province. Cardinal Le Camus made it one of his first duties to find sound directors for his seminary; and Bishop de Roquette eagerly set about building one. Many were the bishops who called on the Lazarists and especially the Sulpicians to assist in the training of their young students for the priesthood.[37] Numerous seminaries began to operate in Italy—at San Miniato near Florence, in Andria, Pistoia, Lareno, San Severo, Catania and Naples. Cavalieri, Vicar-General to Cardinal Orsini and a zealous Dominican, introduced the French type of seminary into Spoleto, Cesena and Benevento, where future clerics remained longer and did not mix with lay students. In German territory seminaries were opened at Wurtzburg and Ratisbon; the same was done at Brixen, Breslau, Vienna, Olmutz, Prague, and in Switzerland at Freiburg. Original foundations should also be mentioned, for even where official seminaries existed private ones were also

---

37. It must be emphasized, however, that it was not yet obligatory in all dioceses for students to pass through a seminary. Where it was the rule, the period of training varied from four to eighteen months. The seminarists paid for their board and lodging, but those who were too poor were allowed to do their own cooking, and they could go into the town to buy provisions. The quality of the buildings varied a great deal. In some cases they were set up in disused inns. Ordinary laymen were generally permitted to join the classes with the seminarists, and in any case to attend divine service with them. One of the rules of the seminary at Coutances provided for a student to take over the duty of "driving away dogs and keeping beggars quiet" during Mass.

established. Among these was the Trente-Mois, which owed its existence to the generosity of the holy priest Claude Bernard. Others were the Presbytery Schools of Pierre Crestoy (1622–1703), parish priest (from 1678) of Barenton in Normandy. They were real country seminaries. The most remarkable of such institutions was that of Claude Poullard des Places (1679–1709), whose aim was to attract to the priesthood young men from the poorest classes. His Séminaire du Saint-Esprit (1702) provided the Church of France with a body of vicars for the poorer districts; they were called "Bouics" from the name of his first successor. These seminaries also provided men of devotion and courage for the most difficult missionary work in pagan lands.[38]

The facts were there to demonstrate the eventual results of these patient efforts, especially in the opposition put up by the general mass of the clergy during the eighteenth century to the forces of unbelief, and the courage shown by the French clergy during the Revolution. Moreover, notable figures stand out from the vast number of good and saintly priests whose names are forgotten. Before Claude Joly became Bishop and Count of Agen he was an excellent parish priest at Saint-Nicolas-des-Champs in Paris; and courageous too, for he dared to tell the Duchesse de Noailles to supervise the conduct of the ladies of honour at court when they came under the eye of young Louis XIV. At Saint-Sulpice, Baudrand de Lacombe, M. Olier's biographer, and La Chétardye, who refused the bishopric of Poitiers in order to remain a parish priest, were other fine examples. Every great Catholic country had its own exemplary priests. Regarding them as a whole we might be justified in taking an optimistic view, but they were badly paid and often despised by the higher clergy, with the result that there developed a social consciousness and a tendency towards dogmatism and insistence on their demands. When therefore the Jansenist crisis occurred the movement assumed considerable importance—a veritable "Catholic Presbyterianism" which drew its arguments from Richer. The movement found a champion in the facetious Abbé Jacques Boileau (who said he wrote in Latin so that

---

38. See *The Church of the Classical Age: The Era of Great Splintering*, Volume 1, Chapter II.

the bishops might not understand!). By 1700 it was powerful enough to send to the astonished Bishop of Chartres a well-considered document inviting him to recognize in priests the same spiritual powers possessed by the bishops—a sign of grave and dramatic antagonism ahead.

The position was also favourable in the religious Orders and congregations, but much depended upon circumstances. Generally speaking institutions dating back to the sixteenth century or the early part of the seventeenth remained efficient forces in the service of the Tridentine ideal. The Jesuits were still a powerful influence; they were made the subject of official inquiries, calumniated and even persecuted in some areas; in others they were praised to the skies, and continued all powerful. They constituted the élite, of the priesthood in every Catholic state, acting as confessors to princes and spiritual directors to countless souls. In 1701 they became publicists and journalists by founding the famous *Mémoires de Trévoux*. All the Generals one after another were excellent men: the German Nickel, the Genoese Oliva, the Spaniard Tirso Gonzalez and the Milanese Tamburini. Despite a little friction resulting from Probabilism, the Society of Jesus, eighteen thousand strong, remained a bulwark of the Church—as Voltaire would find out. The Capuchins were not so far up in the scale, and were therefore less open to suspicion. Their growth was extraordinary: by about 1700 they numbered thirty thousand members, had eighteen hundred houses, and were to be seen everywhere. It was they who maintained the great Franciscan tradition at its liveliest.

Recent institutions were less numerous, but they retained the bloom of youth. Bérulle and his Oratory were much talked about, mainly on account of Mascaron, Massillon and Malebranche, and the Jansenist affair in which the Oratory was somewhat compromised; all of which proves that it exercised a considerable spiritual influence. The progress of the Lazarists continued: "Bestowed upon all, dear to all," runs an inscription on the tomb of one of them in Warsaw. The wise Matthieu Beuvelet, who strove to improve the organization of M. Bourdoise's congregation, was superior at Saint-Nicolas-du-Chardonnet. As for Saint-Sulpice, its renown as a source of seminary teachers was assured. Numerous dioceses asked for Sulpicians; in Canada they were the "Lords of Montreal," and they gave the country that sound body of priests which it has had ever since. The glory of the Congregation at that time was Louis Tronson (1622–1700)—"Monsieur Tronson." He was the third Superior-General and truly representative of its spirit; a corpulent but ascetic man who resigned an attractive post as chaplain to the king, and later refused a bishopric, to dedicate his life to the training of priests. His book *Examens Particuliers* (1690) was the offspring of a fervent soul and long experience as seminary director. The book has remained a classic; some of its precepts may cause a smile, but the high quality of the writing, its delicacy of analysis and its common sense make it an undisputed masterpiece in the training of priests.[39]

Less satisfactory were conditions among the priests and nuns of the old religious Orders. No doubt Bossuet was thinking of them when he wrote to the abbot of La Trappe: "The Church's affairs are in a very bad state..." The *in commendam* principle governing the revenues of unoccupied benefices was still in force, and not even the best people—among them Bossuet, who derived benefit from the custom—found fault with it. We have seen the disastrous effects resulting from the system, which hampered the efforts for reform made during the preceding period. The behaviour of some communities was conspicuously scandalous; the Benedictine nuns at Metz dispensed entirely with communal fasting and took turns, one at a time, to carry out the fast for all the rest. During carnival time they dressed up their porters and gardeners in their own habits. The sons of St. Bernard got rid of the *Histoire générale de la réforme de Cîteaux* from their libraries, because the work laid bare their vices. The Franciscans and Dominicans were hardly better. However, it is unnecessary to stress these known facts.

Furthermore, in one way and another relations between the Regulars and the hierarchy were bad, often because of a clash of interests. "There would be greater spiritual independence," said Fénelon, "if there were no material interests at stake." But the discord was also due to the fact that so many religious of all Orders had lost their sense of discipline. Strife broke

---

39. Jean Gautier has furnished an excellent portrait of M. Tronson in *Ces Messieurs de Saint-Sulpice.*

354   out at every opportunity: in France, in Italy, and even in Poland, where an incident involving the abbey of Andrezejow caused a riot, and in the Low Countries, where a group of Benedictines were in open conflict with all the bishops of the country.

Notwithstanding this picture of decadence there were some encouraging exceptions. In every sphere of religious life attempts at reform met with a measure of success; nowhere, however, was the fundamental issue faced squarely: that is to say, whether the organization of the regular clergy really corresponded with "the needs of an age when the social structure was so varied and centralized State control predominated."[40] In France that question would be put bluntly in 1765 by the public authority.[41] The French Benedictine congregation of Saint-Maur, made famous by Mabillon, was beyond reproach, and a revival was under way at Reichenbach and at Michelfeld in Bavaria. Not all Benedictine nuns by any means resembled those at Metz, who gave so much trouble to the Archdeacon Bossuet. At Faremoutiers, for instance, one of the two oldest convents in France, a splendid spiritual revival developed under the direction of two successive abbesses whose lives were models of holiness. The Carthusians were scarcely affected by the decline. Their Superior-General Dom Innocent Le Masson published an excellent guide to mental prayer in 1695, and he managed the Order with a firm hand. Father Samaniego, General of the Friars Minor, strove bravely to lead the Franciscans back to discipline and observance of the Rule. Among the Dominicans the man who so magnificently embodied the ideal of the reform was Father Antonin Cloche, a lean Gascon from Saint-Sever, who was elected Master-General in 1686. He spent no more than five hours a night in sleep and ate once a day; he travelled continuously, preaching, reviving missions among the people and doing his best to prevent the purchase of titles or their bestowal upon favourites. "The face of the Order has changed," he frequently complained; "its beauty is declining, souls are

---

40. E. Préclin.

41. See *The Church of the Classical Age: The Era of Great Splintering*, Volume 2, Chapter V.

perishing, and I am afraid God will call us to account for it." He was one of those who did not resign themselves to the unhappy situation.

Among the numerous reformers of the Great Century Jean Le Bouthellier de Rancé has an undeniable claim to recognition. His was a strange destiny, as romantic as anyone could wish. His name will always be associated with La Trappe, one of the most original spiritual families in the history of the Church; a family which suggests to the uninitiated the most exacting form of Christian experience and one somewhat contrary to nature.[42]

On April 28, 1657, Jean Le Bouthellier called at the city residence of the Montbazons, with whom he was on familiar terms. It was early in the morning, for he had been worried about the health of the *duchesse* for several days. On the steps he met M. de Soubise, who exclaimed: "It is finished; the play has ended." Le Bouthellier collapsed with grief on the stone steps, making no attempt to hide his feelings.

He was a handsome young man of thirty-one, of brilliant intellect and such wide culture that at fifteen years of age he had published a translation of Anacreon. He was of a violent, impulsive disposition and inclined to extremes in everything. Bremond called him "the thundering abbot." He had already had a dazzling career in the Church; partly through his father's influence and partly through the kindness of Richelieu, his godfather, ecclesiastical benefices had been piling up for him ever since he was eleven. He was a canon of Notre Dame at Paris, chaplain to the King, abbot of Saint-Symphorien-Lès-Beauvais, of La Trappe, of Notre-Dame du Vai, of Saint-Clementin in Poitou, and prior of Boulogne—an amazing achievement, but such was the custom of the age.

When he rose from the steps he went to pray beside the dead body of the woman whom he loved tenderly as a friend rather than as one of his penitents. He spent the whole of the following summer in one of his castles examining his conscience and writing down his thoughts. Had God sent him upon earth to be a worldly priest intent on cultivating useful connections,

---

42. The French word *trappe* also means "trap" and "trap-door," and is therefore liable to create the idea of a trap into which a man may fall and disappear for ever.

surrounded by lackeys, enjoying the pleasures of the hunt and his magnificent carriages? He went through a heartrending spiritual crisis. God seemed to speak to him and reproach him so severely that the deep repentance he felt never afterwards left him. He determined to be as lavish in his penances as he had been in worldly enjoyments. The priests of the Oratory, Pavilion and the austere Bishop of Alet, all set him on the right path, and he determined to follow it to the end.

He suddenly relinquished all his livings: of his titles he retained only that of abbot of La Trappe. The Cistercian abbey of La Trappe was in the diocese of Séez, in Normandy. Like most monasteries of White Monks, it had badly deteriorated. The walls were cracked, the ground overrun with brambles; of the two hundred monks who had once dwelt there only six remained, and they lived like poachers, or rather like thieves. Rancé, the commendatory abbot, set to work; he decided to reform that wretched community and restore life to La Trappe. If it were God's will a salutary influence would spread from this restored community to the others, perhaps even to the whole Order of St. Bernard.

He had to face strain and stress, and even danger, for the six ruffianly monks were capable of using dagger and poison. But "the thundering abbot" held his own. He succeeded in replacing the reprobates by Cistercians of the strict observance, who followed his way of life. Moreover, throughout the Order everyone became seriously disturbed by the prevalence of unseemly ways. Eustache de Beaufort reformed Sept-Fons, near Moulins, with Rancé as its leader. But attempts by the abbot of La Trappe to impose a more strict observance upon every monastery were unsuccessful; the "mitigated" opposed him, and even won over the authorities at Rome. Rancé was not distressed; he would be satisfied if La Trappe became the only community in which God would be served by a life of penance, and his example must prove contagious. After all, everything seemed to show that he was right: vocations were numerous, and often quite surprising—a former seafaring man, an unfrocked priest, the ex-provost marshal of Touraine and so on.

It was the spirit of penance that drew them all to La Trappe—the same spirit that took others to Port-Royal. Rancé progressed passionately along

the path of renunciation, as it was in his nature to do. He did without fish, 357
eggs, butter and wine; he gave up sleeping on his straw mattress. The monks
were no longer allowed to leave the monastery; they maintained perpetual
silence; their lives were governed by the singing of the Office day and night
and the carrying out of heavy manual work. To what limits would the spirit of penance lead this great and terrible abbot? The ordeal of singing the
Psalms standing barefooted on the icy flagstones for ten or twelve hours at
a time seemed natural to him. But it undoubtedly proved too much, and
he had to slacken a little in face of protests and an increase in the number
of sick. La Trappe became, however, the very home of penance, a model
of renunciation carried to the limits of human endurance. Innocent XI
approved the reformed Rule in 1678, and La Trappe became foremost of
all the monasteries of St. Bernard in striving to renounce their former laxity
and adhere to strict observance. So it has remained to the present day.

It has often been said of Rancé, in his own time and since, that his
behaviour was immoderate. It is true that some of the hardships practised
in various Trappist monasteries were beyond the limits envisaged by the
kindly St. Bernard. It is equally certain that Rancé's scorn for the parading
of intellectual pursuits, an attitude that brought about his violent quarrel
with Mabillon[43] and Le Masson, was very different from the attitude of him
who had declared that it was "not becoming for the spouse of Christ to be
illiterate." But it is remarkable that in a century so obviously worldly and
frivolous so many souls turned to La Trappe as to a haven of salvation; that
so many penitents from court and city should have approached the abbot
for guidance in the leading of better lives. One may argue about Rancé, but
there is not the slightest doubt that when he died in 1700 one of the great
spiritual lights of his time was extinguished.[44]

---

43. See *The Church of the Classical Age: The Era of Great Splintering*, Volume 1, Chapter I.
44. In connection with the movement towards reform we must mention a Benedictine
community set up by Peter Mekhitar, an Armenian who came over to Catholicism from
the Greek Orthodox Church. He was driven from Greece by the Turks, and he and his
brethren settled in Venice. The monastery of Saint Lazarus near Venice still houses the
"Mekitarists." The community also has a branch in Vienna and another in Trieste.

10. CHARITY—THE MISSION:
ST. GRIGNION DE MONTFORT

THE spirit of revival in evidence during the first half of the century was just as decisively concerned with charity and the apostolate as it was with reform. But what was its position during the classical age? Here again we should not speak of an eclipse, but rather of a slowing down of creative effort. St. Vincent de Paul was no longer on the scene, but his lessons continued to bear fruit.

The spirit of charity was not wanting during the Great Century. Preachers extolled the virtue in stirring accents. The mystery of the poor (their "eminent dignity," to use Bossuet's phrase) and the duty of the rich to give alms were frequent subjects of sermons. "When God made the rich," said Fléchier, "His purpose was to make them charitable. He chose them to be the instruments of His goodness, the channels along which flow His exterior graces within the Church. He imposes upon them a command and a necessity, not merely a counsel." And Bourdaloue exclaimed: "Why are you rich unless it be for the sake of the poor?" It was not a case of finding a subject for eloquent oratory. Many of those who listened to these admonitions put into practice the precepts they learned, and the example came from those in high places. When members of the nobility died they bequeathed their property to the poor; organizations, such as the Apostolic Association to which we have referred, recruited its members from among the wealthy classes, and continued the charitable work of the Company of the Blessed Sacrament. For half a century laymen had become more and more aware of their responsibilities in relation to charity, and works undertaken by saintly people tended to become organized and formed part of definite charitable enterprises. Governments co-operated with the Church towards the same end. More and more hospitals and hostels were established. To the General Hospital in Paris were added the Val-de-Grâce and Les Invalides. Throughout the French provinces twenty-seven hospitals were opened between 1661 and 1715, in addition to those built during the preceding period. In the territories conquered by the Great King the bishops usually opened a

hospital as soon as they took over the administration of their dioceses (e.g.,
Bishop Choiseul at Tournai). Italy and Austria did likewise. Three hospitals
were built at Turin, two at Milan, two at Venice and four at Vienna.

All the religious Orders dedicated to charity prospered; this was partly
due to the decline of the mystics, for the contemplative Orders lost recruits
to the advantage of active institutions. The splendid community of the Sisters of Charity began to develop at this period.[45] The Brothers of St. John
of God—*Fate bene fratelli*[46]—were also expanding rapidly; in France, Italy,
Spain and even in Spanish America their houses multiplied. Their hospital in
Rome, built on an island in the Tiber, was continually enlarged. The various
Charite hospitals in Paris and in the French provinces experienced the same
growth. The Brothers even established small hospitals in country districts
run by a brother who was a doctor. The Camillians undertook similar work.
All the female Orders and communities devoted to charity were developing
rapidly. New ones were founded with specific vocations: refuges for fallen
women were opened at Besançon, and institutions for Protestant converts
and the *Nouvelles catholiques*, to which the Sisters of Christian Union were
dedicated. Founded by Vachet and his sister Mlle. de Crézé, they opened
eighteen houses in ten years. Prisoners, convicts, condemned criminals for
whom the heart of Monsieur Vincent had bled—none was forgotten. Few
people know that in Italy the great scholar Muratori devoted all the hours
he could spare from his library work to those poor outcasts. Mercedarians,
Trinitarians and, of course, Lazarists were ever mindful of the fate of those
unfortunate people, and the first two institutions established in Spain strove
heroically to ransom those who suffered in the Berber prisons. The former
Hospitallers of St. John of Jerusalem, henceforward known as the Knights of
Malta, experienced a revival and returned to their traditional role.

The charity of Christ was not dead. There was certainly too much dissi-
pation of effort and too little organization, resulting in reduced efficiency;
but the effort was none the less splendid.

---

45. See Volume 1 of this work, Chapter I, p. 41ff.
46. See Volume 1 of this work, Chapter II, p. 114.

The Mission, which was one of the flowers that blossomed during the Great Century,[47] continued to thrive, though less vigorously than in the time of Monsieur Vincent. Of the old team St. John Eudes still remained, and continued to wear himself out during the first twenty years of the personal rule of Louis XIV. The indefatigable Father Maunoir worked on in Brittany until 1683. A way had been found to kindle the spiritual flame in souls; the best bishops were adopting it systematically and establishing numerous diocesan missions. Antoine Pierre de Grammont, Archbishop of Besançon, entrusted the Josephites with a mission to Lyons that lasted two months. He organized in all about a hundred, which were undertaken by Capuchins, Jesuits, Oratorians, Benedictines and a group of secular priests "whose work in the Lord's vineyard," he said, "was very fruitful." At Limoges, Louis de Lascaris d'Urfé sent for Father Honoré, a Capuchin from Cannes, who had preached no fewer than three hundred missions and was therefore an expert. Every important Order and community took part in this great work: the Lazarists with Father Planat, apostle of Auvergne, and Father Bonal, a pioneer from Rouergue; the Capuchins with Father Séraphin of Paris; the Jesuits with Father de Lingendes and Father de la Colombière, a champion of devotion to the Sacred Heart. René Lévêque added to their number his Compagnie des Piétistes de Saint-Clément.

It is a remarkable fact that the idea of the mission spread from France to the great Catholic countries. In Italy its unflagging leader was the Jesuit Father Paolo Segneri, the most famous preacher of his day. There was not a province in the country where he did not preach missions between 1665 and 1692. After his death his cousin and friend Father Segneri the younger and father Pinamonti continued his work. In southern Italy, which suffered great distress, Father Cristofarini laboured in the Abruzzi, and the ascetic Father Ansalone battled for forty years against the vices of Naples. Father Francisco de Geronimo, another Jesuit, also preached in Naples. To assist him he established two lay communities known respectively as the "Two Hundred" and the "Seventy-Two," the latter working in secret. All these

47. See Volume 1 of this work, Chapter II, p. 107.

great Italian missioners were extraordinary men: they used the discipline in
public, preached in the streets, in the squares and before the theatres; they
engaged in violent debate with their opponents and called a spade a spade,
railing against sin in holy anger. They were true men of action. It is said that
during Father de Geronimo's missions he made between one hundred and
five hundred converts yearly.

The mission also progressed in Spain, but it was less vigorous and less
spectacular. Father Tirso Gonzalez was a remarkable missioner before being
elected General of the Society of Jesus. So was the famous Portuguese
preacher Antonio Vieira; he preached a "Station" at the court and journeyed to the West Indies. The missions multiplied in Germany. The Jesuit
Father Schacht laboured in Hamburg, Jemingen in the south, Ampferle in
Breisgau, Scheffler in Silesia; the Capuchins Prokop von Templin and Martin von Cochem were the apostles of the Rhineland. Bishop Fürstenberg of
Paderborn left nearly one hundred thousand *thalers* on his death to finance
missionary work. It would be impossible to overestimate the importance
of this great kneading of the dough of Christianity. It was thanks to the
missions that the canton of Valais was restored, and that the greater part of
the Helvetic canton of Thurgau returned to Catholicism. Protestantism was
repelled in Hungary through the missionary activities of Father Stankoviez
and Bishop Erdoddy.

Towards the end of the seventeenth century and in the early part of the
eighteenth Louis Marie Grignion de Montfort was the embodiment of the
missionary spirit as well as of the spirit of charity and penance. He was a
man of vast energy and a great saint. He stood aloof from his time, a sort
of misfit in the religious life around him, utterly outside the austere and
rather uniform pattern of the existing priestly ideal. We might say he was
an eccentric; but there have been many such in the Church who have none
the less played an important role. St. Philip Neri was one; St. Francis of
Assisi another. Let us say that our saint was "mad about God." Everything
we know of him through reliable witnesses suggests that he was a strange
figure, a ragged and penniless priest who begged his bread and proclaimed
his poverty as others display their wealth. He was a wonder-worker who

healed the sick by laying his hands upon them. He had experience of spectacular and mysterious occurrences: good and bad angels fought for possession of the sinful soul of a dying man, and not without coming to blows. To demonstrate the meaning of charity he would kiss the purulent sores of the sick, as Catherine of Siena had done. Most certainly all holiness is not necessarily expressed in actions of that kind, but they are a manifestation of holiness. Indeed, it was not a bad thing to remind Christians of the Great Century that the ethics of the Beatitudes are not identical with those of human wisdom, and that no scandal ever shocked more than the scandal of the Cross.

Louis Marie Grignion was of Breton stock, Montfort being a village of the old diocese of Saint-Malo. His father was a briefless barrister who had great difficulty in bringing up his eighteen children. When the future saint, whose piety had astonished his masters in the Jesuit school at Rennes, decided to go to Paris to study for the priesthood, he had nothing approaching the three hundred *livres* necessary at that time to enter a seminary, and had to depend upon the generosity of some good friends. Thanks to them he was admitted to the annexe of Saint-Sulpice, where M. de la Baroudière accepted the sons of poor families. He was then twenty years of age, having been born in 1673, and was already well known for the strangeness of his behaviour, the violence of his penances and his thirst for humiliation. This young John the Baptist's continual talk of the Holy Spirit and the end of the world caused a smile at Saint-Sulpice; he was more severe than a Jansenist and had more devotion to Our Lady than a Jesuit. Some strange tales were current about him. Once when he accompanied one of his superiors who had business with a bank, he was found on his knees in the main office among the employees and servants, praying without paying the slightest attention to those around him.

Louis Marie was ordained priest in 1700, and was invited to Nantes by the aged René Lévêque, whose Compagnie des Piétistes de Saint-Clément emulated the Lazarists in preaching missions in country districts. He went about preaching everywhere, and met with success; but his manner did not please the traditionalists. Ten months later Bishop Girard, who surmised

what good a priest of his type might achieve in the denser parts of Poitiers, 363
invited him to that city. Louis Marie Grignion roused the people so effec-
tually that the bishop entrusted him with the chaplaincy of the hospital. It
was a badly run hospital, lacking in generosity and the spirit of dedication;
it therefore provided the saint with his first opportunity to exert his influence. He found the sick neglected, and the nurses, who were lay folk, were
wanting in discipline. The new chaplain took this chaotic little world in
hand. A wonderful and pious idea occurred to him: he decided to associate
the sick with the running of the establishment, especially from the spiritual
point of view. He elaborated his plan, and formed his willing helpers into a
congregation. He gathered his "daughters" together in a large ward, in the
centre of which he stood a cross—he called it the Hall of Wisdom—and he
made them recite the Office as nuns do. News of what he was doing spread
around the city. The daughter of Trichet, a public attorney of the présidial
court, offered to help him; she left the world and donned an ashen-grey
woollen habit, taking the name of Marie-Louise de Jésus. The squalid hospital became a model of cleanliness and the Daughters of Wisdom were
founded. The saint achieved all this in five years. The community was very
small, but today it numbers more than five thousand members.

These achievements were merely a beginning, enabling him to lay the
foundations of his work. The hospital at Poitiers no longer needed him,
but the peasants, whose faith was threatened, were waiting. Louis Marie
Grignion was grieved, as Monsieur Vincent had been, to find that the spirit
of the Gospel no longer lived among the country people. Armed with his
rosary and a great crucifix, which he held above his head as though for
protection, he set out to give his missions. He preached, erected Stations
of the Cross and rebuilt churches. Soon he was in demand almost everywhere in Brittany and Normandy, and even beyond. From Saint-Malo he
went to Saintes, from Saint-Brieuc to Coutances and La Rochelle. Enormous crowds gathered when he spoke, and he brought tears to their eyes
when he talked to them of their misfortunes and Christ crucified. Many
were the cities, market-towns and villages through which this tall, thin
man passed in his ragged soutane. Many were the crowds that succumbed

to the magic of this unattractive orator with gaunt face, large mouth and stubby nose; but his eyes shone, and his voice penetrated to the depths of their conscience. He was also a great walker, trekked everywhere, and made pilgrimages to many shrines including those of Notre-Dame des Ardilliers and Chartres.

His charity became a byword. It is said that while a seminarist at Saint-Sulpice he used to call on the servants of nobles and teach them the catechism. When he was working at his hospital in Poitiers everyone in the city had seen him sauntering along the streets and roaming around the markets leading a donkey carrying baskets for the food he begged. One day, when he came across two swordsmen about to fight a duel, he threw himself between them, grasping the murderous blades in both hands. On another occasion he found some dandies importuning young laundresses; removing the discipline which he always carried attached to his belt, he made such good use of it on their backs that they ran away. His idea of charity obviously did not exclude the use of violence! All sorts of stories were current about him. He even found his way into houses that were so unsparing in their hospitality that it would have been regarded as most unseemly for a priest to be seen there; yet he compelled the guests to leave by talking to them of the salvation of their souls.

His method of saving souls was one of which the authorities did not always approve without some hesitation; at least not until a long time afterwards, when he was canonized. One after another the bishops, even those who had welcomed him to their dioceses, concluded that he went too far. "If wisdom consists in undertaking nothing new for God and in not getting oneself talked about, the apostles made a great mistake when they left Jerusalem; in any case, St. Paul should not have travelled so much, nor should St. Peter have set up the Cross on the Capitol." That is indeed the language of Christian truth; but this difference of opinion gave rise to a great deal of discord from which Louis Marie Grignion drew supernatural lessons: "More than ever am I impoverished, crucified, humiliated; men and devils wage a sweet and agreeable war against me. Let them calumniate me, mock me, tear my reputation to pieces and cast me into prison, for these are precious gifts;

to me they are dainty dishes. Oh, when shall I be crucified and dead to the 365
world?" Most certainly he had no rule of life but the "folly" of the Cross.

Such was the nature of his strong and original spirituality. As a student
of Olier and Tronson, a voracious reader of Boudon, and "Bérullian" in outlook, Louis Marie Grignion added new material to what he had received
from his predecessors, and that material was drawn from his personal experience. He declared that one must "empty oneself of self" and "adhere to
God," as his teachers had said. He demanded of those who listened to him
that they "cleave to God" and practise a "holy slavery." This great ascetic
was a mystic who instinctively reconciled both tendencies. He was a belated
defender of the principle of "pure love." Furthermore, Jansenists and their
supporters held him in great contempt. But this paradoxical saint, who
attempted to manage the world, wished to emphasize one important fact
above all others: God's wisdom in what to men is foolishness, the sublime
absurdity that is the sole legitimate end of the Christian. His remarkable
book entitled *Amour de la Sagesse éternelle* reiterates this principle, "the plac-
ing of all wisdom in the wounds of Christ," the preaching of Christ humiliated, despised and crucified, and nothing else. His entirely Pauline and
Augustinian doctrine compensated for the occasional too human element
in the Christocentrism of the seventeenth century. His teaching, however,
did not cease to address itself to men's hearts; for Louis Marie Grignion not
only pointed to the end, he offered the means to attain it: recourse to Mary,
the sweet Mother, the mediatrix of grace; and such was the purpose of his
moving *Traité de la vraie dévotion à la Sainte Vierge.*

However, this wholly dedicated life exhausted him. His work had
prospered despite every difficulty. He went to Rome—on foot, of course—
where his efforts won approval, and he was given the title of "Apostolic Missioner," a term made famous in the past by Jacques de Vitry. So many people
came forward to help him that he was able to found a community of priests
destined for the mission fields, of which he had dreamed since his early
years as a priest. In 1712 he founded the Company of Mary or Missionaries
of Mary, who carried on and expanded his apostolate of the countryside.
Around them he gathered a group of fellow workers, originally laymen,

366 under the name of Brothers of the Holy Ghost.[48] He allotted them the task of educating the children of the poor, for he was as much concerned with the problem of training the young as with the apostolate. Shortly before his death he sent Sister Marie-Louise de Jésus to open a school at La Rochelle for the daughters of working-class families. But he had worn himself out at an early age by his ascetic life and his superhuman efforts. In 1716, at the age of forty-three, he went peacefully to God.

The Great King had died shortly before, and with the Regency began an era in which Christianity rapidly disintegrated. St. Louis Marie Grignion de Montfort foresaw more than anyone else the march of events leading to that circumstance. He was the prophet of those latter days, the Jeremiah of the dying seventeenth century, and with all his strength he shouted his warnings in moving words: "Remember, Lord. Now is the time to fulfil your promise. Your divine law has been transgressed, your Gospel slighted, your religion rejected; torrents of iniquity flood the earth and there is abomination even in the holy places. Will you remain silent for ever? I appeal to you through your Mother. Remember her compassion and do not cast me aside. Rise up, Lord, in your mercy."

Such was the last witness whom the Great Century had to offer of its faith, its torments and its hopes. The important point is that this barefooted priest, so foolish in the sight of men, but so holy before God, had little or nothing in common with the traditional conception of the "classical Christian."

11. CHRISTIAN EDUCATION: FROM CHARLES DÉMIA TO ST. JEAN-BAPTISTE DE LA SALLE

ST. Louis Marie Grignion was not alone in his anxiety for the education of children: he shared his concern with a number of contemporaries. One, of

---

48. In 1835 they were reorganized as a separate congregation by Father Deshayes, who called them Brothers of St. Gabriel.

course, was Monsieur Vincent, whose saintly followers, led by Marguerite   367
Naseau, became teachers[49]; equally concerned were M. Bourdoise, Pierre Fou-
rier,[50] the Jesuits, the Oratorians, the Ursulines and many others. The education of the young remained one of the major cares of society in the seventeenth
century. That concern, indeed, was among the brighter aspects of the period,
although the attempts made to increase the number of schools and to make
education available to all classes of society are some of its least appreciated
features. Our democratic régimes pride themselves on having made education
widespread, but before them the old Catholic regime, especially in France,
carried on a work that in many respects the former have merely inherited.

About 1660, educational undertakings experienced something in the
nature of a pause following upon a fruitful period; but they soon regained
momentum, and public authorities became interested. The king insisted on
many occasions that every parish should have its school. In 1700 an edict
instructed judges and attorneys to ensure that parish priests checked the
regular attendance of children at school. In this field as in that of charitable
enterprise the State looked to the Church to organize education and provide the means of carrying it out. Moreover, in accordance with the spirit of
the times the two spheres merged; "the exercise of charity and the education
of youth" are two terms which are very often found together in the annals
of the seventeenth century. The provincial assemblies gave the name Office
of Public Welfare to the department which combined matters relating to
relief, education and agriculture. The Church, loyal to a duty it has never
shirked, entered fully into the effort to provide against the inadequacy of
the educational system and to adapt it to the needs of the time. Education,
according to Fléchier, "appertains neither to charity nor to human institutions, but is a divine command and a matter of justice." But the teaching
had to be Catholic, for it was inseparable from a Christian education—a
fact expressly stated in an ordinance of 1698. This is the answer to the legend that the ancient regime of the Church was the myrmidon of ignorance.

49. See Volume 1 of this work, Chapter I, p. 42.
50. See Volume 1 of this work, Chapter II, p. 119.

By 1661 some remarkable results had been achieved in various branches of education. In so far as higher education was concerned, the universities, after a period of crisis, were reorganized during the fifteenth and sixteenth centuries. The Sorbonne retained its high reputation; it was a veritable oracle of Christendom, and its doctors, universally famous, were a closed circle to which it was impossible to gain admittance without strict tests, including the presentation of a thesis which lasted a whole day. But the students' colleges, even the celebrated Collège de Navarre, were dominated by routine, and were out of touch with the educational discoveries of the day. The type of education which might be called secondary approached the higher standard of the universities in so far as the upper forms were concerned, and it tended more and more to remain in the hands of the religious Orders which inclined to this method at the beginning of the century.[51] The education of the children of the nobility and the upper middle class was mostly in the hands of the Jesuits. Their colleges multiplied, not only in France where they numbered about a hundred in 1700, but also in Germany, in Bohemia and Austria (one hundred and one), in Italy (one hundred and thirty-five), in Spain (one hundred and five) and in present-day Belgium (twenty-six). They have often been taken to task for the uniformity and lack of originality in their teaching, as well as for needless insistence on discipline which left too strong an impression on the child. But they produced first-class men, admirably trained in self-control and capable of undertaking methodical work. The colleges run by the Oratory[52] were more modern in their teaching methods and were the only serious rivals of the Jesuits after the Jansenist crisis had almost eliminated the "Little Schools" of Port-Royal. They too were among the élite of educationists, especially in their college at Juilly. As for the education of young society girls, the most prominent teachers were the Ursuline nuns, the daughters of St. Angela Merici.[53] In France alone they

---

51. See Volume 1 of this work, Chapter II, p. 120.
52. See Volume 1 of this work, Chapter II, p. 121.
53. See Volume 1 of this work, Chapter II, p. 121.

had three hundred and twenty houses. They were closely followed by the 369
Visitandines, the Sisters of the Holy Child Jesus,[54] the Dames de Saint-
Maur and many others; and Port-Royal ran schools under the rule drafted
by Jacqueline Pascal.

This was a very satisfactory state of affairs. Elementary education for
girls had been given a strong impetus during the preceding epoch, and
many Orders and congregations were dedicated to that work. The Sisters
of Charity were most prominent, but the Ursulines, the Visitandines and
the Notre-Dame Sisters ran schools for the daughters of the poor side by
side with those for the children of the wealthy. An extremely large number of local congregations and institutes were established and developed:
the Sisters of Providence; the Sisters of Ernemont, founded in Rouen in
1698 by a friend of Renty and Bemières[55]; Grignion de Montfort's Sisters
of Wisdom, a number of whom were dedicated to teaching; the Sisters of
the Holy Family at Besançon; the Filles de l'Enfance, who were forced to
disband on account of their Jansenist tendencies; the Sisters of the Christian Doctrine in Nancy; and the Sisters of the Adoration of the Blessed
Sacrament in the Avignon district. The fecundity of educational establishments during that period is staggering; they were perhaps a little chaotic,
but there is no doubt about the amount of good work done. The fact that
generally speaking more women than men today practise their faith in all
the Catholic countries of Europe is in a large measure due to the work of
the good teaching sisters.

---

54. To be distinguished from the modern Society of the Holy Child Jesus. (Translator)
55. The Sisters of Ernemont were initiated by the Company of the Blessed Sacrament and
the efforts of St. John Eudes; the Baron d'Ernemont was acquainted with them both.
The sisters also fell under the influence of Saint-Sulpice, for one of their early superiors was the Sulpician M. Blain; they were typical of the numerous congregations of
nuns who at that period gave their lives to teaching and hospital work, and embodied
the Catholic spirit of the day. But they were unique in two respects: they were the first
religious congregation of women to be formed by Colbert (1690), then Archbishop
of Rouen, into a congregation taking simple vows, unlike the Daughters of Charity,
whom St. Vincent de Paul made into a Society; in addition, under the spiritual influence of St. John Eudes they were the first to be called "Sisters of the Sacred Heart." On
the eve of the Revolution they had more than a hundred schools and nearly a hundred
hospitals. Cf. Canon Levé's *Qu'est-ce qu'une religieuse d'Ernemont?* (Rouen, 1932).

370   The position in relation to elementary education was not quite the same where boys were concerned. Not that they were neglected; we have seen[56] that "parish schools" and "charity schools" were widespread during the first half of the century. We have also seen how public authorities insisted on the need to open schools and the importance of regular attendance; and the bishops, or at least the best among them, moved in the same direction. At Autun, Gabriel de Roquette drew up a complete plan for primary education, and his successor Colbert, son of the great minister, went so far as to compel parish priests to bring in from the fields children who failed to attend school. Pavilion, Bishop of Alet, allotted seven thousand *livres* from his annual budget of twenty thousand for the education of the poor. Broadly speaking it is correct to say that in France (though much less so in Spain and Italy, and still less within the Empire) the majority of parishes had a primary school which normally depended upon the parish priest. But the problem of teachers still remained unsolved; they were in dreadfully short supply. No religious congregation was entirely devoted to teaching, so that the situation was very different from that affecting girls. The Brethren of the Common Life, the Piarists and the Doctrinarians leaned towards secondary education; the efforts of the Lazarists and M. Bourdoise's priests were limited in scope. In consequence a definite retrogression was noticeable about 1660. When Jean-Baptiste de la Salle arrived in the neighbourhood of Saint-Sulpice only one "charity" school had survived of the thirty that functioned in the time of M. Olier, and with very inadequate teaching staff. Such a deficiency, which could have been made up solely by institutions devoted to teaching poor children, was indefensible.

In 1666 the magistrates of Lyons received a long report under the heading *Remontrances* "dealing with the need for and usefulness of Christian schools for the teaching of poor children." The author was Charles Démia (1637–1689), a young priest of Lyons. He was a former student of Saint-Sulpice, a familiar figure belonging to the group of priests at Saint-Nicolas-du-Chardonnet, where the words of M. Bourdoise were still quoted: "If

---

56. See Volume 1 of this work, Chapter II, p. 120.

THE GREAT CENTURY OF SOULS: *Volume 2*

St. Paul were to return to the world he would become a school-teacher." 371
Démia's memorandum was doubtless read by one or other of the magistrates, but he received no official backing. He therefore decided to begin
alone. The children he wished to reach were the poor, the homeless, those
whose parents could ill afford the expense of education, or who could not
gain admission to the few "charity" schools that existed. It was for them he
created his "Little Schools," admission to which was quite free. The first was
opened at Lyons in 1667, and others soon followed, for groups of pious
laymen took an interest in the enterprise. At Lyons sixteen schools were
opened in twenty-two years, and ten more in the neighbourhood. Démia
established the Seminary of St. Charles to train the teachers he needed.
Families began to ask this splendid priest to do something for their daughters also, and he founded the Sisters of St. Charles. Such work required
proper organization and money. This was taken in hand by the Bureau des
Écoles, composed of priests and laymen; its officers handled the running of
the schools in regard to hygiene and curriculum. The undertaking was so
successful that the archbishop entrusted Charles Démia with control of all
schools in his diocese. Démia's work survived in the district around Lyons
until the Revolution. It was not only as a man of enterprise, a creator and an
organizer that this astonishing man made his mark; everything which today
goes by the name of "modern progress" in our schools already existed in his
achievements, including aptitude tests and career guidance. The extremely
secular Ferdinand Buisson in his *Dictionnaire de Pédagogie* paid homage to
him as the author of "the first attempt at methodical organization" in primary education. If the Assembly of the Clergy, before whom he first laid his
scheme in 1685, had followed it up, France would have been the first nation
to have a Minister of Education, and he would have been a Christian.

Charles Démia was not alone in his vocation. We have seen what was
accomplished by St. Grignion de Montfort and his disciples. Father Barré,
a Minim, a saintly and contemplative man associated with the foundation
of the Sisters of the Holy Child Jesus and the Dames de Saint-Maur, tried
to establish at Rouen, and later at Paris, a community to be known as the
Brothers of the Holy Child Jesus, with the object of giving free education to

372   poor children. In fact he made little progress, but his *Statuts et Règlements* laid the foundation of future achievements. One of his followers, Canon Nicolas Roland, an extraordinary character who at fifteen years of age performed in a play at the coronation of Louis XIV and later sailed in a pirate ship, took up Father Barré's idea and initiated at Rheims a scheme for the education of girls. He intended to establish a college for teachers, but did not live long enough to complete his work. Another disciple of Father Barré was Adrien Nyel, a humble teacher of burning enthusiasm and simplicity of soul. He attempted to set up schools all over France, and he might have achieved a great deal had he been a better organizer. All these efforts were not futile; they prepared the way for one who was a teacher of genius, a methodical organizer and a true saint who reaped the fruit of all that went before: St. Jean-Baptiste de la Salle.

In the spring of the year 1688 the parish of Saint-Sulpice in Paris was in a state of great excitement. From the Rue Dauphine to the Invalides, from the Seine to Notre-Dame des Champs, everyone was talking of the new ideas that were being introduced at the old school in the Rue Princesse, where the poor children of the district had been taught since the time of M. Olier. Some people thought the new master's strange methods absurd; others thought them excellent. He was a priest from Rheims, assisted by two laymen both oddly dressed. His first decision was to exclude Latin from the curriculum, and he abolished compulsory manual work; the whole class received instruction together, not individually. The dunces thought the discipline too severe; the parents thought it too lax. And the parish priest wondered whether he had done right to call on the services of this M. de la Salle.

The charity school in the Rue Princesse was in very poor shape when the new team took over. It was the last surviving school of the thirty functioning in M. Olier's time, and numbered two hundred pupils whom poor M. Compagnon, assisted by a fifteen-year-old boy and a voluntary worker who was a hosier by trade, found great difficulty in controlling. M. de la Salle and his two companions did not easily win obedience from these "wild young animals," as they called them. But apparently their methods were not bad, for order gradually returned to the school in the Rue Princesse. The number of pupils quickly grew, and they worked. The censure of the pessi-mists and everlasting critics came to nothing. The inquiry undertaken by M. Forbin-Janson on behalf of the authorities did not bear out the accusations brought by scandalmongers. Better still, the new parish priest M. Baudrand pressed M. de la Salle to open a new school in the Rue du Bac, and three hundred pupils were accepted. Thus the work prospered.

Who was this M. de la Salle whose methods were so effective? He was a priest of thirty-seven years of age (born in 1651) whose family came from Champagne. They had grown rich in business and rediscovered their ancient nobility in exercising the responsibilities of the magistracy. Intend-ed for the Church, Jean-Baptiste was made a canon at the age of sixteen and thus provided with a sound living. He studied zealously under M. Tron-son at the seminary of Saint-Sulpice. At twenty-seven he was ordained, returned to Rheims and settled down to the life of a well-to-do canon with an income of forty thousand *livres*, acquired quite legitimately. But fate—or rather Providence—unexpectedly brought him into contact with Nicolas Roland, his colleague in the cathedral chapter; later he met Adrien Nyel, who was obsessed with the idea of teaching as a method of reaching souls, and had answered the call of some pious women in the town who wished to open charity schools. Everything happened naturally and inexorably for Jean-Baptiste de la Salle. He was caught as it were in a net, but it was the net of God's will. How could he possibly have escaped the obligation he was under to Nicolas Roland who, on his deathbed, left the care of his orphan-age to Jean-Baptiste? He was equally susceptible to the warmth of Adrien Nyel, who appealed to his charity. To please Adrien he bought a house to accommodate the teachers of the schools for the poor; and he began to take an interest in these good people who had meant little to him and whom he had rather looked down upon from his prosperous middle-class position.

At length he plunged into the work, preaching a retreat to his boarders and providing them with a Rule of Life. Without really intending to do so he found he had created a training college for primary schoolteachers. The teaching profession thus came to him suddenly and unexpectedly. When Adrien Nyel one day went to establish a school at Guise, Canon de la Salle took his place in the classroom. His family thought he was mad, and when he installed the teachers in the family home they were convinced that he was; so much so that his own brothers left home in disgust. Things got even worse when, on the advice of Father Barré, whom he went to consult in Paris, he obeyed to the letter Christ's command to the rich young man. He resigned his canonry and distributed all his wealth to the poor, providing for the destitute during a dreadful famine. Immediately he became poor among the poor, as were the teachers around him and with whom he now felt on close and brotherly terms. His little group was established. It was not yet an institute, much less the congregation to be known as the Brothers of the Christian Schools; but in the sight of God and man it was already in existence on May 28, 1684. About a dozen schoolteachers made a vow to dedicate their lives to teaching the children of the common people, to live as lay religious in poverty and self-sacrifice, with Jean-Baptiste de la Salle as their leader and soul of their little group. A great work was unobtrusively born into the Church.

Jean-Baptiste de la Salle was indeed an extraordinary man. This well-to-do canon of gentle and refined disposition, modest and unassuming in his way, became a stern ascetic, using the discipline, wearing a hair shirt and a painful belt against his skin, sleeping on a plank and fasting more often than the law enjoined. But he was also a mystic, as is clear from his splendid book *Méditations pour le temps de la retraite.* He was a true son of the French school, of Saint-Sulpice and of Bérulle; his one aim in life was, to use the words of his predecessors, to "adhere to God" and to promote His Kingdom. The efficacy of his spiritual life may be compared in some respects with that of Monsieur Vincent's. The influence he exerted, the sweet force that attached men to him, despite his extreme humility, sprang from his interior life. He would, of course, have been the last to regard his work as unique, vastly ahead of his time and stamped with the seal of genius; but it was so none the less.

He devoted his whole life to this unforeseen vocation to teach. He was to be nothing but a pedagogue, but in the noblest and fullest sense of that word. He had the primary and indispensable quality of a teacher, an understanding of children; he knew them and loved them. Moreover, he did not hesitate to lend a hand himself, taking the classes, going from desk to desk pointing out mistakes, and assisting those who were slow. His experience was unrivalled, and his splendid book, *Conduite des écoles*, shows him to have been a brilliant theorist. He regarded the ability to adapt oneself to a child as the foremost quality of a teacher, to be direct and realistic in order to reach the child's understanding. For that reason he did away with the teaching of Latin in beginners' classes, an old and rather silly practice.[57] To create a spirit of competition among students he made them work in teams, correcting each other's work. Before his time the teacher endeavoured with varying degrees of success to give individual instruction to each child in turn. In future the class was taught as a whole, the students following the lessons in a book, each being questioned in turn. This is now the essential principle of modern teaching practice in primary schools, where spelling and arithmetic hold first place.

But many other ideas developed around this central principle. Teachers had to be trained to practise the new method of teaching. His modest institute aimed at providing this type of training; he founded training establishments to which every diocese sent prospective teachers and which eventually became the basis of our teachers' training colleges. And, thought Jean-Baptiste, why should there not be special courses for adults and young people already working? These he organized, and they were the forerunners of our present-day continuation courses, clubs and study circles. The arrangement of special training facilities for difficult and backward pupils—a quite recent undertaking—was also the idea of Jean-Baptiste de la Salle. This great teacher appreciated that Latin was not indispensable to many middle-class children on completion of their primary education; they required instead a knowledge of the sciences and technical subjects. For them he founded the first of what are now our modern technical institutes. So manifest in his achievements are his genius for education and his talent for educational

---

57. This was also the opinion of Comenius in Moravia, but he did not succeed in getting it approved.

technique that even the most secular-minded of our modern French theorists, such as Ferdinand Buisson and Victor Duruy, pay homage to him and regard him as the precursor of modern educational practice.

Such was the man who staggered Paris by his innovations, after trying them out at Rheims and a few small towns. The success achieved in the neighbourhood of Saint-Sulpice gave new strength to the little band. In 1691 he took a large house in Vaugirard, and in October of the following year a training centre was opened with ten young trainees. The time had come for Jean-Baptiste de la Salle to establish his work on more solid foundations, and on June 6, 1694, he and six of his most dependable colleagues made a vow to the Blessed Trinity "to form a society for the purpose of maintaining free schools together and with others." The Institute of the Brothers of the Christian Schools was founded. They were not to be priests, nor even clerics. To enable them to remain loyal to their vocation as teachers they would undertake no ministry. They would pursue only the ideal of the Christian teacher, subordinating every purpose to the formation of children—a sufficiently vast and noble ideal in itself. Their attire, adopted at Rheims where it caused great amusement among those who were ill-disposed towards them, was a cassock of rough serge, a white collar turned down, a three-cornered hat and a large cloak with loose sleeves similar to the one then worn by working people. As news of their success spread, this garb would be seen more and more frequently in French towns. Mme. de Maintenon's confessor, Godet des Marais, invited the Brothers to teach at Chartres, and the Duc de Béthune established them in Calais at his own expense. Soon they were at Troyes and Avignon, in Normandy and Burgundy. Wherever bishops or governors desired to open schools they called on the Brothers: Mende, Alès, Grenoble, Valence, Moulins, Boulogne-sur-Mer and even at Versailles. Wherever Protestantism still remained strong the authorities relied upon the teaching of the Brothers to instill faith into the minds of the children.

Such success was not attained without provoking violent opposition; the life of Jean-Baptiste de la Salle was indeed a perpetual cross, as is the privilege of all great pioneers. Desperately he fought all who stood in his way and whose rule-of-thumb methods he upset. The "master writers" and schoolmasters who earned their living by teaching the children of those who could pay were furious at the development of an institute whose members offered education without payment. There were even incidents in which the schools were ransacked and the Brothers maltreated. A few bishops, either prompted by these people or perhaps to avoid trouble, refused to accept the Brothers even when they themselves had sent for them. Strange and sometimes sordid intrigues were instigated against the great pioneer; legal proceedings were instituted in which justice was thwarted to the end that he might lose his case. He also had to defend himself and safeguard his work against those who endeavoured to take it over and use it for purposes different from his own: the Jansenists, especially in the south of France, showed excessive interest in the schools and the Brothers, and when their founder reacted against their schemes their wrath exploded, and they set out to destroy his work. In the face of countless and never-ending trials Jean-Baptiste de la Salle's weapon was a sublime confidence in God and humble submission to His will. The internal crises which shook his Institute caused him the greatest pain; they were perhaps the normal teething troubles of a new enterprise, but they were to him the source of intense suffering. There came a day when he had doubts about himself, his vocation and the usefulness of the work he had undertaken. St. Teresa had also experienced similar moments of black despair.

But his soul was too magnanimous and too strong to yield to discouragement. The great majority of the Brothers remained loyal to him, even when, almost outlawed, he was forced to leave Paris; even when a tactless bishop endeavoured to have him replaced as Superior of the Institute; even, above all, when an attempt was made to break up the Institute and distribute its fragments among the dioceses. There exists a letter of matchless beauty signed by the directors of all his houses, begging their old superior, indeed commanding him "in the name of the society to which he had promised obedience," to return and place himself at their head and save the work he had undertaken. He obeyed and came back; that was in 1714. The reign of the Great King was nearing its end; but St. Jean-Baptiste de la Salle had

378   given his Institute, tormented though it was by so many formidable forces, the means of preserving Christianity in the souls of the children of the common people, even after the outbreak of the Revolution.

When he died on April 7, 1719, the Brothers of the Christian Schools numbered two hundred seventy-four members. By 1900, the year of their heroic and illustrious founder's canonization, they numbered twenty thousand, with over three hundred fifty thousand pupils in their schools.

12. AN UNFULFILLED HOPE

DESPITE such figures as Jean-Baptiste de la Salle, Louis Marie Grignion de Montfort and Margaret Mary Alacoque, not forgetting Rancé and the glorious pulpit-orators, there remained aspects of the classical age which did not encourage optimism. From some points of view the outlook was distressing. At the end of the sixteenth century the Church had hoped that simultaneously with the work of order and renovation the work of reconquest might proceed, for she was not content to abandon for all time to the Protestants the territories in which they had settled. Unfortunately, the "Counter-Reformation" did not continue during the reign of Louis XIV. There were two methods envisaged by Catholics to reconquer lost souls, and they attempted to put both into effect together: conversion and the use of force. Both methods, demonstrated respectively in St. Peter Canisius and the Battle of the White Mountain, seemed condemned to failure.

During the first half of the seventeenth century high-minded men considered that a reconciliation between Catholics and Protestants was possible.[58] These men were to be found in both camps, and serious efforts had been made towards reconciliation without worthwhile results. The Lutheran Calixte, the master of Helmstedt, was criticized both by his co-religionists and by Catholics, and the great Capuchin Valerio Magni was eventually thrown into prison. The idea of reunion of the Churches was not however

---

58. See Volume 1 of this work, Chapter III, p. 207.

abandoned: it was taken up again during the last thirty years of the century
and actively pursued. The situation appeared favourable, for the early fanaticism of the Reformation had seemingly diminished and various princely
families of the Empire had returned to Catholicism. The various shades of
Protestantism were more or less in the throes of a crisis and incapable of
organizing a Church[59]; they were uneasy about the progress of Socinian-
ism[60] and worried about the growing power of the princes.

It was considered that a skillful policy of maintaining contact and a
disposition to make concessions might furnish good results, and this was
attempted in 1665 by Cristobal de Rojas y Spinola, a zealous Franciscan,
more subtle, skillful and conciliatory perhaps than he was prudent and
thoughtful. He was, nevertheless, a true apostle of reunion. As Bishop of
Tina in Dalmatia, later of Wiener-Neustadt and confessor to the empress,
he persuaded Rome that only he could bring about a *rapprochement*. Innocent XI, who was grieved by the Turkish threat and the great rift between
Christians, put whole-hearted trust in him, and the Emperor Leopold
firmly supported him. Armed with this twofold mandate, Spinola visited
the various states of Germany, called on the princes and made numerous
contacts with theologians of the reformed Church. The Papal Legate Bevilacqua was sent especially to follow up his efforts, and the ardent Spaniard
imagined that victory was in his hands. He felt convinced of the early conversion of the Elector of Saxony and the Elector Palatine; in Hanover, in
any case, John Frederick, won over to Rome, was assisting the Capuchins
and Jesuits to convert the masses, and abjurations were so numerous that
Rome appointed a Vicar Apostolic. A wave of optimism spread despite the
pessimistic reports of the Nuncio at Vienna. It was at this juncture that the
Dane Niels Stensen (or Stenon) became a convert, was ordained priest and
eventually consecrated bishop. Molanus, the Lutheran abbot of Lokkum,
appeared to be on the point of recanting. When Spinola went to Rome in

---

59. See *The Church of the Classical Age: The Era of Great Splintering*, Volume 1, Chapter
    III.
60. See Henri Daniel-Rops, *An Age of Renewal: The Catholic Reformation* (Providence,
    RI: Cluny, 2023), Volume 2, p. 290.

1678 to give an account of his mission his infectious enthusiasm influenced well-intentioned people, including the Pope, into believing that they were on the eve of a great victory.

In actual fact, when it came to the preparation of a plan for reunion, matters appeared less straightforward. In 1683, after many discussions, Spinola and his questioners agreed upon the following points: Rome would concede the marriage of priests, Communion under both species for the laity, and approve a German liturgy; in consideration of which the Lutherans would recognize the Pope. Other points of doctrine would be submitted to a new council; meanwhile the Tridentine decisions would be held in abeyance. By all appearances Spinola went too far, and the Holy Office, despite Innocent XI, who continued to rely upon the generous Franciscan, was right to protest. Further, two questions remained unanswered: one concerned Catholic property which had been secularized, and the other concerned the role which the princes had assumed within the Churches. It soon became clear that the latter was the stumbling-block. In Hanover, John Frederick's successor proved hostile to every approach. Everywhere else, in Sweden, Denmark and Brandenburg, the situation hardened. It was the same in Catholic countries: in France, where the Edict of Nantes was about to be revoked; in Bohemia, where the saintly Cardinal von Harrach, a great pioneer of missionary work, was being more and more hampered in his activities; in Hungary, where the Primate of Gran continued to effect conversions by the use of force, exile and the galleys. Repudiated by Rome, thwarted in Germany by vested interests, Spinola continued in vain, though tirelessly, his travels in search of reconciliation. When he died in 1695 he had achieved nothing definite.

While Spinola was active in the practical sphere, theoretical discussions began between the Catholics and the Lutherans. The Lutheran representative was Gottfried Wilhelm von Leibniz (1646–1716), an encyclopedic genius, learned in literature and science, theology and history, philosophy and law; a remarkably engaging personality, thoughtful, shrewd and generous. His splendid qualifications were the result not only of vast erudition, but also of his travels in Europe, where he had made the acquaintance of

such men as Malebranche, the great Arnauld, Newton and Huyghens. Leibniz was a member of the Aulic Council at the court of Hanover, that is to
say one of the most active centres of irenicism. He had an intense desire for
unity; he revived the grandiose ideas of Sully and Grotius, and dreamed of
rebuilding the unity of Europe through the creation of a Christian republic.
To him Christianity was one and the Church was one; one in her belief in a
few great fundamental truths that guaranteed salvation; one in the love that
united all her members. Leibniz was by no means hostile to the Catholic and
Roman Church. He admired her discipline and her religious Orders, whom
he called "a saintly, a heavenly host." He even understood the customs, liturgy, ceremonial and music of the Church. He reproached her, however, for
being loaded with too many corrupt practices, for being intolerant—in his
eyes excommunication was as reprehensible as schism itself—and with cling-
ing to useless dogma. Moreover, Leibniz did not regard Protestant churches
as being universal either; they were individual churches, just as intolerant
and just as intractable in their dogmatism. In short, the author of *Traité de la
Souveraineté*, *Essais de Théodicée* and *La Monadologie* demanded the adherence of all Christians to an invisible Church built on charity and faith, while
adherence to a visible Church might be maintained by diversity within unity.

About 1680 intellectual circles of Christian Europe were giving Leibniz's ideas serious attention. The Holy See was slightly misled by the terms
he used in referring to the religious Orders, the Blessed Virgin, the saints,
and even papal authority itself; it saw him as a messenger of reconciliation,
so much so that it offered him a post as librarian at the Vatican! He maintained relations with the Archbishop of Mainz, the Papal Legate Bevilacqua,
Father Malebranche, and even the Nuncio in Vienna. But his relationship
with Bossuet was the closest of all. From his early youth Bossuet had always
enjoyed discussions with Protestants. He embarked upon them loyally and
seriously, certainly with the firm intention of winning Protestants over to
the Catholic Church, but he was equally determined not to yield on basic
principles. When Bossuet published his *Explication de la doctrine chrétienne*
Leibniz assured him that he had an extremely high opinion of his work;
similarly Bossuet's later book, *Histoire des variations*, claimed the attention

of the German philosopher. In 1692 there began a correspondence between the two which, with a short interruption, lasted until 1702. Both these brilliant men passionately defended their respective points of view, utilizing all their resources of knowledge and logic.

But it soon became as clear as day that their two concepts were irreconcilable. To begin with, how could a Catholic, a member of the Roman Church, accept Leibniz's theories as to the very meaning of "Church"? Leibniz, logically pursuing his arguments, rejected the ecumenical character of the Council of Trent, while Bossuet rightly claimed that the Tridentine decisions constituted the very bases of the restored Church because they were the genuine voice of Tradition. An even more profound difference between the two minds lay in their conception of faith, where there was no possible chance of agreement; here Leibniz claimed liberty of thought, while Bossuet stood for full adherence to the truth of the Church. When Leibniz broke off the correspondence in 1702 under the pretext that "he found the peremptory tone of his correspondent discouraging," it was in fact because, as the Duke of Hanover's representative on the Aulic Council, he could not continue to discuss a reunion which must deprive him of his rights, since the duke expected to become King of England on the death of Queen Anne. The relationship had at least proved that no compromise was possible between two absolutely incompatible doctrines. It meant the end of the conciliatory discussions. A few intrepid souls continued indeed to labour the subject, but they were modest attempts with no far-reaching consequences. On the threshold of the eighteenth century it became clear that Catholic propaganda was no longer gaining any ground from the various branches of Protestantism.

Hopes that Catholicism might recover some territory in the East, in the areas of schismatic "Orthodox" Christianity, were also dashed. More serious still, the Uniate Church was threatened. Reunion had been the means of leading back the Christians of Lithuania and the Ukraine[61] to the Catholic fold in 1596, enabling them to reform and reorganize their Church, which

61. See *An Age of Renewal: The Catholic Reformation*, Volume 2, p. 443.

was then declining. The hostility of the Orthodox, culminating in the mur-
der of St. Josaphat Kuntsewycz in 1623, continued, and the conflict broke
out again between the Metropolitan Orthodox and the Uniate bishops. The
reunion was honoured under the authority of the energetic Metropolitan
Peter Mokyla, but the Cossack Wars continually weakened it. In 1705 Peter
the Great himself caused Uniate priests to be put to the torture; others were
exiled to Siberia. Worse still, Catholics of the Latin rite treated their Uniate brethren badly on account of their particular form of liturgy, the marriage of their priests and the fact that they used leavened bread for the Holy
Eucharist. The nobles and the Catholic bishops excluded the Ruthenian
bishops from the Polish senate. The situation had become so tense by 1714
that the Metropolitan Kiszka, assisted by the Nuncio at Warsaw, undertook
to call a synod at Lemberg in an attempt to "Latinize" the Uniate Church,
but there was little hope of saving it.

The situation was nowhere very satisfactory among the Orthodox. The
Patriarchate of Constantinople (which was under Turkish rule) continued
to argue peevishly over the validity of the Latin form of baptism and tran-
substantiation as understood by Rome. In Serbia, Catholics were so badly
treated that about forty thousand of them crossed over to Hungary, and
the Orthodox clergy attempted to use force against those who remained. In
Romania some Catholic nobles managed with the aid of a few bishops to
reconstitute a church, but it remained under threat from both the Turkish
authorities and the adherents of Orthodoxy. It did not become established
until about 1730. The only serious attempt made by Catholicism to penetrate the Orthodox zone was that undertaken in Russia by the Croat Kri-
janich and a few Jesuit missions. The pan-slavism of Peter the Great offered
them little hope of success. It seems that everywhere we look we see the
work of peaceful reconquest and expansion being brutally arrested; and this
at the very moment when the quarrel of Chinese Rites was undermining the
work of missionaries in Asia.[62]

---

62. See *The Church of the Classical Age: The Era of Great Splintering*, Volume 1, Chapter
II.

13. A WASTED PAST: THE POLITICAL
COUNTER-REFORMATION

THE halting of the century-old dream of *political* Counter-Reformation—the attempt to reinstate Catholicism by force—was just as brutal. This attempt was, as we have seen, halted at the beginning of the century,[63] but the spirit that inspired it still survived, though of a very different quality from what it had been. In consequence, its efforts resulted only in failure.

Was it only to serve the interests of Catholicism that Louis XIV used coercion in his dealings with the Protestants,[64] ultimately revoking the Edict of Nantes? Was it not rather with the intention of pressing his principle of unification to its logical conclusion? At all events, it is plain that his severity, which drove so much excellent material from the country and caused the bloody revolt of the "White Shirts," did not succeed, for it had to be replaced by more tolerant methods.

A comparable policy within the Empire had even worse consequences. In the hope of achieving in Hungary what it had done in Austria, and making general use of the coercive measures adopted by Cardinal Pazmany,[65] the Imperial Government destroyed the *modus vivendi* so painfully established with the Magyar Protestants. Profiting by the impetus derived from victory over the Turks[66] the Government quartered German troops in the land of St. Stephen, and rebellion ensued. Following the proclamation of Croatia-Zrinyi, in answer to the call of the son of Raköczy, and more especially of Imre Tökölli, fighting began around the Danube similar to that carried on by the "White Shirts" in France. It was savagely suppressed; the rebel bands were easily overcome by the Austrian regular army. Most of the leaders were captured, and others took refuge with the Turks. Their pastors were condemned as heretics and traitors, their temples were closed, and the Grand

63. See Volume 1 of this work, Chapter III, p. 193.
64. See above, Chapter IV, p. 259.
65. See Volume 1 of this work, Chapter III, p. 203.
66. At St. Gothard; see below, p. 393.

Master of the Teutonic Order became governor of Pressburg. The reaction was so violent and so obviously intended to smother Hungarian nationalism as much as Protestantism that the rebellion broke out anew with even greater fury. This time Catholics and Protestants united, which resulted in a bitter struggle with cruel fighting on both sides. The Hungarians stood alone against the enormous power of the Empire, and history has recorded the courage and tenacity of their resistance. The struggle was carried on by Imre Tökölli, assisted behind the scenes by France, and even supported by a revolt of the Czech peasants. Finally, appreciating the hopelessness of his position, he appealed to Turkey as a last resort; and the Sultan replied by launching a gigantic army against Vienna. Such was the consequence of the so-called Counter-Reformation conducted in the worst possible manner. When the Turks were driven out, Buda and the Danubian fortresses recaptured and Hungary completely subdued and systematically Germanized, the unifying authoritarianism of the Hapsburgs triumphed, but not Catholicism.

In England an attempt to reinstate Catholicism was crushed even more decisively, for the outcome resulted not only in political defeat but also in the final eradication of Catholic traditions. For a time, however, it seemed that the country might return to its former loyalties. For as yet there was no real concord within the ranks of Protestantism itself[67]; a struggle went on more or less openly between Anglicanism and each of the other reformed sects with the object of imposing their respective creeds upon the country. But the one point on which all these hostile brethren were agreed was that Popery must be eliminated; not on any account were the "Jesuits" to regain a foothold. Cromwell's Commonwealth led, in fact, to a Puritan dictatorship under which Catholics were denied every right. The restoration of the monarchy under Charles II (1660–1685) in no way changed the situation, despite his own leanings towards Catholicism and pressure from his mother

---

67. Concerning events in Protestant England and the consequent crises see *The Church of the Classical Age: The Era of Great Splintering*, Volume 1, Chapter III; Volume 2, Chapter IV.

and sister, the two Henriettas. His Declaration of Indulgence, under which priests were authorized to celebrate Mass in private houses, provoked such a furore in Parliament and had such a bad effect on public opinion that he was forced to hurry through Parliament his Test Act (1673), under which all persons holding office were required to take an oath of supremacy, recognizing His Majesty as supreme head of the Church. The king's brother, the Duke of York, a convert to Catholicism, renounced all his appointments, including the post of High Admiral of the splendid fleet he had created, in order to avoid taking an oath which he regarded as blasphemous. But even those measures proved insufficient. Hatred of Catholicism was shared by every shade of Protestantism. The Popish Plot, fabricated by the ageing Anglican minister Titus Oates, was believed without question: the Jesuits were supposed to be organizing a new Gunpowder Plot, Catholics to be awaiting the landing of French forces and Ireland to be implicated. Six Jesuits and nine other priests were hanged; two thousand Catholics were either thrown into prison or compelled to flee the country. The question of depriving the Duke of York of his right of succession was under consideration.

In the midst of this tempestuous atmosphere the Duke of York became king as James II (1685–1688). The English people had such unpleasant memories of Cromwell's Commonwealth that their loyalty to James overcame their religious bigotry, and he was accepted without demur. James was courageous, upright and virtuous, but stubborn and narrow-minded. No sooner had he become king than he thought it his duty to restore Catholicism by law. He openly attended Catholic services, received Holy Communion and surrounded himself with Catholic advisers; and with such inordinate haste that Innocent XI advised prudence. Monmouth, an illegitimate son of Charles II, landed in Puritan Scotland, and the country rose up in response to the call of Argyle, son of a Protestant executed after the restoration of Charles. Monmouth was defeated at Sedgemoor, and Lord Chief Justice Jeffreys was sent to punish the insurgents at the "Bloody Assize." James II set up a court of ecclesiastical commission and prepared the way for a return to Catholicism. In 1687 he annulled the Test Act; Father Petre, S.J., was given a seat on the Council; the Archbishop of Canterbury and seven Anglican bishops were committed to the Tower. It was at this time 387 that Dryden, a convert to Catholicism, wrote his strange poem, "The Hind and the Panther," glorifying the Roman Church. The king considered he did a wise thing when he issued his Declaration of Indulgence, the aim of which was to link Non-conformists, Baptists, Presbyterians and even Quakers with the Catholics against the Anglicans. Staunch Protestants were suspicious of such company, and public opinion was roused when all Anglicans were gradually excluded from important official appointments. Parliament refused to approve the Declaration in favour of the king's "innocent Catholic subjects"; a jury acquitted the seven bishops of seditious libel, and the stage was set for revolution. Protestant England had tolerated her unpopular king for three years in the hope that he would soon be succeeded by his elder daughter Mary, a Protestant, who had married the Protestant William of Orange. Their fury burst when a Catholic heir, James Edward, was born in the palace. James II prepared to retreat before the growing storm.[68] William landed his Huguenot army at Torbay. His standards carried the legend *Pro religione protestante*. With the flight of James II Catholicism had lost the day.

Henceforward the small band of English Catholics, numbering about a thirtieth of the population, diminished in importance. They were treated as inferior citizens and barred from posts of responsibility; they alone among the "non-conformists" were refused religious freedom. The Declaration of Rights (1689) allowed freedom of worship to all others who recognized the schema of Christian faith as laid down in the Thirty-Nine Articles; the only bodies excluded were the Catholics, the Unitarians and the Jews. Harsh measures were taken against all Papists, and the "crime of the Mass" was again punishable. It is doubtful whether William and Mary (1689–1702)

---

68. The extent to which public feeling had been roused is suggested by a curious incident which took place on December 22, 1688. On learning that the king had left the palace Londoners became panic-stricken. It was rumoured that the Irish were attacking London. There was a beating of drums, a great bustle of muskets and pikes; the streets were illuminated and barricades were set up. A state of uncertainty reigned, but nothing happened after all. Someone shouted, "No popery!" and the crowd flung itself upon all Catholic embassies. The incident became known as the "Irish Night."

themselves approved of this fanaticism, but they were compelled to yield to public opinion. Anne Stuart (1702–1714)—"Good Queen Anne"—second daughter of James II and wife of Prince George of Denmark, treated the lower Anglican clergy kindly, but continued to apply to Catholics the full rigour of the penal laws. The Act of Settlement passed by Parliament in 1701 excluded all Catholics from succession to the throne, and Anne, who would gladly have bequeathed her crown to her half-brother James Edward (James III), was obliged to sign the Act. She was succeeded in 1714 by her cousin of the House of Hanover, who became George I, a moderate but thorough-going Protestant. No further hope remained to the Catholic cause in the land of St. Edward and St. Thomas à Becket.

The Counter-Reformation in England was therefore not only a conspicuous failure, but it brought about a very strong Protestant reaction. A similar reaction was experienced elsewhere (e.g., in Scandinavia). In Denmark, after Christian V's *coup d'état* of 1660, all previous anti-Catholic enactments were collected together as a code of laws and enforced (1683). Priests entering the country were liable to execution; anyone converted to popery ran the risk of banishment and confiscation of property. When the French ambassador claimed the right to build a Catholic chapel he had to undertake not to allow any Danish Papist to enter it. Furthermore, the vitality of the Catholic faith in Denmark definitely languished, despite the notable conversion of the savant Niels Stensen, who was appointed Vicar Apostolic but was forced to live in exile; despite also the secret missions financed by the Bishop of Fürstenberg and organized by the Jesuits at Münster. By 1715 the Catholics of Denmark numbered no more than one in five thousand.

The position was no better in Sweden. The conversion of Queen Christina[69] had created a sensation, but none had followed her example. Her cousin and successor, Charles XI, strengthened the anti-Catholic laws, and from 1686 onwards they were precisely the same as those of Denmark. Converts were banished and their property confiscated, and priests could enter the country only secretly. So great was the distrust of anything akin

---

69. See Volume 1 of this work, Chapter III, p. 206.

to popery that Ussadius, a venerable champion of Lutheranism, was condemned to thirty years' imprisonment for having dared to teach that works
were useful towards salvation. Only in the last twenty-five years of the
eighteenth century, under the philosopher King Gustavus III, was it possible for Oster, the Vicar Apostolic, to reinvigorate the unhappy Catholic
Church in Sweden.[70]

In Germany the position was not much better, though legal measures
seem to have been less severe in certain areas. Many German states, such as
the episcopal electorates and Bavaria, remained absolutely loyal to Catholicism, as did the ecclesiastical principalities of Fulda, Münster, Ratisbon
and Würtzburg. In Hesse and the Palatine a *modus vivendi* was established
between Catholics and Protestants; while in Saxony, Frederick Augustus,
converted to Catholicism and elected King of Poland, came to an arrangement under which Catholics were given the right of private worship. Everywhere else, however, notably in Prussia, Protestant reaction was violent,
either openly or beneath the surface. The Grand Elector Frederick William
proved tolerant, but from 1688 his successor Frederick III was relentless,
encouraged as he was by those French refugees who had settled in Prussia
after the revocation of the Edict of Nantes. In any case, Frederick entertained rather extravagant ideas: he desired religious unity in his states, but
his readiness to reach an agreement with Rome was dependent upon the
Pope's agreeing to crown him king. When his plans were frustrated he withdrew from Catholics the right to practise their religion, and reinforced the
old decrees, which resulted in persecution and the expulsion of the Jesuits.
The Catholic population of all the Prussian states scarcely exceeded three
percent and was definitely on the decrease.

In some parts of Europe the situation was even worse, and Catholics
were severely persecuted—in the Low Countries especially, though here
Catholicism put up a vigorous defence. Since 1648[71] Catholics had been
continually frustrated, and they were suspected of being pro-French. The

---

70. See *The Church of the Classical Age: The Era of Great Splintering,* Volume 2, Chapter V.
71. See Volume 1 of this work, Chapter III, p. 196.

falsity of this accusation was proved by their staunch loyalty in the struggle against Louis XIV; nevertheless they were treated as enemies of the State and forced to lead a more or less underground existence. Officials were forbidden to visit them; their votive chapels and crosses set up on the highways were demolished, and they were unable to protest. Many priests and religious were exiled, but the Church, though virtually outlawed, struggled on in grim determination. Mindful of the lessons of Rovenius, they bribed Protestant officials into allowing them to practise their faith; they educated their young, and trained their priests in Germany. About 1671 there were ten thousand Catholics in Amsterdam and eighteen "houses of prayer"; by 1715 there were approximately three hundred thousand Catholics in the whole of Holland. The deplorable affair of the Jansenist schism in Utrecht[72] severely hampered the forward movement of Dutch Catholicism, but only for a while.

Nowhere in the whole of the West was Protestant savagery more in evidence and Catholic resistance more heroic than in Ireland. The religious and political aspects of the conflict combined to render it implacable. Since the days when Cromwell's Roundheads subjected Catholic Ireland to English discipline by means of barbarous repression, that country, though reduced almost to helplessness, had continued to strike fear into her executioners. To the Irish people loyalty to the Catholic faith and to her national consciousness were inseparable. She defended both freedoms with her blood. It was not surprising therefore that the Irish interfered in England's politics, were hostile to her Anglican kings and allied themselves with her Catholic pretenders. But this confusion of interests could result only in more harsh repression. When under Charles II tempers were roused in consequence of the consternation provoked by the "Popish Plot" fabricated by Titus Oates, the Irish were the first to be accused of having fostered the conspiracy. Oliver Plunket, Archbishop of Armagh and Primate of Ireland, was sent to the gallows at Tyburn in order to satisfy public opinion. Peace returned to the Emerald Isle during the very short reign of James II; the Irish Catholics

---

72. See below, Chapter VI, p. 531.

recovered under the vicegerency of Talbot Tyrconnel—"Mad Dick"—and 391
were allowed a measure of autonomy. But the revolution of 1688 plunged
them into misfortune. They rose against the Protestant monarchs William
and Mary, and assisted James II to land at Kinsale with five thousand men
whom Louis XIV had placed at his disposal. James was defeated at the battle
of the Boyne (1690) and returned to France. The Irish fought their last desperate battles, and were forced to yield at Limerick (1690). The subsequent
treaty promised them freedom to practise their religion, but William and
Mary, under pressure from the Protestants, were unable to keep their word.
Persecution was quickly resumed. Catholics were excluded from Parliament;
they were forbidden to have priests, to carry arms or to open schools. They
were literally blockaded in their island, and any man who sent his son to be
educated on the Continent was forced to pay a fine of one hundred pounds.
They were treated as inferiors and obliged, on pain of a fine of sixty pounds,
to assist at Protestant services. Many were driven from their estates, which
were taken over by their enemies (a total of one million acres were thus confiscated), and they were the victims of any extortions that the English cared
to impose upon them. Terror reigned throughout the country; as cruel as, if
not worse than, that experienced by the French Protestants after the revocation of the Edict of Nantes. But their resistance did not weaken. Patrick
Donnelly, assisted by seventy-seven priests, twenty-two religious and nine
nuns, journeyed from place to place throughout the country. Mass was celebrated at secret meeting places upon an altar-stone, the *corrig-an-aifrion*.
Donnelly was eventually captured, and most of the bishops had to flee to
France and Portugal. Many, however, with the aid of French bishops, opened
seminaries on the Continent for training young priests who would continue
the struggle. The eclipse of the Catholic Church in the land of St. Patrick was
merely apparent: Ireland was not conquered; she was not even discouraged.

Poland, another bulwark of Catholicism at the other end of Europe,
appeared on the point of collapse. For a long time the country had been a
source of grave anxiety to the Church,[73] but she remained as magnificently

---

73. See Volume 1 of this work, Chapter III, p. 200.

loyal at the end of the seventeenth century as she had formerly been. The dramatic events of 1655, when the monks of Czestochowa repulsed the Swedes, seem to have had the effect of sublimating their faith. Nowhere was the Church surrounded with more love and veneration; nowhere were the feasts of Christmas and Easter celebrated with greater devotion, or the prayers said to Our Lady more fervent. And nowhere were the clergy more powerful. They owned eight hundred thousand serfs, and one archbishop was the proprietor of sixteen towns. All the Orders, including such new French congregations as the Lazarists and the Sisters of the Visitation, were active, and mission work was in full swing. Yet the position of Poland was extremely dangerous, squeezed as she was between schismatic Russia and Protestant Prussia and Sweden, and unable to communicate with the Catholic West except through Bohemia. At home she was in even greater peril from the elective monarchical system, from the ambitions and incurable anarchy of the nobles, and from the underlying disagreement between the different regions and classes of the population. This state of affairs whetted the appetites of her neighbours, two of whom—Prussia and Russia—were rapidly expanding. King John Sobieski (1674–1696) halted the march of decadence; on his death a Frenchman, Louis de Conti, victor of Steinkirk, was elected king, but England and Brandenburg-Prussia opposed his nomination. The Elector of Saxony therefore became king and reigned at Warsaw as Augustus II. The War of the League of Augsburg, the Great Northern War and the War of the Spanish Succession isolated Poland and deprived her of the support of France. Bordered by Russia, Sweden and Saxony, lacking a strong army to safeguard the integrity of her frontiers, torn more and more by the forces of anarchy, the unhappy country could only await the edicts of Peter the Great, communicated to her through the Russian ambassador. The tragedy of partition already loomed on the horizon.

It was indeed a far cry from the time when the Catholic world, led by the newly born Tridentine Church, seemed on the point of overcoming her adversaries; the days of the White Mountain and the political "Counter-Reformation" seemed very far away. The spirit of reform, however, the same spirit that had made possible the victory at Lepanto, still survived, and it

found expression in the sphere in which it had met with its greatest success. Christendom, if we may still use the word, was threatened not only by
internal dissension; another and a very old peril had just raised its head in
the East—the Turkish threat. An offensive had been preparing since 1656,
when the Albanian Köprili, Grand Vizir of Mohammed V, took control of
the Ottoman Empire. In 1663 it was unleashed against the Danubian territories. Hungary, the bastion of the Cross, was the victim of brutal anti-Prot-
estant measures devised by the emperors, and many Hungarians had thrown
in their lot with the Turks. Faced with this danger, the Papacy assumed its
ancient role and called for a crusade. In 1664, responding to an appeal by
Alexander VII, an international army under the command of the Italian
Montecuccoli halted a Turco-Tartar army two hundred thousand strong in
the neighbourhood of the St. Gothard monastery on the Raab, where a con-
tingent sent by Louis XIV and including the flower of the French nobility
fought with great distinction. But the threat of the Crescent was not thereby repelled, because the Emperor Leopold was in too great a hurry to sign
peace through fear of his Hungarian subjects, and also because Hungary
had been ravaged by war for many years. The Turks then launched a new
attack, this time against Crete, a dependency of Venice. Despite Clement
IX's earnest appeals and the help sent by Louis XIV, Candia was compelled
to capitulate (1669). A second Turkish assault upon the Danube was made
in support of the Hungarian rebel Tökölli, who had asked for their help. A
complete rout followed. Two hundred fifty thousand soldiers of ten nations
flung themselves upon Vienna and its fifty thousand inhabitants, and the
dawn of the year 1683 seemed to herald the end.

But once again the Pope acted. Innocent XI begged all Christian states
to abandon their internecine quarrels and unite against the advance of Islam;
Louis XIV alone of the great Catholic princes of the West remained deaf
to his entreaties. In Vienna labourers, middle-class citizens and students,
inspired by the eloquence of a Capuchin, Marco d'Aviano, fought side by
side at the barricades under the command of Roger von Stahremberg. Meanwhile the counter-offensive was under way. As the sixty thousand imperial
troops commanded by Charles de Lorraine were of poor quality, the Pope

394   sent financial assistance together with an army of twenty-five thousand crack troops led by John Sobieski, King of Poland; it was their heroic charge against the slopes of Kahlenberg that saved Vienna. The Turkish retreat began. The fact that the Polish forces had saved the day humiliated the emperor; he showed his resentment towards Sobieski and declined even to thank him for his support. The emperor reorganized his army, putting excellent generals in command, and once again took the offensive. One after another the fortified towns of Hungary were captured, and in 1686 the fortress of Buda, "the shield of Islam," which had been held by the infidel for one hundred forty-five years, was reoccupied. A Holy Christian League organized by Rome, and joined by the czar despite his contempt for it, carried the war into the Ottoman Empire. It invaded Zante, Cephalonia and Leucade, and captured Corinth. When the League bombarded Athens, the Parthenon, used by the Turks to store gunpowder, was blown up and suffered irreparable damage (1697). Prince Eugene and the Venetian Morosini won great glory. The Sultan was forced to sign the peace of Carlovitz, under which he abandoned Transylvania and the whole Hungarian plain. All that remained to him was Temesvar, from which he was later driven by Christian forces at the request of Clement XI. The peace of Passarovitz (1718) confirmed the overthrow of Turkish power in the Balkans. This was the first step in a long series of events that was to continue into the twentieth century, and eventually brought about the downfall of the Sublime Porte. It is doubtful, however, whether we may regard this achievement as a Christian victory, a crusade. Christian principles played very little part in the emperor's Hungarian policy or in the Venetian campaign of pillage which destroyed so many monuments of ancient art. The spirit of Lepanto was no more. The defence of religious interests was no longer at issue; there were other interests to defend.

14. THE TROUBLES OF THE PAPACY

WHAT was the position of the Papacy during this momentous period in which the Church, while apparently enjoying a glorious present, had cause

to be uneasy about the uncertainties of the future? We have seen with what
an admirable sense of duty she conducted the struggle against the Turks. The
victory of St. Gothard could never have been achieved without Alexander
VII; the victory of 1683 would not have been so outstanding without the
enormous amount of money collected by Innocent XI to finance Sobieski's
expedition; and behind the military achievements of Prince Eugene in 1715
and the Christian counter-attack in Morea lay the diplomatic skill of the
wise and energetic Clement XI. But did all this mean that the Papacy had
regained its authority, that it was in a position to resume its former role as
leader of the Christian world?

It is certainly true that the Church was no longer governed by unworthy
popes. The seven pontiffs of the classical age may have been very different
from each other (Alexander VIII and Innocent XII were far from agreement on all points); but all were worthy of esteem and two of admiration.
None could certainly be compared with Julius II or a Borgia.

The strong and courageous Alexander VII died in 1667 after a troubled
pontificate,[74] sad at heart because of the humiliations inflicted upon him
by Louis XIV,[75] and immersed towards the end of his life in a gloomy piety.
He left behind him the memory of indomitable energy, a good life and an
upright character. Clement IX (1667–1669), who occupied the Chair of St.
Peter for less than three years, was a shrewd and wise Tuscan, hard on himself and kind to others; *aliis, non sibi clemens* was his motto. He strove with
remarkable determination to fulfil his duties, and was the very embodiment
of charity, a spirit of conciliation[76] and courage—as on the occasion when
a decision had to be made to snatch Crete from the clutches of the Turks.
The aged Cardinal Altieri was next elected Pope after the interregnum of
five months. The election was marred by disputes arising from the fact that
the new Pope was eighty-four years old, and his reign seemed certain to be

---

74. See Volume 1 of this work, Chapter II, p. 158f.

75. See above, Chapter IV, p. 273.

76. It was in connection with his efforts that the expression *Pax Clementina* came into
    use; he arranged a temporary settlement of the Jansenist affair (see below, Chapter VI,
    p. 459).

396 ineffectual. He wept bitterly before agreeing to accept the heavy responsibility, but after his coronation as Clement X (1670–1676) he proved to be anything but incompetent. He worked extremely hard on behalf of the Missions, resisted Louis XIV in the affair of the *régale*, and helped Poland with subsidies to maintain the struggle against the Turks. Deep down in that soul inspired by the spirit of reform dwelt a degree of holiness badly needed by the age.

With Innocent XI (1676–1689) sanctity returned to the Chair of St. Peter, such as had not been seen since Pius V a century earlier. The Christian people had acclaimed him as a saint long before his beatification by the Church in 1956. His name was Benedict Odescalchi; his family came from the shores of Lake Como in the north of Italy. He was a noble figure with all the solid qualities characteristic of men from that part of the country: tenacity, courage in the performance of duty, frugality and a love of discipline. According to his portraits he was slim and rather delicate looking, with a long nose and face, elongated still further by a goatee beard; there is a look of thoughtfulness on his face, anxiety even. His biographers relate that he experienced such emotion when he said Mass (which he considered himself too unworthy to do every day) that he often shed tears at the altar. He was a model of piety, austerity and simplicity of life—the perfect example of an utterly dedicated priest who has renounced all things. But his personal austerity was accompanied by infinite tactfulness towards others. As Papal Legate at Ferrara, and later Bishop of Novara, he was already well known for his unbounded generosity, his visits to the sick, the criminals and the destitute. Innocent X who, despite his weakness, was a good judge of men, gave him the cardinal's hat and entrusted him with tasks at the Vatican that were subsequently included in the duties of the Secretariat of State—an appointment that struck fear into the hearts of many of the Roman nobility, the ladies of fashion, and even the superiors of religious congregations.

Everyone had good reason to beware, for Innocent XI attacked abuses of every description from the moment he was elected Pope. He abolished sinecures, and none of his nephews received advancement. The regular clergy were strictly controlled and led back to the discipline of their Rule, especially the Dominicans and Cistercians. Before appointing a bishop the Holy Pontiff made a very thorough personal investigation into the candidate's spiritual qualities and the extent of his learning. Parish priests were called upon to preach, to be "simple and pious," to teach the Catechism, reside within their parishes and conduct themselves properly. The behaviour of Roman ladies of fashion was censured; many of them objected to the Holy Father's regulations concerning dress as their husbands did to his decrees on the subject of gambling. Some have accused Innocent XI of Jansenism, because of the severity with which he defended morals. Though he attacked the Quietism of Molinos[77] and gave his whole-hearted support to Father Tirso Gonzalez, the great adversary of all Laxists and Probabilists, he showed no sympathy whatever with the doctrines of Jansenius; it was moreover during his pontificate that Port-Royal disintegrated. Benedict Odescalchi was no great theologian, but he was a defender of the faith.

He was an equally forceful defender of the rights of the Church and the Catholic world. It is touching and even paradoxical that a man physically frail and whose life was so deeply spiritual could fight so fiercely. He was the one Pope who stood firm against the might of Louis XIV, even to the point of excommunicating the French ambassador Lavardin; rather than yield, he preferred to see his Avignon estates seized by French troops.[78] By sheer energy and diplomacy he succeeded in forming the coalition against the Turks, and was therefore the real victor of Kahlenberg. All these courageous achievements were in harmony with the charity that he evinced to the end of his life. When he was compelled for political reasons to refrain from condemning the revocation of the Edict of Nantes, he approached James II of England on behalf of the unhappy Huguenot refugees. Even at the height of conflict with the Turks he found time to interest himself in a field hospital which he had sent with Sobieski's forces and which may be considered the forerunner of Catholic Red Cross work. When Innocent XI died on August

---

77. See below, Chapter VI, p. 471.
78. See above, Chapter IV, p. 283.

12, 1689, the whole of Rome flocked to watch the funeral *cortège* as it proceeded from the Quirinal to the Vatican. With difficulty the hearse pushed its way through the eager crowd striving to touch the coffin with a piece of material or some other object to be kept as a relic. No Pope of that period had such a deep and lasting influence upon events.

The brief reign of Alexander VIII (1689–1691) was very different. Not that this shrewd Venetian was unimportant; he was proficient in canon law, very well acquainted with ecclesiastical administration, and had acted as adviser to seven Roman congregations. His foreign policy too was praiseworthy, for he worked to restore peace with France. But while Rome rejoiced at the revival of those ostentatious and licentious festivals which Innocent had forbidden, she was angered by the new Pope's weakness for all his relations. The nepotism of the Ottoboni was soon as proverbial as had been that of the Barberini; but it did not last for long.

When Cardinal Pignatelli became Innocent XII (1691–1700) it was not without good reason that he took the name of his saintly predecessor. Beneath a gracious exterior he retained the severity of an inquisitor, which office he had previously held. His harsh measures against nepotism created a deep impression, and he made it clear to priests, bishops and even to cardinals that they must preach by example. He attacked Quietists and Jansenists alike; but he also knew how to care for the poor and the orphans of Rome with the tenderness of a father. His death in the middle of the Jubilee Year came as a surprise, and saddened the Catholic world.

He was followed by the first Pope of the eighteenth century, Clement XI (1700–1721), who proved a worthy successor. He was an eminent jurist and a former governor of the papal cities of Urbino and Rieti; he had such an impressive personality that he was unanimously elected by the Conclave despite the fact that, though a cardinal for ten years, he had been ordained and had said his first Mass only two days before the Conclave. Immersed in countless political problems, he maintained against the emperor and the Duke of Savoy the same firm attitude he had adopted towards Louis XIV. It came quite naturally to that kindly and erudite Umbrian, the friend of art and literature, to defend the Church against Christian princes as against the

Turks: he was likewise the champion of morals, of the spirit of reform and 399 of the true faith. The Bull *Unigenitus* was his work.

This impressive series of popes has earned much unfair criticism from French historians, who have resented the Holy See's opposition to the policies of Louis XIV. It is therefore imperative to emphasize their qualities, for they were imbued with the true Christian spirit. In those days not every aspect of Roman life was commendable, whether we consider the papal *entourage*, the religious Orders or even the Sacred College. The secret dispatches of the nuncios and the Secretariat of State suggest that there was some truth in the bantering satire of Saint-Simon. Fabio Chigi, Pope Alexander VII, made no secret of his opinion of his namesake, Cardinal Sigismund Chigi, whose gay parties and quail-shooting set tongues wagging. Neither had Ginetti, Mellini or Bassadonna much regard for their purple. So many rumours circulated concerning Cardinal Carpegna that Innocent XI instructed another cardinal, the virtuous Casanetta, to hold an inquiry. These imperfections, so close to the Apostolic See, saddened and disturbed the saintly Pope, and Cardinal d'Estrées records that he heard him deplore them. When a cardinal died the Pope deliberately refrained from appointing a successor until twenty-four vacancies remained in the Sacred College; he thus reduced the number of cardinals to fifty in the hope that he might improve their quality. When Cardinal Maidalchini had himself ordained a priest the Pope forbade him to celebrate Mass! But the existence of a few black sheep should not lead us to exaggerate the evil; many of the clergy were excellent and worthy of the greatest praise. Blessed Gregory Barbarigo was a model of zeal, charity, piety and learning. Cardinal Bonvisi, Nuncio in Vienna, the Spanish Cardinal Saenz d'Aguire and the Austrian Cardinal Leopold von Kollonitz were no less virtuous. After Innocent XI an intense effort was made, especially by Innocent XII and Clement XI, to refine the Sacred College and combat every abuse.

The struggle against nepotism, which had been a veritable scourge of the Holy See during the preceding epoch, is typical of the efforts made in this direction. If we exclude Alexander VIII, not one of the pontiffs we have just mentioned permitted himself to yield to this very natural but disastrous

400 tendency. Urged by Bonvisi, Kollonitz, Saenz and Albani (who became Clement XI), Innocent XII decided to strike an effective blow against these long-established abuses, and in 1692 published his Bull *Romanum decet Pontificem*, under which the Canons forbidding bishops to enrich their near relations with ecclesiastical property were applied also to the Holy See. "Popes may appoint one nephew only as cardinal. Under no pretext whatever may they give money, property or responsible posts to their relatives. If any of their relatives are without means, Popes may assist them as they would help any poor people. If a relative of the Pope becomes cardinal as a result of personal merit, his emoluments shall not exceed twelve thousand Roman crowns." At the same time this energetic Pope abolished all appointments, whether civil, military or ecclesiastical, that were traditionally granted as sinecures to the relatives or agnates of the reigning Pope.

These and similar gestures had a far-reaching effect. It is interesting to note that in the great doctrinal disputes of the period (Jansenism and Quietism) Rome always had the last word in the long run. Even Louis XIV had willy-nilly to reach an understanding with the Pope in order to settle the question of Port-Royal. In the Church of the classical age everything pertaining to the permanence of the spirit of reform depended upon the popes and had their support. This was just as true of Rancé and his Trappists as it was of Father Cloche and his Dominicans. We shall see[79] evidence of the personal intervention of the popes, often a deciding factor, in overseas missionary work. It is also interesting to note the number of saints canonized and beatified by those pontiffs, especially by Clement X and Alexander VIII. Among those canonized were men who reflected the priestly ideal, such as Francis Borgia, Laurence Giustiniani and Pius V; such reformers as Cajetan of Tiene; such great missionary figures as Louis Bertrand, Francis Solanus, Rose of Lima; souls utterly dedicated to God, such as John of the Cross, Peter of Alcàntara, Mary Magdalen dei Pazzi. There existed an undoubted relation between the choice and the purpose.

79. See *The Church of the Classical Age: The Era of Great Splintering*, Volume 1, Chapter II.

It stands to reason that this determined effort to give back to the Papacy its position of authority increased its prestige. Even when, politically speaking, things were going badly for the Pope, Louis XIV was careful to show him great personal respect. The respectful manner in which public figures spoke of or to the popes during that period was not in the least comparable with their former treatment (e.g., at the beginning of the sixteenth century). The deference with which the sacred office of Pope was surrounded was plain for all to see; there existed a real distinction between the man and his position. Everyone knew that papal elections were the occasions of all kinds of political schemes, and that pressure was brought to bear on behalf of various interests. It was often said of a cardinal that he was "of the crown," meaning that in the Sacred College he was less a man of the Church than the representative of some monarch. In this connection Mme. de Sévigné wrote: "You have only to read history to appreciate that a religion which owes its origin and its survival to a permanent miracle cannot be regarded as a figment of man's imagination. Believe me, despite all that goes on in Conclave, it is always the Holy Ghost who chooses the Pope." The crowds who flocked to Rome from the four corners of the earth during the great Jubilee Year of 1700 did not, of course, concern themselves with such questions; at other periods in history, less propitious as far as the Holy See was concerned, such manifestations always drew the crowds, for the glory of Rome and of the Vicar of Christ has always been resplendent. It is none the less important that thinking Catholics should be aware of the facts.

The idea of Papal Infallibility began to make positive progress during the seventeenth century, although the age appeared to have surrendered to victorious caesaropapism. It is true that the old conciliar theories were still occasionally advanced, even by Bossuet; but no one took them seriously any longer. Papal Infallibility had not yet been defined as a dogma, and still had numerous enemies, but the fact seemed to be gradually forcing itself upon men's minds. A great impression was created by St. Robert Bellarmine's comment in his splendid treatise on the Roman Pontiff, referring to Christ's words in the Gospel of St. Luke: "But I have prayed for thee that thy faith fail not: and thou being once converted, confirm thy brethren" (Luke

22:32). In fact, no one questioned the sovereign right of the Vicar of Christ to make laws. On that point even Jansenius entertained no doubt. During the period 1703–1705, when the French bishops endeavoured to oppose a procedure that tended to reserve to the Holy See alone full and exclusive jurisdiction in doctrinal matters, Clement XI retorted bluntly: "Who made you judges? The bishops hold their prerogatives from the Roman Pontiff alone. The Pope has no use for their opinions; he calls upon them to obey." Public opinion approved language of this kind. The doctrine of Infallibility was demonstrated more and more ably by the works of Viva, Billuart, Kilber and Orsi in the *Biblioteca Pontificia Maxima*, and later on in the treatises of Petitdidier and Fénelon; but its elements were still not precisely defined. Fénelon saw Infallibility as the privilege of the Roman Church, Billuart as the personal prerogative of the Sovereign Pontiff; but, in any case, the idea was on the way to becoming common doctrine.

However, this lovely picture contained dark shadows. Here, as in every other field, the Great Century, especially the classical period, was remarkably less as an era of perfect stability than as a time of grave crisis during which dogged and courageous attempts were made to maintain the ever-threatened order of things. The Papacy was very well aware that formidable forces were ranged against it: absolutism, Erastianism and Gallicanism.[80] All three endeavoured to impose the notion of complete independence of the monarchs in relation to the spiritual power, and even to justify the ascendancy of the State over the religious sphere of influence. It is to the glory of Innocent XI that he boldly threw the whole weight of papal authority against the Great King's caesaropapism which had been so cautiously handled by his predecessors. It was the Holy See that finally won the battle against Gallicanism, although Louis XIV took cunning revenge by publishing his Fifty Articles. The same problem arose in all other Catholic countries. The Pope protested to the emperor concerning the handling of Peter's Pence. In Spain there was ceaseless argument about levies and taxation; indeed the dispute became so acrimonious under Philip V that diplomatic relations between

---

80. See Volume 1 of this work, Chapter III, section 12: "Towards Absolutism in Europe."

Madrid and Rome were broken off. Similar problems arose in Bavaria and   403
Poland. But it was not simply a question of money. As in France, where the
affair of the *régale* precipitated the Gallican conflict, the underlying issues
were everywhere much more serious than a mere matter of finance.

In the sphere of international politics the Papacy was not only attacked
by hostile forces; she was nearly defeated. She never recovered her position as
arbiter of the Christian world. The fact that the Pope's representatives were
excluded from the negotiations at Osnabrück and Münster, where the treaties of Westphalia were agreed upon with complete contempt for the interests of the Church, confirmed the political eclipse of the Papacy; in other
words, all hope of securing the triumph of a Christian political morality was
killed. Not that the Popes did not seek to resume their ancient role. Alexander VII and Clement IX endeavoured to unite Catholic states against the
Turks; Clement X worked for peace between Genoa and Savoy, and offered
to mediate between Paris and Vienna; Innocent XI devoted himself body
and soul to the reconciliation of nations; and Clement XI embarked upon
similar negotiations. On the whole all these efforts proved unsuccessful; the
secularization of international policy continued. In vain, for example, did
Innocent XI take it upon himself to guide the conscience of Louis XIV, to
remind him, often in moving terms, of his duties as a Christian.[81] Henceforward decisions were reached on all important political matters without
consulting the Holy See or taking any account of the higher interests of
Christendom. On the threshold of the eighteenth century states even disposed of the Pope's fiefs, under the treaties of Utrecht and Rastadt, without
the least consideration for his sovereign rights. The political eclipse of the
Holy See reached a climax with the criminal partition of Poland while the
popes looked on helplessly.

A similar eclipse took place in the field of ideas. The novel trends invad-
ing minds and consciences[82] no longer took account of papal views—a fact

---

81. See above, Chapter IV, p. 291.
82. See *The Church of the Classical Age: The Era of Great Splintering*, Volume 1, Chapter
I.

which emphasizes yet another weakness on the part of Rome towards the end of the seventeenth century. Did they appreciate the gravity of the crisis and the importance of the issues at stake? Did they lack the ability or intelligence to anticipate the future? Their usual approach to subversive doctrines was to counter by condemning them. But was it sufficient to place on the Index the *Provinciales*, the *Discours de la methode* (subject to amendment), Fontenelle's *Histoires des oracles*, Bayle's *Dictionnaire*, and even the biblical works of Richard Simon? Twentieth-century Popes, including Pius XI and Pius XII, have realized that mere condemnation of modern errors is not sufficient in the war against them; the world and its problems need to be "rethought" from genuinely Catholic viewpoints. This the popes of the seventeenth century scarcely understood, and their silence was disturbing.

The popes of the classical age, infinitely more praiseworthy than their immediate predecessors, do appear to have made a valiant attempt to lessen the effects of the contemporary crisis, but we cannot refrain from thinking that they might have achieved more in the circumstances. The eighteenth century could not deny the temporary eclipse of papal power.

15. CHRISTIAN ART DURING THE GREAT REIGN

WAS it coincidental that the classical age corresponded with a lowering of vitality in religious art?[83] From 1670 to 1680 the fact was obvious. Borromini died in 1667, Bernini in 1680; and during the year 1682–1683 Louis XIV became established in Versailles. The climate had changed. Clement X erected the two fountains in the piazza of St. Peter's and planned the Ponte Sant' Angelo. Clement XI encouraged tapestry and mosaic, thus enabling Rome to compete with the schools of Venice and Ravenna. Generally speaking, however, the popes were occupied with cares of a different nature, and were no longer deeply interested in art. Even in France, at that time resplendent as the home of all the arts, very few works can

---

83. See Volume 1 of this work, Chapter II, p. 147ff.

be considered distinctively Christian. Churches already in course of con-   405
struction were completed, among them Saint-Sulpice, whose architect, Le
Vau, who died in 1670, had been able to finish only the choir, the transept
and a small portion of the nave. But very little new work was commenced.
The masterpieces of religious architecture during the Great Reign were the
dome of the Invalides and the Chapel of Versailles, both of which tended
to the glory of the king as much as to the glory of God. The vast work
undertaken at Saint-Denis under the direction of Robert de Cotte towards
the end of the reign was destined to receive the body of the all-powerful
monarch himself.

These facts do not by any means imply that the artists of this period were
less imbued with faith than their forbears. The solid sense of Christianity
that we have seen so firmly rooted in the souls of other men during the Great
Century was just as much alive and exacting among painters and sculptors.
Le Brun, Puget and Girardon each devoted part of his fortune to the building of a chapel in his favourite church; the first at Nicolas-du-Chardonnet,
the second at Saint-Madeleine de Marseille; the third at Saint-Landry in
Paris. Jacques Courtois, nicknamed "the Raphael of Battles," was among the
famous converts of the day, and he became a Jesuit. Even Coysevox and Watteau, who left to posterity the pagan grace of *Vénus à la coquille, Aphrodite
accroupie* and *Embarquements pour Cythère*, were none the less sincere Christians who seemed in no way to suffer from the distinction between their profession and their spiritual life. "Rigaud's last painting," observes Langevin,
"when he was rich in years and blessed by fortune, is one of the only two
religious pictures we have from his brush; I refer to his *Presentation in the
Temple*, which re-echoes so clearly the artist's *nunc dimittis*."

The fact that Christian art did not occupy the eminent place it had held
formerly did not point to a diminution of faith, but rather to a change of
attitude on the part of society towards art. Society was invited less frequently to praise God, because it was expected to exalt man, especially through
the apotheosis of kings. The amount of money devoted to the building of
churches during the reign of Louis XIV cannot be compared with the sum
spent on Versailles. The vast hall of the Great King's palace, in which he

406   received the homage of his loyal subjects, was perhaps the true sanctuary rather than the chapel. This trend is not noticeable in France alone; in Prussia, Portugal, Austria and Poland princes followed the example of Versailles. It has been estimated that thirty thousand sumptuous town and country houses were built throughout Europe between 1660 and 1715. Secularization was therefore evident in art as in all other fields. Towards the end of the reign it developed into a process of sensualization confirming that final breach with faith, as we shall see when dealing with the eighteenth century. It may be said therefore that immediately on the death of Louis XIV the sails were set, as in Watteau's picture, in the direction of Cythera.

But Christian art did not cease to exist. When the vast assets of states and the capital of wealthy patrons, so essential to the development of architecture, were diverted from the building of churches,[84] religious art turned towards painting and sculpture to adorn existing churches or to decorate private chapels. Pierre Puget (1622–1697), the genius who carved *Milo of Croton*, also sculptured the wonderful *Stoning of St. Stephen* at Aix and the moving *Magdalen's Communion*. Girardon (1628–1715), on the recommendation of Le Brun, dedicated to the memory of Richelieu the sensitive mausoleum in the chapel of the Sorbonne. Coysevox (1640–1720) compared very favourably with him as the sculptor of Mazarin's tomb, but excelled him in his *Descent from the Cross* in the chancel of Notre Dame at Paris. Nicolas Courtois (1656–1719) commemorated in marble the vow made by Louis XIII. Finally Sebastien Slodtz (1655–1726) was responsible for the statue of Faith, a little-known masterpiece in the chapel of the palace at Versailles.

During that period painting was more fashionable than sculpture. The taste spread both from Flanders and from Italy, and churches everywhere teemed with paintings. They covered walls, overcrowded chapels, and attained enormous dimensions. Vicarages, cathedral chapters, confraternities, the residences of nobles and wealthy citizens—all wanted paintings. At the

---

84. This does not include abbeys; a good number of abbots, whether commendatory or regular, put in hand repairs or rebuilding in the classical style of architecture, which resulted in edifices of great dignity. A splendid example is the Premonstratensian abbey of Mondaye, in Normandy, which has often been imitated.

church of Saint-Germain l'Auxerrois the pictures were changed throughout the year according to the feasts! The guild of goldsmiths and silversmiths at Paris ordered every year a gift for Our Lady, and it usually took the form of a huge painting. This genre produced its own specialists; among them were Philippe de Chennevières, who painted a large number of such pictures, and Sacquespée, who was seven times prize-winner of the "Palinods de Puy de l'immaculée Conception." But the masters who won fame in profane art had Christian pictures also to their credit: Le Brun (1619–1690), his *Triumph of the Virgin*, *Martyrdom of St. Stephen* and *Elevation of the Cross*; Mignard (1610–1695), a friend of Molière, his graceful *Virgin with Grape*, which hangs in the Louvre, and among many other works, his amazing *Baptism of Christ* in the church of Saint-Jean. There were also the two Coypels (father and son), de la Fosse and Jouvenet (a student of Rubens and the Carracci), all less famous but far from inconsiderable. We have already referred to Rigaud, but we might also mention Largillière's *Offering of St. Genevieve*. It must not be forgotten that all these artists took their religious paintings seriously. Lomazzo's book, *The Temple of Painting*, read at that time in a French translation, warned painters that before beginning to portray a Christian subject they should ascertain from theologians "how to represent God, the angels, the soul, the devil, the saints and heaven; their appearance, colours according to their functions, and, generally speaking, any pious stories attached to them." And no one failed to follow the injunction. Le Brun based his work on these principles when he attempted to express the theology of his master M. Olier.

Though fewer churches were built in the classical age, the period remained fertile in religious art, thanks to painting and sculpture; not only, of course, in France, but in every great Catholic country. To place all this work under one heading and label it "classical art" is hardly satisfactory. It seems to flow from two great sources. Baroque on the one hand had its hour of glory during the preceding period, and continued along its course. It produced no more masters of Bernini's eminence, but a multitude of talented votaries. From the Tyrol to Sicily, from Portugal to Bohemia, and even as far as Latin America, hundreds of churches and chapels were still being built and decorated in that style. Swept along by its strange genius, Baroque

408   became more and more luxuriant, more complicated and over-elaborate, perhaps even wanton and artificial. Rocaille and Rococo began to make their appearance, and the form retained very little Christian inspiration.

The other trend was altogether different. A reaction set in against the excesses of Baroque, and an attempt was made to subject art to rules and standards, to logic and a more ordered taste. No more church façades resembling drapery lashed by the wind; no more naves overladen with ornamentation. From the models of antiquity artists selected the austerity of their colonnades and their harsh equilibrium. Henceforward the taste was for façades of orderly appearance, whose beauty emanated from the strictly mathematical harmony of their parts; naves that were spacious, cold and naked, whose glory proceeded from the quality of the material, depending no longer upon the lavishness of their decoration. Such a conception of art corresponded to a very formal religious expression linked with an all-powerful monarchical system: the religion of such a man as Bossuet.

This opposition between two trends of Baroque was purely theoretical; it had no foundation in fact. A great deal of Baroque survived even in the great classical art of the age of Louis XIV; it was apparent in the component members of architectural types. Were the colonnade and the dome borrowed from antiquity or from Baroque? Was not the influence of the "Jesuit churches" and Bernini's colonnade considerable? But decoration owes more to Baroque than one usually cares to admit. This applied to altar-pieces, which, as we have seen, were so ornate and so often exhibited the influence of the Carracci and Rubens. Baroque also were those characteristically "classical" sculptures, in which marble was shaped in a manner to suggest the pliability of cloth. Baroque was the reredos, which in so many churches rose up behind an equally Baroque and lavishly decorated altar. The arrangement of sumptuous funerals was similarly affected. When illustrious personages were to be buried the nave was hung with voluminous black draperies ornamented with braid and silver tears, accompanied by symbolical figures, torches and ornamental chandeliers. In some way the sense of the grandiose, the ostentatious and the majestic visible in classical art was not inconsistent with Baroque tradition, but was rather a direct continuation of it.

Briefly, we might almost say that Christian art in the Great Century was
"classical" as to its exterior structure, but retained much that was Baroque
in its interior arrangement. It is astonishing that this blend did not result in
lack of harmony; but the artists of those days, thanks to good taste and an
innate sense of proportion, apparently knew how to harmonize elements
that were naturally opposed. But did not the spiritual life of that time inherit
the lessons of the Council of Trent and the French School? Is it not possible
to feel the tension between opposing tendencies? Not only did Baroque and
the Classic coexist, but the faith of Rancé and Bourdaloue coexisted with
that of Bossuet and Fénelon, because the religion of that day was vigorous.

The two aspects of classical religious art may be considered in what are
perhaps the only two French monuments dating from the reign of Louis
XIV which achieved fulness of expression: Saint-Louis des Invalides and
the chapel of Versailles. The value of the first lies in its purity of architectural
line, the perfect balance in the colonnades of the façade, the majestic thrust
of the dome set so firmly upon its drum. It is the Christian masterpiece of
Mansart (1598–1666), wherein he displayed the "classical" in the most formal sense of the term. In style Mansart stands out as the heir of antiquity;
indeed this architect, who must have read Descartes, brought antiquity back
to life. The beauty of the chapel of Versailles lies in its interior decoration, so
rich in detail, so graceful and of such remarkable freedom of touch; austere
restraint is certainly not its overriding quality. Both these works are typical
of France under Louis XIV, and are in keeping with the religion of the Most
Christian King and his age.[85]

Music was equally wedded to the glory of the Great King.[86] One cannot
imagine the festivities of Versailles without the accompaniment of orchestras
scattered about the gardens, and human voices mingling with the *arpeggio*
of the fountains. The reign of Louis XIV was the period when opera, which
had recently known such rapid development in Italy, took France by storm;

85. See V. L. Tapié's excellent book, *Baroque et classicisme*, mentioned in the bibliographical notes.
86. See Volume 1 of this work, Chapter II, p. 153.

it was the age when the instrumental concert that came to the fore about 1660 became rooted in the life of the nation. But there was clearly nothing specifically Christian about that.

Religious music was not, however, omitted from society's infatuation with musical expression. Every great master of the day included sacred music in his compositions. Even Jean-Baptiste Lulli (1632–1687), a free-thinker from Florence (and probably an atheist), wrote a *De Profundis,* a *Miserere* and a number of motets, apart from his successful operas. Among other composers of motets and similar works of Christian inspiration were J.-B. Moreau, the author of the two choral works *Esther* and *Athalie,* Clérambault, Couperin le Grand (1668–1733) and Rameau (1683–1733), most of whose compositions were adjuncts of secular entertainment during the Regency and the reign of Louis XV. Moreover, the king himself was interested in music. The standard of performance at the chapel of Versailles, in which Du Mont and Lalande won fame, was extremely high. The organs at Versailles, the Invalides and in the more important provincial cathedrals were first-class instruments. Sung Masses with organ and orchestra achieved beauty that still has power to move us; those of Du Mont and Couperin le Grand have a worthy companion in Lalande's *Office of Tenebrae.* Motets were likewise enormously popular. Lully wrote twenty-three, which, though they lack feeling, reveal an occasional upsurge of fervour and magnificence. On the death of Lalande, Louis XV commanded that his forty motets be published in collected form. Apart from the formal type of music, in which Lully (and after him Lalande) was a sort of dictator, there were some ingenious Psalms by André Campra. Marc-Antoine Charpentier (1634–1704) drew on sacred history for subjects from which his strange genius produced such masterpieces as *The Prodigal Son* and *St. Peter's Denial.*[87]

In Italy too profane music began to develop rapidly. Every little court had its theatrical company for the purpose of presenting opera. Venice

87. It must not be forgotten that great missioners—among them St. Grignion de Montfort—composed canticles that are not lacking in quality.

outshone them all; but there also religious music benefited from the vogue.
Operatic orchestras played at High Mass; the Sistine Chapel was celebrated on that account as well as for its *castrati*. The fashionable oratorio and
motet continued to flourish side by side with Masses, of which Alessandro
Scarlatti wrote no fewer than twenty. The oratorio was the favourite form of
Carissimi, and of the venturesome Stradella, whose style was elegant, lucid
and precise. Immensely successful was the cantata, in which solo and choral
vocals alternated; popular too was the recitative, invented by Alessandro
Grandi in 1620, shortly before his untimely death.

The same forms were adopted in Germany. Hitherto the German-speaking world had been relatively unproductive in other spheres of art; but now,
under some mysterious influence, Germany revealed herself as the land of
music, and above all of religious music. She came into her own in the biblical atmosphere of Protestantism, and ultimately produced such illustrious
men as Bach and the exuberant George Frederick Handel.

16. THE DAWN OF A NEW CENTURY

THE period known as the classical age could not last for ever; and, as in
the case of all great eras, it closed at a time when society appeared to have
attained a state of fulness and stability. It is not man's destiny to achieve
a permanent synthesis of passions and principles, interests and ideals. The
century of Pericles was doomed to pass; so was that of Augustus, and the
century of Louis XIV was no more eternal. In every field classicism reveals
a courageous and determined attempt to impose order upon the forces of
destruction which cruelly tormented the age. For a short time the attempt
succeeded; an unhoped-for harmony was achieved. The political regime
became an integral part of spiritual aspirations, and the social element
endeavoured to identify itself with the religious ideal. But that stability,
splendid though it was, was condemned to impermanence, for it depended
upon circumstances and the presiding genius of a few men. Time would
challenge its constancy.

412   Thus the end of the reign of Louis XIV marked a turning-point. After the melancholy events and the pressure of the preceding ten years a reaction was inevitable. It occurred during the Regency and the reign of Louis XV, and was as much a moral and intellectual reaction as it was political. Indeed, premonitory signs might have been detected almost throughout the reign, certainly from 1680 onwards, when the principle of kingship by divine right began to be questioned at the very height of its triumph, and when the coalition of European states threatened the ascendancy of Louis XIV. At the time of the despot's death thirty-five years later the threats had become more alarming, and the menace of disintegration loomed on all sides.

By a strange coincidence, just as a change of political climate occurred in the entire West at the very moment when Louis XIV assumed personal control of affairs, so did his death seem to be irresistibly significant; for the seventeenth century died with him. In every sphere and from every point of view the eighteenth century was clearly destined to be different. What had happened to the theory of divine right in England, where on two occasions—when the crown was given to William of Orange and then to George I—the "right" was exercised by a perfectly human will? And what was it worth to the House of Brandenburg and the House of Savoy, who owed their leadership of Germany and Italy respectively solely to their own courage and ingenuity? A transformation had taken place in social life; those classes that were deemed to be at the bottom of the ladder began to question the right of the hierarchical system which placed them there. The economic evolution of the West tended to challenge the old order of things; capitalism was born, money increased in importance at the expense of land, and the role of bankers was magnified.

But there were other more disquieting signs. At that period, as always when great changes are imminent, the true causes of the crisis lay in man himself. He questioned his very conception of life and of himself. Very early in the seventeenth century indications of this "crisis of the European conscience" were evident. The crisis, which according to Paul Hazard began around 1675, was really an indissoluble blend of crises relative to the intellect and the moral conscience. Furthermore, a spirit of libertinism manifested itself early—a growing cleavage between faith and life, the first satanic attack in the revolt against God. Many leading figures noted these evident signs—even Bossuet, who was seldom endowed with the gift of prophecy. They were the source of the great onslaught soon to be made against the concepts under which the world had hitherto been governed, and against the human powers that controlled it.

That onslaught would be directed likewise against divine authority, for the Church was deeply involved in the impending crisis. She was intimately linked with the principles of statecraft and the organization of society during the classical age; she sustained and buttressed the entire system. If the regime were threatened how could the Church possibly avoid involvement? We appreciate that this relationship was essentially provisional; the Church, the spouse of Christ, the trustee of an eternal message, was bound to the regime only in that sense. In no other sense was she tied to any particular form of civilization. She was capable of dovetailing into any transitory system that history might produce without changing her destiny, which transcends time. There was a Church in pagan times and in medieval times; there was even the Church of the Renaissance and of Humanism. The Church of the Classical Age might in her turn drift towards the abyss; but "the Church" as such must always survive.

To enable that to happen it was essential that the sap within her remain vigorous enough to engender future growth, that those in authority become quickly aware of gathering clouds, and do not confuse the transitory with the eternal in relation to the promise. They must be capable of distinguishing between a moribund world and one about to be born. That twofold function was magnificently fulfilled by the Church from the fifth to the tenth century, when she created the civilization of cathedral and crusade out of the bloody chaos of a barbarous Europe. We shall see her faced once more with the need to exorcize it again in modern times.

Several questions therefore present themselves. How did the Church react to the crisis of mind and conscience, and was she aware of what was at stake? Would she manage to give the correct answers to the questions men were asking themselves in the name of intellectual progress? Had she

414 anything to offer beyond overruling authoritative statements by way of reply to a change of intellectual outlook that cast doubt upon her tenets? These questions constitute one of the serious problems facing the Church on the threshold of the century of Voltaire and the Revolution.[88]

Another question that was already being posed in a different form around 1660 was whether the Church had the energy and vitality required to renew herself while restoring the world. No doubt splendid work had already been done by saints and men of faith and talent to impregnate the marrow of society with the spirit of Christianity. It could not be said that the Church had failed to accomplish the mission imposed upon her from the beginning to raise up the baptized but sinful masses. Yet the fact remains that there was still a great deal to be done; that pure lustrous and radiant Christianity of which the greatest Christians have dreamed, a religion sufficiently robust to counter the difficulties of new times without harm, was still far from being a reality. By the end of the century there were many signs of an impending landslide: fewer missions, fewer books of instruction, and a return to many abuses. Furthermore, the Church herself experienced internal crises which shook her severely, one of which had not been disposed of by the beginning of the eighteenth century. These crises so reduced her power and prestige that she was unfortunately unable to face the storms of tomorrow with her forces intact.

---

88. See *The Church of the Classical Age: The Era of Great Splintering*, Volume 1, Chapter I.

CHAPTER VI

The Doctrinal Crises of Jansenism and Quietism

1. A THEOLOGICAL ALLIANCE

AT the end of summer, 1621, two friends, both priests, met at the college of Sainte-Pulchérie in Louvain. Both had formerly been pupils at the city's university, one of the glories of the Church for nearly two centuries and an important cultural centre made famous by Erasmus, Latomus, Busleyden and Justus Lipsius. The university was also the centre of disputes and brawls, frequently occasioned by theological discussions.

It was a long time since the two friends had left college. One of them had returned to the Flemish city to become president of the college, in other words superior of the seminary. The other had come from Paris, where he resided. The younger was a Dutchman born in 1585, in the village of Accoi near Leerdam. He was lean and gaunt, all bone and muscle; the type of Dutchman whom the Spaniards had found unconquerable in Holland's struggle for independence. He was tall, with a long, slightly aquiline nose and a high brow; his chin jutted out, and his pointed, goatee beard made it seem even longer. His biretta gave him the appearance of a fighting man rather than a man of prayer. His eye was keen, and through the apparently unbroken calm of his features might be glimpsed an occasional flash of subdued storm. Those who knew him well were aware that his imperturbable air concealed intense emotion and a spirited character.

The Dutchman's parents were very poor, but he turned to Holy Orders, following in the footsteps of an uncle on his father's side who had succeeded in becoming Bishop of Ghent and a delegate at the Council of Trent.

He had a brilliant career at the university, obtaining a first in literature and philosophy and a mastership in theology. He began by seeking admission to the Society of Jesus, but was rejected for some obscure reason, probably because he was ill-suited by disposition to a life of absolute obedience. Having returned to Louvain after a long absence in France he enjoyed a considerable reputation on account of his learning, piety, eloquence and strong principles. His name was Cornelius Jansen but, in the manner of the Humanists, he used the Latin name Cornelius Jansenius.

The Frenchman, whom Jansenius welcomed with open arms before the fine marble statue of Our Lady which adorned the entrance to his seminary, was a very different man. This restless little Basque was prematurely bald, deeply lined and of stocky appearance; he had an ardent and pained expression which was both disturbing and fascinating. His name was Jean-Ambroise Duvergier de Hauranne, and at that time was forty years of age. Born in Paris in 1581 of a well-to-do family, he received the tonsure at the age of ten, and was educated by the Jesuits under the care of Bishop Bertrand d'Eschaux whom Henri IV held in high esteem. A rosy future faced the young man. At twenty-five he was given the well-endowed parish of Ixtassou, and in the following year a canonry. It seemed therefore that he was destined to lead the easy-going life of a rather worldly minded cleric, of whom there were so many at that time. But that was not to be. He had within him a hunger and thirst which the pleasures of the age could not satisfy; neither could the intellectual attainments which had come to him so easily in Paris and Louvain. His soul pined for God, reaching out to an inaccessible holiness. Indeed, he was a strange and extraordinarily complex man whose character was made up of obvious contradictions. Quarrelsome, bitingly and passionately critical of everything, he adopted the discourteous and domineering air of a prophet; yet he was capable of gaiety and tact, and displayed a winning simplicity and an almost Franciscan charity. Undoubtedly this engaging personality, this unfinished genius, could have been a saint. A few months before the Frenchman's journey to Louvain the Bishop of Poitiers, who admired him, presented him with a wealthy abbey which rendered him secure from all material cares; in accordance with the custom of the times he assumed the title of his living—Abbot of Saint-Cyran.

It is very likely that these two men became acquainted at Louvain, in the library or during one of the study-courses. They certainly met again between 1604 and 1606 in Paris, as former students of the same faculty; a little lost perhaps in the big city and rather unwelcome at the Sorbonne where the theological tenets of the Louvain Jesuits were not highly esteemed. They must have passed the long evenings debating many a great problem during the interminable discussions which were the joy of student life. The Dutchman Jansenius was well acquainted with the problems of Protestant reform; and they no doubt touched upon the different spheres of ecclesiastical and lay authority as expounded by the Gallican professor Edmond Richer[1] whose courses they were following. As former students of the Jesuits they both shared an intense and bitter antipathy towards their old masters, which possibly explains the harsh judgments passed upon them by the Jesuits. Temporarily separated, the two friends were later able to renew their frequent discussions when Jansenius stayed five years in the Basque country, first as director of the college of Bayonne and later at Camp-de-Prats, the family estate of the Haurannes, where Jean-Ambroise's mother, "the lady of Hauranne," treated him as a son. The two young men had reached a point in their relationship when feelings were subordinated to their common search after vital truths, neither really knowing what part each played individually in their work. Later they parted once more, one going to Louvain and the other to Poitiers and then to Paris. But distance was no barrier, for they maintained a communion of souls and minds by means of a continuous flow of letters written in the rather affected style of the time.

In September 1616 Cornelius sent Jean a particularly important letter; he told him of an intellectual revelation he had had, the truth of which he considered to be of such grave significance that he felt compelled to inform his friend at once. With passionate insistence he returned to the subject in

---

1. See Volume 1 of this work, Chapter III, p. 224.

letter after letter. Eventually the abbot of Saint-Cyran shared his friend's mental anguish: he became convinced that Jansenius was right. Surely it was absurd to occupy themselves with Greek and Latin authors, the Fathers of the Church, and even probing the Scriptures as they had both been doing up to then, while neither of them had found the reply to the fundamental question that tormented every Christian—"Shall I attain salvation, and how must I attain it?"

After a meeting with Father de Condren, the celebrated Oratorian, Saint-Cyran had become "converted," in the Pascalian sense of the term, and he was ready to devote his whole mind to this single problem. Was it possible that his friend had indeed found the solution? Without delay he set out for Louvain.

The problems of divine grace and free will were among those that had racked men's consciences for twenty centuries, especially in the West, where personal salvation had always been regarded as the supreme problem. In the East, the East of Arius and Nestorius and metaphysical discussion, controversy had always raged around the dogma of the Blessed Trinity and the two natures of Christ. It was on such problems as the former, those stumbling-blocks that straddled the paths of faith, that Martin Luther had come to grief. Free will, man's helplessness, efficacious grace and sufficient grace— over these terms theologians were still in conflict even though the Council of Trent had formulated precise Catholic definitions. Thirty years earlier, in Louvain itself, Michel de Bay, nicknamed Baius, master and subsequently chancellor of the university (he died in 1589), endeavoured to reconcile Protestant concepts with the teaching of the Church. He was, however, condemned by St. Pius V in 1567 and by Gregory XIII in 1579, and he submitted. But his ideas survived him, and his friend Janson, professor of Holy Scripture at Louvain, maintained them, though cautiously through fear of the Holy Office, and they continued to be held. Others circulated similar ideas; among them the Irish Franciscan Conrius, whose courses, definitely Augustinian in character, created a sensation among the students. It became clear that the controversy relating to grace was not at an end when the Jesuits and the Dominicans confronted each other over Father Luis de Molina's

book[2] *Concordia*, which dealt with the problem of reconciling grace and
free will. The strict Thomists led by Bañez strenuously opposed it on the
grounds that, apart from other defects, it led to a too facile moral outlook. A
special Congregatio de Auxiliis was instituted by Clement VIII in 1597 to
settle the controversy—which it declared itself unable to do. As bitterness
increased Paul V forbade all theologians to refer to the matter publicly. But
how was it possible to prevent Christians from discussing in secret, and to
enthuse over and devote their life to questions which concerned issues most
vital to man?

Jansenius, therefore, wrote to his friend that the only subject worthy
of their complete attention and their whole existence was that of grace; in
other words, salvation. And he added that he thought he had discovered
the unique solution to its most complex problems, a solution that would
reconcile all opposing theories, and provide the answer for which all men
of faith were waiting.

But how, and where? Jansenius declared that the essentials of his discovery came from his reading of St. Augustine. He was sure that within the
voluminous and inexhaustible writings of the Bishop of Hippo everything
was to be found—every question and every answer. Was he not called the
"Doctor of Grace"? He it was who had mapped out the right path through a
maze of errors; he had defended God's rights against Pelagius and the rights
of man against the Manichees. St. Augustine! He was far and away superior
to all those babblers who entangled themselves in Molinism and the arguments of the Schoolmen. Jansenius was quite definite: all truth dwelt in the
inspired works of the African bishop.

Such was the subject of the ardent discussions of the two friends
during the ten or twelve years that Jean Duvergier resided at the college of
Sainte-Pulchérie. Undoubtedly Jansenius sketched out for Saint-Cyran the
main points of the doctrine he had evolved and of which, as he considered,

---

2.   He was a Spanish-Jesuit who died in 1600, and must not be confused with another
     Spanish priest, Molinos, whose theses gave rise to the Quietist crisis. Molina's system
     is known by the name Molinism; but Molinosism is used with reference to the theo-
     ries of Molinos.

420   St. Augustine would furnish the proofs. They discussed them together, while the naturally critical acumen of the little Basque raised objections to which the Dutchman was forced to reply.

Together also they grew excited over the grandeur and beauty of their discovery. What great service they would render the Church if they formulated in precise terms, with incontrovertible arguments, the doctrine they glimpsed!

Thus their great scheme was developed. Jansenius would devote himself to probing St. Augustine in order to extract the substance of the work. He would read through the books on grace ten times, fifty times or more if necessary. He would write a commentary worthy of that genius; a work so profound, so perfect that it would meet with the approval of all enlightened minds. Thus their doctrine, their solution, would penetrate deeply into innumerable souls, passing into the very marrow of Catholicism. Saint-Cyran would assist him by research, criticism, testing the force of Jansenist arguments on this and that person, and generally paving the way for the spread of their doctrine. They had to be careful however; precautions were necessary to prevent their undertaking from encountering the same fate as that of Baius. But they intended to keep the secret until the moment when the bomb would burst. Accordingly they perfected a code—admittedly a little childish—to prevent their design from becoming known if their correspondence should be read. The code name for their great project was "Pilmot"; Jansenius called himself "Boèce" or "Sulpice," and his friend "Celias" or "Solion." The Society of Jesus was dubbed with the rather disagreeable name of "Gorphoroste," and its members were "Les Fins." St. Augustine himself was given the pseudonyms "Seraphi," "Aelius" and "Leoninus." Other personages referred to occasionally were given esoteric names; for example, Richelieu was "Purpuratus," Bertille "Rougeart," and the King of Spain "Carpocre." As for the Protestants, for some unknown reason they were called "Cucumer."

Having thus perfected their great scheme and the details of their code, the two friends separated after agreeing not only to write to each other but also to meet periodically in order to acquaint each other with the work's

progress. Jansenius remained in Belgium, at first in Louvain, where he was
given the chair of Holy Scripture, and then at Ypres, of which he became
bishop in 1635. He rarely left the country, except for a mission to Spain and
a few brief visits to meet Saint-Cyran. In 1627, having no doubt sufficiently
read and re-read St. Augustine, he began to draft his celebrated commentary
Augustinus. He had just finished it in 1638 when death overtook him. He
died in dispositions of great piety, submitting his book to the decisions of
the Church and entrusting it to his chaplain Lamaeus with instructions to
publish it after his death.

Saint-Cyran left the theoretical aspect of the undertaking to his friend
and devoted himself to the practical side. He settled in Paris, where he
endeavoured to win influence. He was acquainted with Richelieu, who
publicly referred to him as "the most learned man in the world." He struck
up a friendship with Father de Condren, Cardinal de Bérulle, the energetic
Adrien Bourdoise and even with St. Vincent de Paul. As a spiritual director
he guided the souls of a large number of men and women, most of whom
belonged to the fashionable world. The doctrine in which he instructed
them was solid, exacting and imbued with the spirit of reform, such as was
taught by the leading spiritual men of that earnest epoch. Bishoprics were
offered to him on several occasions, but he refused them: he was satisfied to
remain the living conscience of his day and to exercise his influence discreetly. The attitude he adopted in public was a skillful one; he wrote a crushing pamphlet condemning the somewhat farcical apologetics of the Jesuit
Father Garasse, thus bringing the laugh to his side. The works he published
under the name "Petrus Aurelius" (Petrus after the apostle, and Aurelius
after Augustine!) secured him the goodwill of the Gallican bishops. The
plan was therefore well on the way to realization; and it seemed likely that
the young community of the Oratory, won over to the influence of Saint-
Cyran, would serve as the vehicle for the new ideas. Indeed, Jansenius, as
Bishop of Ypres, had already helped the Oratory to found houses in Belgium. Thus, little by little, and even before it was known, "Pilmot" emerged
from the confines of intellectual conception and tended to become a religious movement capable of attracting souls. And the abbot of Saint-Cyran

had already discovered the most appropriate centre from which to raise up the movement and disseminate its doctrine: the abbey of Port-Royal.

2. PORT-ROYAL AND THE ARNAULD FAMILY

PORT-ROYAL, an abbey of the Bernardines, situated in the valley of the Chevreuse, about six leagues (between sixteen and seventeen miles) from Paris, was founded in 1204 by the wife of a soldier of the Fourth Crusade to obtain from heaven the safe return of her husband. It stood in the hollow of the narrow valley, and the hills cut off the horizon on all sides: a melancholy region, in which a state of meditation and prayer seemed to come naturally to the soul. For a long time the abbey had sheltered pious women, living in seclusion, unknown, but following steadfastly the rule of Citeaux. Since the end of the Middle Ages its discipline had become relaxed as in so many other convents of every Order. The nuns' way of life was not actually scandalous, but they had certainly become worldly. They were not enclosed; anyone who wished could enter the convent, and the religious could go out whenever they so desired. As a recreation these rather foolish virgins organized masquerades; their servants did likewise under the direction of the chaplain. The latter, a Cistercian, could not even translate the *Pater Noster*, and the convent's library contained but one spiritual book—a Breviary. In forty years the nuns had not heard more than seven or eight sermons.

On the threshold of this abode so ill-disposed to receive grace there suddenly appeared one day a new face—a child of eight. Her father, very much in favour with King Henri and naturally anxious to see his six daughters established, had secured Jacqueline's appointment as coadjutrix of Port-Royal, while her younger sister, aged five, was appointed to Saint-Cyr. Such were the lamentable customs of the times.

When the abbess died three years later (1602) Jacqueline, who had become Mother Angélique, succeeded her. On one and the same day she made her First Communion and was solemnly blessed as abbess. It seemed that very little could be expected from this eleven-year-old mother superior.

She found the convent very boring, and was so terrified at the thought of having to pass her life there that she fell sick. But there was no way of escaping her fate; the abbatial Bull under which she was appointed had been duly sealed, and by a piece of trickery, for the authorities in Rome had been informed that she was eighteen years of age. And her dreadful father, taking advantage of her weakness, persuaded her to sign a document renewing her solemn vows. "Bursting with spite," she obeyed him.

But God, of course, makes use of everything, even of the most unlikely instruments. Though this abbess had no vocation she had within her the seed of sanctity; and here, where she expected perpetual boredom, grace lay in wait for her. At the age of seventeen she already gave evidence of those qualities which she exhibited throughout her life: depth of soul, a tendency to impulsiveness, a virile strength of purpose even in the midst of intense suffering; but she lacked perhaps that true simplicity of heart which might have placed her among those pious women who approach near to God. During Lent in 1608 a certain Franciscan Father Basile, a wandering monk of doubtful morals,[3] preached such a moving sermon at Port-Royal that the young abbess was deeply stirred. While she listened to him speaking of the self-abasement of Christ, she gradually came to perceive in an agony of grief the wretchedness of the worldly life of her convent, and she decided to change it.

She began to effect reform by reforming herself. She dressed in a habit of coarse wool, bathed the loathsome sores of a sick novice, returned to the practice of rising at night for prayers and the use of the discipline morning and evening. She grouped around her a nucleus of sisters as determined as herself to change their mode of life. The movement gained ground. Assisted by a visiting Franciscan, the young abbess persuaded her sisters to return to strict poverty. They all laid at her feet their small personal treasures, their fine linen, their jewelry and caskets, and decided unanimously to re-impose strict enclosure. September 25, 1609, was a dramatic and splendid day—the

---

3. He gave up the priesthood and became a pastor, but later returned to the bosom of the Church.

424 "Day of the Grating"—which remained famous in the annals of Port-Royal. Mother Angélique refused her own father admission to the convent, and closed heart and ears against his indignant protests; she even remained inflexible to her mother's entreaties and went away victorious, though almost at the end of her tether.

This young woman of steel belonged to an old Auvergnat family of parliamentarians and lawyers named Arnauld, who, though tainted with an hereditary strain of pettifoggery, were not without merit and talent. Jacqueline's grandfather, a Huguenot, had rejected Calvinism after the Massacre of St. Bartholomew. Five years later he was raised to the peerage. Her father Antoine, who became successively Commissioner of Audit and Public Attorney, was finally called to the bar, and became famous for his lawsuits against the Society of Jesus, which was at that time in conflict with the university. Her mother, Catherine Marion, was the daughter of an Advocate General in the Parliament de Paris. Thus the family belonged to the upper legal class, and were elbowing their way towards the peerage. Antoine Arnauld had twenty children, of whom ten survived him. Mother Angélique was the third; the eldest, Robert Arnauld d'Andilly, was the father of the Marquis de Pomponne, minister of the Great King Louis XIV; the sixth, Henri, became Bishop of Angers. His other five daughters, including the widows, took the veil at Port Royal; and the youngest son, Antoine, born in 1612, became the "Great Arnauld."

When the Arnauld family recovered its equanimity, they looked a little more kindly upon the courageous act of the young abbess. Her father, no doubt recognizing his own qualities in this display of character, changed his attitude. He accepted the situation and lent his influence in support of the reform undertaken by Mother Angélique. Rumour reached Paris of the splendid happenings at Port-Royal. The Great Century had just begun, and all that was best and loftiest in the Church was ready to grow enthusiastic over such a creditable enterprise. Instead of an illiterate Bernardine or a visiting Franciscan, Port-Royal could now have first-rate men, even saints, as its spiritual directors, among whom were Father Archangel of Pembroke, a celebrated Franciscan and a real mystic, and Sébastien Zamet, the admirable

Bishop of Langres. Other welcome visitors were the Fathers of the Orato-   425
ry, even Bérulle himself and more frequently Condren. St. Francis de Sales
also, while staying in Paris, desired to visit the good nuns in the valley of the
Chevreuse. Mother Angélique made a general confession to him, and after his
return to Annecy he continued to correspond with her on spiritual matters.

Flattering reports concerning Port-Royal eventually reached the ears of
Louis XIII, who instructed the intrepid abbess to go and reform the royal
convent of Maubuisson, near Pontoise, which another Mother Angélique,
sister of Gabrielle d'Estrées and her brilliant rival in intrigue, had allowed
to fall into a lamentable state. In the face of violent opposition, even armed
opposition on the part of the deposed abbess, Jacqueline Arnauld more or
less succeeded in her difficult task, an achievement which put the finishing
touch to her reputation.

It is almost impossible to imagine the fame that surrounded this twenty-year-old girl. When she returned from Maubuisson, accompanied by
thirty nuns who had refused to leave her, Port-Royal became an important intellectual centre that drew a vast number of souls yearning for a life
of renunciation and absolute mortification. Yet one of the most touching
features in the character of Mother Angélique was her constant longing to
retire still further from the world and bury herself in a life of total renunciation. She asked St. Francis de Sales to receive her into his community as least
among his Visitandines, but he refused her request.

There is one black spot in this wonderful story. The valley in which the
monastery was situated was very unhealthy. Many of the religious died from
fever; and while Mother Angélique gladly accepted this as the will of God it
disturbed her. She therefore took a decision which circumstances seemed to
demand: they must leave the valley. At Saint-Jacques, on the very outskirts
of Paris, her mother bought her the "Hôte Clagny," which she pulled down
and replaced by a spacious convent. It became the Port-Royal of which a
Parisian boulevard still bears the name and of which the building has been
used as a maternity hospital since 1814. Suddenly the centre of activity was
transferred to the very gates of the capital, and the influence of the reformed
community increased still further. Port-Royal became fashionable; all the

426   "devout" people of the city, the nobility, judges, priests and religious of all Orders, gathered there to pray.

What is more, the strict and powerful gentlemen of the Company of the Blessed Sacrament, that celebrated lay body whose activities could be traced behind every reforming effort of the day, took notice of those nuns whose ideals were identical with their own. They even thought of selecting some of them to establish a new contemplative Order—the Institute of the Blessed Sacrament—more or less directly attached to themselves, the members of which would dedicate themselves to continual prayer in order to bring down God's blessing upon France. The idea won the enthusiasm of Mother Angélique, who agreed to leave her convent and go to the Rue Coquillière to manage the new foundation; but all her sisters, "because of their great devotion to the Blessed Sacrament," asked to join the new Order. They decided that henceforward their convent would be called "Port-Royal of the Blessed Sacrament," and that they would bear on their white scapular a large red cross. In any case, Mother Angélique did not long remain in the Rue Coquillière because the worldly success of the convent displeased her, and she returned to her beloved community in the *faubourg*.

And so about 1630 Port-Royal had every appearance of being the very model of reformed monasteries, ideally conducted according to the spirit of the Council of Trent. In the eyes of countless Catholics the habit of the Order, which so many young girls longed to wear, seemed to be the symbol of Christianity restored to its full splendour. There was obviously no question so far of doctrinal deviation, still less of heresy and rebellion; and if anyone had dared to tell Mother Angélique and her daughters that one day they would be condemned by the Church they would have died of grief. Yet the danger was already on their doorstep.

3. PORT-ROYAL AND THE ABBOT OF SAINT-CYRAN

SOME time in 1620 Jean Duvergier de Hauranne met Robert Arnauld d'Antilly at the house of a friend, and they discovered that they had a lot in

common. Jacqueline's elder brother closely resembled her: eager, forceful,   427
inclined to solitude and prayer, and obsessed by life's great problems. He did
not, in any case, find peace of mind until he left the world in 1646 and retired
to Port-Royal. A strangely intense friendship developed between the two
men, and Robert Arnauld often spoke to his sisters of the brilliant spiritual
qualities of his friend. At that period the influence of the abbot was growing
perceptibly. His reputation for mortification gave him a halo of glory. The
words he uttered were on everyone's lips: "God has made it known to me
that His Church ceased to exist five or six hundred years ago"—a statement
which allowed it to be understood that he would remake it. All his penitents
sang his praises. Why should the nuns of Port-Royal, themselves aspiring to
sanctity, hesitate to place their souls in the hands of this new Augustine?

And that is precisely what happened as a result of a fortuitous circumstance. Mother Agnès, the younger sister of Mother Angélique, had long
since left Saint-Cyr for Port-Royal, where she wrote a short work containing sixteen meditations in honour of the sixteen centuries since the foundation of the Holy Eucharist. Her work, entitled *The Secret Chaplet*, was
a pious treatise, obviously over-sublimated and weak in theology, though
not much fault could be found with it as to substance. Sébastien Zamet
and Father de Condren approved it; in consequence of which M. de Bel-
legarde, Archbishop of Sens, envious of the influence of his colleague the
Bishop of Langres in the Institute of the Blessed Sacrament, referred the
work to the Sorbonne, which found therein "several instances of nonsense,
irrelevance, error, blasphemy and impiety." The Jesuit Father Binet took the
same view. It seemed that a great fuss was being made over such a little book,
but behind the criticism of Mother Agnès the real purpose was probably to
attack Father de Condren and the Oratory. This was a fairly common procedure among theologians.

There suddenly appeared in Paris a little pamphlet entitled *Apologie
pour servir de défense au Chapelet*, and it soon became known that Saint-
Cyran was the author. The famous abbot stated that, having examined the
sixteen meditations with the greatest care, he could find no fault with them;
on the contrary, he admired their doctrine. He went further: he won the

support of his friends in Belgium, and had the work approved by Jansenius and Froidmont, eminent masters of Louvain University. Finally Saint-Cyran wrote a crushing reply to the criticisms of Father Binet. The gratitude of the Arnauld family was overwhelming, as well as that of the Institute of the Blessed Sacrament, the whole of Port-Royal and, of course, Sébastien Zamet.

Zamet was so grateful that he entrusted Saint-Cyran with the spiritual direction of his nuns, on the grounds that he himself lived so far from Paris that he could not give the task his uninterrupted attention. Thus arose a delicate situation fraught with possibilities. On either side of the grille in the parlour of Port-Royal, Angélique and Saint-Cyran, the two great protagonists in the drama, faced each other—"the flint," as Sainte-Beuve put it, "which would eventually throw off the spark." From the very beginning complete harmony existed between the abbot and Mother Angélique. In a short time he became the spiritual director of all the nuns at Port-Royal, and he suggested to them that the method followed by M. Zamet was much too easy-going and should be changed. These holy women were seized with a veritable craze for mortification. The "supereminent ideal of the primitive Church" became the sole topic of conversation at Port-Royal. The Bishop of Langres bitterly resented seeing himself utterly superseded. The community's official preacher for Lent 1635 was Saint-Cyran, who had now become the master of Port-Royal.

Master not only of the monastery that bore the name, but also of the circle of people that henceforward thronged around those sacred walls. The radiance of Jean Duvergier continued to extend. A youngster of twenty, precocious and burning with the love of God, became the abbot's disciple as soon as he made his acquaintance, and under his instruction launched into the study of St. Augustine, assisted by little books of commentaries that arrived from Louvain and later from Ypres. That young man was Antoine Arnauld, the Benjamin of the Arnauld family. Serious-minded men of "great intellect, learning and virtue," men of good standing in the world, voluntarily grouped themselves together on the advice of the reformer; they took no religious vows, but agreed to lead a life of silence, work and prayer.

Among them were Catherine Arnauld's son Antoine Le Maistre,[4] a celebrated barrister who suddenly renounced the world and built himself a little
hermitage in the garden of Port-Royal; his brother, Le Maistre de Séricourt,
an outstanding military officer; de Bascle, a member of the nobility; and
M. Vitart, a member of the upper middle class whose sister had married
a gentleman named Racine. There were also two clerics: Claude Lancelot,
a student of Bourdoise and sub-deacon in the community of Saint-Nicolas-du-Chardonnet, and Antoine Singlin, who, having become a priest on
the advice of St. Vincent de Paul, abandoned the Lazarists to join the ranks
of the Solitaires of Port-Royal. In order to assist the further development
of his group by drawing to himself the young, Saint-Cyran put into effect
a plan to set up *Petites Écoles*—"Little Schools"—based upon a new educational system and intended primarily to form character. The execution of
this project was entrusted to Lancelot, and pupils began to come in.

The plan outlined by the two friends at Louvain fourteen years earlier
appeared therefore to be a success. They had both worked hard, each in his
particular field. It was now time to instill the great theories of the Bishop
of Ypres into the minds most capable of receiving and disseminating them.
Saint-Cyran, disturbed by certain rumours that had come to his ears, left
Paris and retired for a while to his abbey at Poitiers. Although Jansenius
died about that time it seemed certain that their ideas would triumph.

4. THE THREE STAGES OF JANSENISM

AUGUSTINUS was published at Louvain in 1640, in flagrant violation
of papal instructions forbidding any public statements concerning grace.
While the work was being secretly printed the Jesuits succeeded in obtaining a number of pages and requested the Internuncio to warn Rome, so
that publication might be forbidden. Despite this, the enormous volume
came off the press duly authorized and dedicated to the Cardinal-Infante,

---

4.   Or Le Maître. Both spellings are to be found in documents of the period.

430 governor of Belgium. It seemed to appear everywhere at once. In September 1640 copies were sold at Frankfurt fair. In Holland the Calvinists were enraptured with it—an anagram of the name Cornelius Jansenius produced *Calvini sensus in ore*. So many people read the book in France that it had to be reprinted at Paris in the following year, and at Rouen shortly afterwards. One cannot but be astonished at the success of such a book; it was written in Latin, extremely bulky and made such heavy reading that the very sight of it would discourage Christians of our time. Publicly, Saint-Cyran was enthusiastic about the work, though he had personal misgivings as to the wisdom of certain expressions. He did, however, declare with the air of a prophet that it was "*the* book of devotion of this last age," "a book that would endure as long as the Church," and "it is the kind of book that can never be destroyed, despite King and Pope."

What then was the doctrine expounded by *Augustinus*? In order to obtain a true picture of that doctrine, it should be studied in relation to theories which had already been subjects of controversy within the Church; for the aim of Jansenius was to formulate a solution that would reconcile opposing tenets and put an end to disputes. The basis of the Catholic faith is that man, having lost his original state of innocence through sin, cannot be saved without God's help, without grace. But this divine support is related to man's freedom, and man must strive to save himself. It is extremely difficult to reconcile these two means of salvation. To allow too much to grace might destroy man's liberty; to exaggerate the role of liberty might result in denying grace its proper function and power. Hence the doctrinal deviations in one direction or the other that arose during the course of centuries.

Already during the fifth century the Breton monk Pelagius had stated that man was entirely free by the exercise of his will to do right or not to do right; to save his soul or to lose it—free to say yes or no to God.[5] In other words, original sin had not prostrated man irrevocably. According to Pelagius divine grace is nature itself, and man possesses it because he has reason

---

5.   See Henri Daniel-Rops, *The Church in the Dark Ages* (Providence, RI: Cluny, 2023), Volume 1, p. 37.

and can choose his destiny. In such a scheme of things man depends entirely 431
on himself. "By free will man is emancipated from God": so said the Pela-
gian Bishop Julian of Eclanum. It follows, therefore, that Redemption has
no meaning, and Christ ceases to be necessary. St. Augustine devoted four
large works to the refutation of this heresy concerning free will.

The great doctrinarians of the Protestant Reformation,[6] Luther and
Calvin, held the opposite view: they rejected free will, and denied man any
positive action in the work of his salvation. They considered that salvation
depended solely on grace and the will of God, decided from all eternity by
the infinite but inscrutable wisdom of God. Predestined man could do practically nothing of himself in order to be saved or to avoid damnation.

The teaching of the Catholic Church over the centuries is to be found
between these two extreme systems; it refuses to make everything dependent upon free will, but it does not leave everything to grace. Such problems
were considered as early as 853 by the Council of Quierzy-sur-Oise, which
made this profound statement: "To those who are saved salvation is a gift
of God; but those who perish are lost through their own fault." Here grace
and liberty are reconciled; it is an agreement in principle, which leaves a vast
field for discussion. This had become very clear from recent controversies in
which the Molinist Jesuits laid greater emphasis on free will, with the object
of building up a moral effort on man's part; while the Dominican Thomists
stressed the importance of grace in order to extol faith. Because the Congregatio de Auxiliis established for the purpose of settling the dispute had
declined to make a decision, both theories could be taught from the pulpit
in Catholic churches. Who then would put an end to this quarrel? Jansenius
declared that he would; he, and he alone, was the authoritative interpreter
of St. Augustine!

According to Jansenius no one before him had discovered in the work of
Augustine the synthesis of the demands of both grace and free will. Original

---

6. Two chapters of Henri Daniel-Rops, *A Religious Revolution: The Protestant Reformation* (Providence, RI: Cluny, 2023), Volume 2, are devoted to the study of Luther and
Calvin.

432   sin created an abyss between man's first state and the fallen state that followed. Man was entirely free in his state of innocence, and his will tended naturally towards what was right. In his fallen state he was no longer free but a slave of sin, for ever dragged along by earthly delights; all that he did led him to the abyss of corruption. But, argued Jansenius, God in His goodness offered humanity a chance to snatch itself from the abyss. Through Christ's merits He gave man efficacious grace, which ennobled the human will. Those who possessed it were indeed free, delivered from the slavery of sin, and the grace in their souls coincided with man's interior demand for the good. But nothing could be done for those who did not possess it; they were without hope. Even the just could not obey the divine commands without grace— St. Peter, for instance, denied Christ before Pilate's judgment-seat. Grace, however, Jansenius declared, was not given to all humanity. Many are called, but few are chosen. Only a few exceptional souls were capable of exercising free will in regard to salvation. As for the rest, God did not condemn them, but, because grace has not been given to them, they remained *in massa damnata* as a result of original sin. The Jansenist synthesis, at least as far as the word was concerned, recognized free will in man, but limited it to those few who received grace—a doctrine which parted company with Protestantism in its first assertion, but drew close to it in its second. It rejected the Catholic doctrine which teaches with St. Paul that God "will have all men to be saved" (1 Tim. 2:4), and gives everyone sufficient grace to enable him to carry on the struggle for salvation. Perhaps it would be an exaggeration to describe Jansenism as a "rehash of Calvinism," as has so often been done. It would be more accurate to describe it as a kind of semi-Protestantism.

Such was the substance of Jansenius's vast work *Augustinus*, the essentials of what we might call "doctrinal Jansenism," speculative and metaphysical, born "in the library of an intellectual," as Bremond so rightly said. But when the theories of the Bishop of Ypres were injected into the atmosphere of Port-Royal they assumed a totally different character, and found expression in moral directives applicable to the daily life of the Christian. Thus a "moral Jansenism" developed and asserted itself, to which real Jansenism gradually gave way. The term "Jansenist" in our day has come to signify

almost exclusively an excessively severe moral attitude. The relationship   433
between these two aspects of Jansenism was not binding. The Jansenist doctrine of grace no more demanded a stricter form of moral behaviour than
did Luther's Protestantism (as was very evident in Germany). For if man is
not granted efficacious grace, if, despite his efforts, he is to remain *in massa
damnata*, why should he strive to live according to the Commandments?

But the *milieu* in which the doctrine was disseminated was already predisposed to apply the most "Jansenist" interpretation to the bishop's ideas.
The people of Port-Royal were inclined towards austerity; they entertained
a gloomy and tragic outlook on Christian life. But the austerity of Port-Royal was not unique; quite the contrary. The writings of many prominent
Catholics of the day, including among others St. Vincent de Paul, Bérulle,
Olier, and even the gentle St. Francis de Sales, contained statements that
the solitaries of Port-Royal would gladly have claimed as their own. Mother
Angélique's reformed nuns were not alone in refusing all compromise, all
worldly entanglement. Nor was the Jansenist Pascal the only one to suffer
spiritual torment in wrestling with great problems. The early intentions
and the first leaders of Port-Royal were beyond criticism—"Everything we
admire in them," said Bremond, "is Catholic."

Deviation came later, and it happened through Saint-Cyran. There is no
doubt whatever that doctrinal Jansenism developed into moral Jansenism
in the soul of that ardent, immoderate mystic to whom Mother Angélique
had entrusted the spiritual direction of her community. In fact, Saint-Cyran
selected from *Augustinus* its moral and practical conclusions only. But he
cogitated upon his friend's transcendent ideas in order to adapt them to a
novel spirituality suggested to him by his personal experience. He had most
definitely a keen and harrowing sense of man's misery as a sinner. What had
undoubtedly moved him most of all in St. Augustine was the idea of the
"cruel war waged between the two men within me," that exhausting conflict
which man, without God, is doomed to lose. Jansenist theories confirm his
tendency towards rigorism, an austere and gloomy religion. Already in his
Apologie pour le chapelet secret he had written: "We have within us a perpetual source of sin flowing towards everlasting death, unless God places

within us the fountain of life that flows into life eternal." These few words embody the whole Jansenist doctrine on grace. When Saint-Cyran reminded his penitents "that the judgments of God are terrible," that all men are wretched sinners, that no one can be sure of salvation even though he strive doggedly to that end, he was repeating truths that many other preachers had proclaimed in his time and before him; but he gave the words a doctrinal background that came from Jansenius's book.

It is easy to understand how, with the best intentions, the pious daughters of Mother Angélique, and even the solitaries, were able to drift into doctrinal deviation; and that so many souls should have yielded later on, drawn by the movement's spirit of mortification, its "most deadly talisman," as Sainte-Beuve says. It was quite easy to go astray; the Jansenists used the same language as St. Charles Borromeo, St. Vincent de Paul and Bourdaloue. Indeed, Bossuet saw clearly that "this severity puffs out presumption, fosters an arrogant sorrow for sin and a spirit of ostentatious singularity." Such faults would become more and more apparent as the various episodes in the history of Jansenism unfolded.

For Jansenism was not to remain merely a doctrine of grace bound up with a complete, coherent and rigid conception of religion and strict morality. It was a subject which had cropped up under different forms throughout the Church's history, and it soon concerned itself with matters of discipline as much as it did with doctrine and morals. A third aspect of Jansenism was soon added to the other two: we might call it "sectarian Jansenism." Its origins were complex. They may be traced through the arrogance of the Arnauld family, proud of its triumphs, and later on of the holiness of so many of its members. "To acknowledge the name of our family," said Mother Agnès boldly, "is almost like acknowledging God." Its origins are also evident in the undeniable pride of Saint-Cyran, in his "haughty and insolent zeal" to which Jean-Jacques Olier referred; in his immovable conviction that he and Jansenius alone could claim to represent true Christianity. They may also be traced to the polemical and quibbling tendencies of the sect—especially of the Arnaulds, who were professional lawyers— and a reluctance to accept humbly the decrees of the Church and submit to

her judgment. From the very beginning Jansenism was on excellent terms   435
with Gallican circles in the parliamentary field, which were anti-Rome on
principle and anti-Jesuit by temperament; there Jansenism gained numerous adherents. It won friends among other classes of society, especially the
lower clergy whose "presbyterian priesthood" Jansenius extolled as the
trustee of grace on equal terms with the hierarchy. A Jansenist "party" was
thus established—in the sense in which the word "party" was then used.
Its members became less and less concerned with Augustinian doctrines
relating to grace, but increasingly interested in the triumph of their side. It
is well known that great doctrinal struggles tend more and more to develop and consolidate the sectarian spirit. Thus, during the hundred and fifty
years of its history Jansenism, having commenced as a doctrinal deviation
on grace, merged into an exacting conception of Christian morality, then
gradually became a heresy against the Church, even going as far as to ally
itself unintentionally with the enemies of Christianity itself. We may feel
justified in thinking that this eventuality was not foreseen by Jansenius,
Saint-Cyran or Mother Angélique.

5. THE ATTITUDE OF CARDINAL RICHELIEU

WHEN *Augustinus* was published the battle of Jansenism had already
entered upon its first skirmishes, and the abbot of Saint-Cyran was in prison. Enlightened people had for some time been forming guarded opinions
of the celebrated spiritual director. Father de Condren, who had known
him since the beginning of his career, said of him: "He has an inaccessible
mind; he loves novelty, and has an inordinate leaning towards the eccentric."
Sébastien Zamet, Bishop of Langres, enlightened by the bitterness of his
experience at seeing himself thrust from Port-Royal by his former protégé,
described him as "an insulting and violent personage, without the slightest respect for those who in any way disagree with him." As for Monsieur
Vincent, saint that he was, he bore with humility his being treated by Saint-
Cyran as an ignoramus when he gently reproved the abbot for claiming to

save the Church single-handed. "Ignorant? I am even more ignorant than you think ..." he replied with a pleasant smile. But he remained aloof from Saint-Cyran, and saw less and less of him.

Richelieu shared that mistrust, though his reasons were not entirely praiseworthy. At first the proud cardinal endeavoured to lure this new force into his own service, but Saint-Cyran refused to be drawn. He was not a man to be bought. It then came to the all-powerful minister's ears that words of criticism had been uttered concerning governments "that desired to have none but minions in their service." The cardinal's opinion of the reformer suddenly changed; he was no longer "the most learned man in the world," but a "visionary," an unbalanced, headstrong man. Before long His Eminence declared that he regarded Saint-Cyran as "more dangerous than six armies"; an obvious exaggeration. It is very doubtful whether the master of Port-Royal did in fact plot against the cardinal, but it cannot be denied that his behaviour was that of a conspirator. He wrapped himself in mystery, instructed his correspondents to burn his letters and continually influenced people and events. Richelieu might have believed, or given a convincing impression that he believed, that Saint-Cyran was capable of the "most evil designs" (to use Bremond's words), and that he exercised control over a sect as dangerous as the Protestants. In fact, these two men were absolutely incompatible. "There is not a potentate in the world," declared Saint-Cyran, "who is more naturally qualified to rule than I am." "Purpuratus," as Saint-Cyran and Jansenius had nicknamed Richelieu, was not the man to make allowances for people with pretentions of that nature.

Various incidents brought his anger to a head. Jansenius, whom everyone knew to be Saint-Cyran's friend, published from Louvain a pamphlet entitled *Mars Gallicus*, a bitter condemnation of Richelieu and his policy of alliance with the Protestants. And when the cardinal had the marriage of Gaston d'Orléans and Marguerite de Lorraine annulled, Saint-Cyran publicly declared that his action was a disgraceful scandal—which incidentally was quite true. Finally, when a certain Father Séguenot of the Oratory published a commentary on St. Augustine's treatise *De Continentia*, the inquiry instituted to examine the work, on the grounds that it contained a

number of unreliable statements, revealed that it had been directly inspired
by Saint-Cyran.

On May 14, 1638, a week after the death of Jansenius, the king's police arrested Saint-Cyran, and confined him in the Château de Vincennes. The least one can say about the ensuing trial is that it was hardly a fair one. The defendant's old friends and even his confessor were questioned. Sébastien Zamet accused of heresy the man whose theology he had praised to the skies a short time previously. Saint-Cyran's letters containing spiritual advice to the sisters of Port-Royal were seized by the police and read in court. And Father Joseph, "the Grey Eminence," worked efficiently in the background. There is no doubt whatever that the trial, conducted by the State, was canonically illegal; for only an ecclesiastical tribunal was competent to try Saint-Cyran, who was indicted solely on his religious opinions. St. Vincent de Paul had the courage to state this fact clearly in his evidence; he refused to incriminate his old friend, and pressed for acquittal pure and simple. Despite everything Saint-Cyran spent five years in prison.

The ordeal was very painful to him; but not physically, for Richelieu saw that the prisoner was treated with consideration. He allowed him to receive visitors, to correspond with his friends and even to write and publish books. This enabled Saint-Cyran to remain the leader of the movement, to continue to guide numerous souls and even to effect conversions among the imperial officers who were at that time prisoners in Paris. But morally he suffered a great deal; so much so that he experienced a dramatic spiritual crisis during which he asked himself whether he was right after all, whether his opinions were justified and whether his boldness was not merely empty foolhardiness.

His captivity, however, raised him still higher in the esteem of his followers. Port-Royal had a martyr! "Remember," exclaimed Mother Agnès, "that the abbot of Saint-Cyran is confined to prison only because he pointed out the true way to penance." Neither his spiritual daughters nor his friends intended to yield to persecution. In vain did the authorities suppress the "Institute of the Blessed Sacrament"; the house of "Port-Royal of the Blessed Sacrament" still remained a centre of mystic fervour. Nothing was achieved by the disbandment of the solitaries. Driven from Port-Royal-des-Champs, where they had settled, they returned without any fuss, continued to recruit adherents and calmly set up their "Little Schools."

While all this was going on, *Augustinus* was published, and it created a tremendous sensation. In Louvain the Jesuits set about its wholesale destruction. In Paris the diocesan theologus Habert attacked it violently from the pulpit of Notre-Dame. In Rome the aged Pope Urban VIII, an advocate of the policy of appeasement, having tried at first to impose and maintain silence, was forced under pressure from the Jesuits to sign the Bull *In Eminenti* (March 1641). Publication was none the less delayed for two years. All these events were mere skirmishes; preparations were being made for more strenuous conflicts ahead.

When Richelieu died, Mazarin, who was more conciliatory, agreed in February 1643 to set Saint-Cyran free. His nuns, the solitaries and friends in every walk of life welcomed him with idolatrous demonstrations. At the convent of Port-Royal the abbess announced the news to her nuns by loosening her girdle, thus avoiding a breach of silence. As soon as he became free Saint-Cyran began to write against the Protestants, probably to gain the goodwill of the queen mother and the court. But a few weeks later he died, a tired man. His zealous followers shared his body amongst them, everyone wishing to keep some member as a relic; the less fortunate had to be satisfied with pieces of linen steeped in his blood, or a little of the dust "that was made when his head was sawn off." This ardent leader, this disturbing and fascinating mystic, vanished from the scene at the critical moment of the conflict, aware that he left behind a successor capable of continuing and developing his work still further. That man was Antoine Arnauld.

6. THE "GREAT ARNAULD"

THE youngest child of the famous Arnauld family was at that time just thirty years of age, but physically and intellectually he appeared much older. He had a little, wiry, energetic body that always seemed about to leap. His

features were swarthy, rather ugly and with large wrinkles, and he had an   439
unshapely nose. But his eyes glowed like embers; they looked straight into
a speaker's face, reaching to the very soul. A strange power emanated from
this ungainly man; it might have been irresistible had he possessed warmth
of heart and some hidden tenderness. Antoine Arnauld was a brilliant dialectician and polemist who gave the impression not so much of embodying
his convictions as possessing a capacity for establishing their truth and setting them out as dogmas. In that role he excelled.

From his childhood his own family had treated him as an infant prodigy. His mother guided his steps towards the priesthood, and from 1638
to 1641 he presented his four set theses before the assembled bishops and
judges at the Sorbonne, who applauded his work. Moreover, "Jansenist" tendencies were already noticeable in his outlook. He had studied St. Augustine and extracts from the work of the Bishop of Ypres, but he had not yet
found his way into the movement. His nephews in the Le Maistre family,
the solitaries, who were older than he, were disturbed to see him so satisfied
with his efforts, content to ride in his stately carriages and eagerly pursuing
worldly success. But like all the Arnaulds he had a craving for things divine;
and Saint-Cyran, a profound psychologist, suspected as much. Once, when
Saint-Cyran was visited by the young theological student in his prison at
Vincennes, he induced him to confide in him and talk about the "perpetual state of lethargy" in which he had so far lived. He warned him against
pride, and persuaded him to restore himself spiritually by solitude, prayer
and fasting—advice that he offered his penitents. The last of the Arnaulds
responded admirably to the master's expectations as the rest of the family
had done, and entered joyfully into the exercise of mortification and austerity of life which "Jansenism" had now become. Saint-Cyran had no equal
in his ability to lead people along the one path that enabled them to give of
their best. It did not take him long to ascertain the part this slim boy might
play, endowed as he was with the intelligence that the conflict demanded.
While still in prison Saint-Cyran wrote to his pupil on February 1, 1643:
"The time has come to speak out; it would be a crime to remain silent." Thus
he who was to become the "Great Arnauld" entered the lists.

The field selected—no doubt by his master rather than by himself—had nothing to do with the theology of grace, but concerned morals and practice. Perhaps it was one way of distracting men's minds from the criticisms that were being hurled at *Augustinus*; and, more precisely, a means of attacking Jansenius's adversary, the Society of Jesus. It was in fact a Jesuit, Father de Sesmaisons, who permitted his penitent the Marquise de Sablé (a lady on good terms with Port-Royal) to attend a dance on the day on which she had received Holy Communion. Saint-Cyran had forbidden his penitent the Princesse de Guéméné to do that very thing. This mundane incident inflamed the theologians in both camps, for the moment was ripe for an explosion. On August 25, 1643, Antoine Arnauld published his *De la Fréquente Communion*, in which, taking the Fathers, the popes and the councils as his authority, he claimed to restore the true doctrine concerning reception of the Sacraments. This doctrine, he asserted, had been vitiated and corrupted by Jesuitical laxism. The pamphlet was not without merit. Its language was lucid and precise, its arguments solid, and the work contained some very beautiful passages and sublime thoughts on the Holy Eucharist, expressed with impressive piety. Hence its success. But Arnauld maintained some curious opinions. Instead of regarding Holy Communion as a means of acquiring spiritual sustenance and increasing grace, he presented it as a sublime reward to be obtained only at the cost of strict mortification and, in any case, to be received very infrequently. In other words—and here we have the ideas of Jansenius—only those should communicate who felt the definite call of divine grace. Not to communicate became a sign of exemplary piety and profound humility. Before confessors permitted their penitents to approach the Blessed Sacrament they should impose on them long waiting periods and severe penances. It was possible to reconcile all this with the intention of the Council of Trent to restore to the Holy Eucharist its former dignity; but Arnauld's treatise clearly ran counter to the tendency of the times, which was to present the Sacred Host as the soul's sustenance. But this emphasis upon the rigorous, rendered inhuman by dint of mortification, was discouraging to poor sinners who constituted the majority of Christians.

The reaction was lively; and not only among the Jesuits. St. Vincent de
Paul remarked that anyone reading Arnauld's book on frequent Communion was forced to ask himself "whether there could be any man on earth
who held such a high opinion of his own virtue as to believe himself worthy to receive Holy Communion." St. Paul would have dreaded the idea
of doing so. "None the less," added St. Vincent mischievously, "Monsieur
Arnauld boasts that he says Mass every day." It seemed obvious that such a
book would turn the faithful away from Holy Communion, and encourage
weakness and apathy. In fact, a few years later parish priests drew attention to an impressive drop in religious practice among their parishioners.
"If this book," to quote Monsieur Vincent again, "has benefited a hundred
people by making them more respectful towards the sacraments, it must
have done harm to more than ten thousand by drawing them away altogether." But not everyone was as far-seeing as Monsieur Vincent. Highly
placed prelates such as Bishop Caulet, Bishop Pavilion and many others
approved the book. In Rome the Jesuit Cardinal de Lugo hoped to put an
end to the dispute by suggesting a simple censure of the body of the work
while condemning the preface because of a clumsy paragraph in which St.
Peter and St. Paul were treated as equals within the Church. Despite these
pacificatory intentions the brawl developed. When the first Jesuit was put
out of action, Father Pétau launched a pamphlet entitled *La Pénitence
publique et la préparation à la communion*, a well-thought-out work but
so badly written that the Jansenists were able to say that the good Father
"knew every language except his own." M. Olier intervened publicly, and
he was joined by the whole of Saint-Sulpice. At the other extreme every
Gallican and anti-Jesuit at the Sorbonne and in the Parliament de Paris
bestirred himself, even urging Arnauld to appeal against his indulgent
condemnation by Rome. This he wisely decided not to do. The quarrel
over *Fréquente Communion* was at its height when the controversy over
Augustinus entered a new phase.

7. THE "FIVE PROPOSITIONS"

THE Bull *In Eminenti* hardly affected the prestige of *Augustinus*, which continued to be read and remained a subject of controversy despite the interdict. In 1644 Father Pétau launched against it two weighty treatises in Latin; though extremely erudite they were the despair of his publisher, the bookseller Charmoisy. Arnauld replied with two works under the title *Apologies pour Jansénius*, which had a very wide circulation as a result of the vast success of his *Fréquente Communion*. But a young and talented Jesuit, Father Deschamps, a more powerful fighter than the excellent Pétau, dealt a stinging blow against the late Jansenius by proving from a comparison of texts that his book revived the theories of Baius which had been condemned by the Sorbonne in 1560. Now at last the anti-Jansenist offensive began. Habert, a former lecturer in theology at Paris who had been appointed Bishop of Vabres, in Tarn, led the attack. A group of Jesuits joined in. Then Arnauld committed the greatest mistake of his career, and it was to do great harm to his side.

When Father Véron, a notable preacher, publicly referred to the Jansenists as Calvinists, they denounced him to the Sorbonne and demanded redress. Nicolas Cornet, doctor of the Faculty of Theology and an extremely just man, decided to deal with the matter personally. He read *Augustinus* carefully, and extracted from it, by a method very common in theological discussions of this kind, a certain number of "propositions" which, it appeared to him, summarized the whole conception of Jansenius. On July 1, 1649, he submitted them to the judgment of the Sorbonne. Arnauld and his friends suddenly became uneasy, and obtained a ruling from the Parliament to forbid examination of the case. Nicolas Cornet and his fellow theologians were indignant; they passed the "propositions" to the Assembly of the Clergy with the suggestions that they be submitted to Rome. A petition drafted by Habert was presented to all bishops. Under it the Pope was requested to give "a plain and explicit judgment." St. Vincent de Paul was terrified by what he learned at that time concerning the Jansenist peril and the falling away in the practice of religion in the parishes; he therefore

lent the whole weight of his authority to the proposal, and pleaded per- 443
sonally for signatures. Eighty-five bishops signed the petition. In spite of
the fact that eleven Jansenist prelates drew up a counter-petition requesting
Rome to refrain from passing judgment, Innocent X accepted the appeal,
and appointed a commission consisting of five cardinals and thirteen con-
sultants to settle the question once and for all.

The case dragged on for two years; innumerable influences were at work
in one direction or another, both sides having dispatched qualified representatives to Rome. The Jansenists subsequently took revenge when they
attempted to have the judgment modified by publishing a lively account
of the gossip which had surrounded the affair; but that had no effect on
the ultimate decision. On May 31, 1653, the Bull *Cum occasione* was signed
by Innocent X formally condemning the "Five Propositions." All five were
declared heretical, and in addition several were described as "blasphemous,
impious and an insult to divine mercy." In substance the first four propositions expressed the idea that efficacious grace was indispensable to salvation,
but that God did not give every man sufficient grace. The fifth affirmed that
Christ did not die for all men; He did not shed his blood for all.

The condemnation of Jansenius and his theories was thus precisely
stated. What were Antoine Arnauld and his friends to do? Nine years earlier the condemnation of a passage from the preface to his *Fréquente Communion* had driven the hot-headed polemist to take shelter "beneath the
wings of God"; that is to say, he buried himself in a château belonging to the
Princesse de Guémené. Since then, however, the position had appreciably
changed. The Jansenist movement had spread and had grown more powerful; the "Jansenist party" was a body of some consequence. To begin with,
vocations continued to increase in the convent. In 1648 it became necessary
to reopen Port-Royal-des-Champs, which had become less unhealthy since
the solitaries had had the low-lying ground drained. And the little band of
solitaries grew; the six original residents had been joined by many learned
men who had abandoned the world to come and pray, sing canticles, dig the
land and write books. Robert d'Andilly, the oldest member of the Arnauld
family, was among them; he cultivated beautiful pears, and sent Anne of

444   Austria the "blessed fruits" from his espaliers; there was his son Arnauld de Luzancy; and Pallu, a doctor who was followed by Hamon, another doctor. Among the clerics were Manguelain, Giroust and Duchemin, and even a bishop named Listolphe de Suzarre, and Pierre Nicole, the most eminent Latinist of his day. Finally there was Antoine Singlin, a former pupil of St. Vincent de Paul. Singlin began by deputizing for Saint-Cyran as spiritual director of the whole of Port-Royal, and eventually took his place. He had an equally deep understanding of souls, but he was wiser and more gentle than Saint-Cyran. But the "Great Arnauld" became the real master.

The second generation now occupied Port-Royal; and being, as is usually the case, more committed than the first, they were tougher and more daring. Among the nuns was a daughter of Robert d'Andilly, Mother Angélique's niece, a young girl of twenty who, because of her brilliant gifts, had been appointed novice mistress. She had a most unusual disposition; apart from her burning enthusiasm, she was extraordinarily energetic, and her frigid air of composure concealed the most intense feeling. Her name was Mother Angélique de Saint-Jean. Among the men of that second generation was Blaise Pascal. As a preparation for the future Port-Royal had had its Little Schools since 1638, to which Lancelot, Nicole and Le Nain de Tillemont dedicated their lives. These schools were destined to compete with the Jesuit colleges and rival those of the Oratory. A new teaching technique was developed, based upon example and mutual confidence between child and teacher. For the first time in the history of education the French language became a distinct subject in the school's curriculum.[7]

The nuns also took boarders into their convent school. Sister Sainte-Euphémie who, before she took the veil, was Jacqueline, sister of Blaise Pascal, watched over them with zeal and tenderness.

The "Jansenist Party" developed out of the publicity attaching to the dispute. Its adherents came from the legal profession and from parliamentarians, supporters of the freedoms of the Gallican Church and hostile to Rome on principle, and even from members of the nobility who hated the

---

7.   See Volume 1 of this work, Chapter II, p. 121.

cardinal-minister on the rather doubtful grounds that he was the Pope's man. Jansenism was in very good odour among the supporters of the Fronde. To obtain an idea of the network of influential members of society that the party included throughout France we have only to quote the names of some of the fashionable women who, from far and near, flocked to Port-Royal: Anne de Rohan, the Princesse de Guéméné, Elizabeth de Choiseul, the Comtesse de Plessis-Guénégaud, Madame de Souvre, the Marquise de Sablé, the Duchesse de Longueville, Louise Marie de Gonzague, future Queen of Poland and friend of Monsieur Vincent, the Duchesse de Liancourt, the Duchesse de Luynes, and even Madame de Sévigné who, as Sainte-Beuve remarked, was "an amateur Jansenist" just as she was a "volatile friend."

Knowing, therefore, that he had the advantage of strong support Arnauld could not avoid the temptation to resist his condemnation. It was a difficult decision to have to make; for Mazarin was about to set up a council of letters-patent to make the Bull law, and was even then calling together the bishops then in Paris, to instruct them to accept the Bull. In fact, all the French bishops, including the Jansenists, did accept it. Even at Port-Royal, hesitation predominated: Mother Angélique, despite occasional sudden and violent outbursts against Rome, was inclined to silent submission; Singlin and Nicole were similarly disposed. Had Saint-Cyran still been there, he too might have chosen that way out of the impasse, for notwithstanding his faults he was a high-minded man and not given to subterfuge. But Antoine Arnauld thought he could hedge and evade the issue.

Hence the famous distinction between "fact and law." Arnauld adopted the attitude that the Pope had quite rightly condemned the "Five Propositions." They were monstrous heresies; but the propositions were not to be found in the *Augustinus*. They were a complete forgery by people inimical to Jansenius and his doctrine, and they distorted his ideas. It was a clever line of argument, but dishonest. Not one of the sect's representatives had raised the point during the discussions in Rome. It reeked of the spirit of double-dealing, the cunning of the quack lawyer. Arnauld, however, adopted that line of argument even though he may not have invented it. Nicole may have put it into his head, but Arnauld clung to it with characteristic determination.

The brawl became more violent than ever. Were the Five Propositions really contained in Jansenius's work? In 1654 the Assembly of the Clergy solemnly confirmed that they were, and a brief statement from Rome said so even more expressly. But were the bishops qualified to settle a point of fact (which any intelligent person could decide for himself) as to whether this or that statement was to be found in a book? Was the Pope really infallible when he set himself up as a judge as to whether a thing was or was not? The way which led to the answer to such questions might also lead to open revolt, even to schism. Whatever the position might be, many upright people were profoundly disturbed. Before giving absolution confessors would ask their penitents if they rejected Jansenist ideas and whether they accepted the Bull. Father Picoté, a Sulpician, refused absolution to a very prominent personage, the Duc de Liancourt, because he stated that the Five Propositions were not to be found in *Augustinus*. Thereupon the Great Arnauld flew into a passion, and retorted with two letters which he published; one to "this Monsieur Picoté" and the other to his superior, M. Tronson, and the whole of Saint-Sulpice. The letters created a great stir, but produced a brusque reaction from his adversaries. The Sorbonne took the matter up, examined the letters, which it declared to be "scandalous and an insult to the Pope," and then disposed of the question of "fact and law" in two well-defined judgments. Arnauld became extremely apprehensive. He drew up two statements which his opponents might have found it easy to accept as a withdrawal had tempers not been over-heated. His enemies intended to make him bite the dust—a fact which shows that not all the faults were on his side. The Sorbonne condemned him, and even threatened to have his name struck from the list of Doctors of Theology if he did not submit formally. All his friends at the Sorbonne could do was to make an impressive exit from the hall as a sign of protest. Even the Parliament dared not accept the appeal lodged by Arnauld.

The Jansenist position appeared to be critical. Rome, the King, Mazarin, the Jesuits, Saint-Sulpice, Saint-Lazare and nine-tenths of the bishops were against Arnauld. They constituted a formidable mass of enemies, and Arnauld felt the approach of disaster. He was obliged to go into hiding, and was able to leave his retreat only at night. For twelve years he led a wandering life, continually changing his hiding-place. Then occurred a sensational circumstance that brought up the whole question once again.

8. BLAISE PASCAL AND THE "PROVINCIALES"

ON January 23, 1656, the very day on which the sixty Jansenist doctors walked out of the Sorbonne to avoid taking part in the condemnation of Arnauld, a pamphlet appeared that was pounced upon by all classes of society in Paris. The style was incisive and satirical; the arguments vigorous and striking. It was written in the form of a letter to the Jesuits and to an imaginary person living in the provinces, and the subject was the policy and morals of the Jesuits. Police inquiries failed to reveal how this little leaflet had been prepared, printed and distributed. Other "Provincial Letters" appeared at irregular intervals during the succeeding months. Altogether eighteen were published up to the middle of 1657, when they were collected and published in one volume. The third letter bore the signature of Louis de Montalte; either a misleading attempt to be precise or intended to arouse a little more curiosity. The reading public thought it must be a pseudonym; Monte Alte might come from *mons altus.* Could the author be Clermont d'Auvergne?

Be that as it may, Mazarin devoured the *Provinciales*, and "laughed heartily over them."

To those in the know there was no mystery about the person hiding behind the pseudonym. He was a close friend of Antoine Arnauld and under the spiritual direction of M. Singlin. His father, a superintendent of taxes in Normandy, was himself a friend of the movement, and one of his sisters was a nun at Port-Royal. The writer's name was Blaise Pascal (1623–1662). He was a young man of thirty-three whose influence was out of all proportion to his age. He had a lean face, an aquiline nose and long, thin

448   lips. The interior fire that burned within him lit up his delicate features, and his restless look seemed to be continually questioning life and peering into its mysteries. Everything in him betrayed an extreme and poignant tension, the strain endured by a sick man who, in order to create and to live, had to overcome continually the pressure of trifles; he had the troubled look of a genius to whom the abyss speaks. At twelve years of age Pascal rediscovered alone all the theorems of plane geometry; at sixteen he composed a treatise on conical sections; at nineteen he invented a calculating machine, and had since given ample proof of an intellect of which the scope, power and penetration staggered those who knew him. In 1647 his *Nouvelles expériences touchant le vide* aroused the enthusiasm of scientific circles, but his eager mind was already moving in another direction. Until that time he had shown very little interest in religious problems. But a year earlier he had made the acquaintance of two doctors from Rouen—De la Bouteillerie and Deslandes—in attendance upon his father who had injured his leg. These gentlemen were enthusiastic Jansenists. Everyone in the Pascal family had read the works of Jansenius, Saint-Cyran and Arnauld, and Blaise also was much impressed by them. The result was a sort of "first conversion," which is apparent in the famous *Prière* he composed for the use of sick people and the excellent letter he wrote to his elder sister Mme. Périer on the death of their father. For the time being things went no further than that, and while his younger sister Jacqueline took the veil at Port-Royal, Blaise was leading a fairly worldly life, mixing with people of fashion, riding in his six-horse carriage and apparently quite unconcerned with questions of grace and salvation.

But God evidently lay in wait for him. Once when he was crossing the bridge at Neuilly he came very near to death. His two leading horses bolted and plunged into the Seine. He experienced a mysterious interior stress in which physical pain (of which he always had his share) played as great a part as metaphysical misgivings. He was thus slowly drawn towards that "night of fire," November 3, 1654, that darkness pierced with light, when his beloved Christ imposed upon him His presence, His truth and His message never again to be challenged. Henceforward his irrevocable choice was

made; with all his being he believed. Obedience to the demands of Christianity meant staking everything on victory at the moment of death without
risking any loss. Converted at last, he placed himself in the hands of M.
Singlin, who sent him to Port-Royal-des-Champs to make a retreat.

Thus Blaise Pascal was introduced into the headquarters of Jansenism
at the very moment when the crisis was at its most serious. The indomitable
Arnauld, after a brief period of anxiety and weakness, decided to resume the
struggle. It now became for him not so much a question of St. Augustine,
of grace, of God's rights, but rather of knowing who would prevail—the
representatives of true Christianity or the Jesuit clique. It was imperative to
return to the contents of the letter which the Sorbonne had recently condemned, but they had to be handled in a different, a cleverer and a more
efficient way. Arnauld determined to try. But one may, as Henri Bremond so
nicely put it, be a "theological machine-gun" and yet be a mediocre polemist. When, therefore, Arnauld read the new draft to his assembled colleagues
he was forced to recognize that their enthusiasm had waned. "I do not think
you find this piece of writing very effective," he declared, "and I believe you
are right." Mme. Périer said of him: "He was not the kind of man who thirsted for praise."

Arnauld turned towards Blaise Pascal. "You are young," he said. "You
certainly should do something."

A little over a week later that "something" was done: Pascal produced
his first *Provinciale*.

"Excellent!" exclaimed Antoine Arnauld. "That will be appreciated; we
must have it printed."

Whether or not this dazzling polemist who within eighteen months
brought men's minds back to the subject of Jansenism actually agreed with
all its concepts has always been, and perhaps always will be, a matter of controversy.[8] All we really know of Pascal's religious convictions is gleaned from

---

8. Before forming an opinion on this subject one might well read Maurice Blondel's
    excellent article, "Le Jansénisme et l'antijansénisme de Pascal," in *La Revue de
    Métaphysique et de Morale* (April–June 1923).

450   fragments, the *disjecta membra* of a great unfinished work. It is not even certain whether some of his short notes express his own opinions or those he intended to refute. The discreet Nicole has assured us that Pascal "thought many Jansenist writings were in need of some slight adjustment." The moral climate of Port-Royal, its lofty and exacting demands, its atmosphere of sombre austerity, together with its undeniable dignity, were qualities that were bound to appeal to a convert like Pascal who was continually rent with spiritual torment, haunted by the anguish of his misery and unworthiness, seeing himself as a mite hopelessly remote from God. But did he really accept the doctrine contained in *Augustinus*? He told Nicole that if he were one day to write about grace "he hoped he would succeed in divesting it of the fierceness that had been given to it, and make the doctrine so commendable that it would suit all types of people." But Pascal was not a theologian; he was therefore amenable to the influence of any theological theories that he might admire; he might even overcolour their expression. At the same time, as a result of this ceaseless and dramatic dialogue that he maintained within himself, he was often led to adopt a very different attitude. Perhaps it was the Jansenist in him that led him to declare among other things that "without grace man is merely a creature filled with natural and ineffaceable error"; that to "people deprived of faith and grace" there remained nothing but "uncertainty and darkness"; that "to find God a mediator is necessary." But from Pascal's pen flowed other sentiments that had no Jansenist flavour: "I thought of you in my agony; I shed that drop of blood for you,"[9] or, "I love you more ardently than you have loved your stains"; such expressions as "God perceptible to the heart," "the heart bowed by God." Pascal also extols "the Pope who comes first," the "trunk" of the tree which is the Church. Though we may not say with Blondel that "Pascal showed himself to be extremely anti-Jansenist," we may agree with Bremond that "beside, or perhaps beneath, this Pascal more or less intoxicated by the theology of his masters, there existed another who escaped from them and whose influence

---

9.   This expresses the very opposite thought to that contained in the condemned "fifth proposition."

was one day to lead innumerable souls back to the bosom of the Catholic
Church."[10]

Why then did he join in the controversy and embark upon a work so far removed from such sentiments? It could not have been entirely due to the influence of those whom he followed as his true guides, or to a young man's pride in being associated with his elders in a struggle. He quite sincerely hated those whom he regarded as public dangers, corrupters of the hearts of Christians—in other words those who supported the easy-going moral attitude that he had learned to hate within himself. What was that violence if not the reaction of an exacting soul against her own inner complicity? A taste for battle did the rest, together with his temperament, less impartial than his intellect, which never yielded but was rather stirred to further activity by contradiction. He believed that he should not obey his own convictions only, but also become the mouthpiece of the group, the appointed advocate of theories with which he did not altogether agree. When Madame de Sablé asked him one day "if he was quite sure of everything he put in his letters," he replied that "he was satisfied to avail himself of the reports with which he was provided; it was not his responsibility to examine whether they were factual." Pascal the physicist would never have argued thus in connection with his experiments on the void!

From the very first *Provinciale*, it seemed that the Great Arnauld's prophecy would be realized; the work was appreciated. Its literary beauty alone would have guaranteed its success. The harmony between matter and form, its supreme facility and its absolute simplicity were remarkable—"the only modern work worthy of the ancients," as Bossuet, an excellent judge, described it. All the experts admired "Louis de Montalte"; it was impossible for him not to continue.

At first he lived near the Luxembourg and the gate Saint-Michel (there were two entrances to the house),[11] and later, under the name of M. de

---

10. From the splendid chapter entitled "Religion de Pascal," in vol. 4 of Bremond's work. See also *En prière avec Pascal* (Paris, 1923).

11. He spent eighteen months there. It can still be seen at No. 54 Rue Monsieur-le-Prince. Cf. J. Mesnard, "Les Demeures de Pascal à Paris," *Mémoires des serv. Hist. de Paris*, t. 4.

Mons, he retired to an inn under the sign of King David in the Rue des Poirées, facing the Collège de Clermont—a Jesuit establishment! He spent the whole of 1656 writing his pamphlets, and wherever Jansenists were to be found in France they distributed them, happy in the knowledge that every blow went home and that their adversaries betrayed signs of the fact.

Furthermore, how could Pascal doubt that he was right when heaven itself gave him a sign? On March 24, 1656, four days after the publication of the fifth *Provinciale*, a miracle occurred within Pascal's own family. It was the Friday of the third week in Lent, the day on which the Church sings at the Introit: "Show me a token for good, that they who hate me may see and be confounded." A precious relic, a thorn from the Crown of Thorns, was exposed for veneration at Port-Royal de Paris, and a little girl of ten who suffered from a dreadful weeping ulcer of the eye prayed fervently before the relic that she might be cured. Her name was Marguerite Périer, the daughter of Pascal's elder sister. She was cured, and the prodigy was duly confirmed by the community, the secular power and the doctors, among them Guy Patin, who could hardly be considered credulous. It created a great sensation, the more so because other wonders followed at Port-Royal, as though the efficacy of the relic were reserved only for the Jansenists. The hero of the "night of fire" could not have failed to see this Miracle of the Holy Thorn as a sign of encouragement.

Thus the offensive developed before a public that was no less amused than enthusiastic. For it very soon became an offensive in the grand style, conducted with the object of creating a diversion, deflecting criticism from Port-Royal so that it might fall back upon its opponents. The first three *Provinciales* sought to defend the Augustinian theses on grace, to justify Arnauld and lacerate the doctors of the Sorbonne who "considered it easier to censure than to assess, because it is so much easier for them to find monks than reasons." From the fourth, and especially from the fifth *Provinciale*, it was no longer a question of defence but of attack. The real heretics, the true poisoners of the public mind, were not the saintly people of Port-Royal but the Jesuits, "who put cushions under the elbows of sinners," and made the Christian religion "indulgent and accommodating" in order to recruit

adherents, a religion in which the scandal of the Cross was abolished, and   453
the sacrifice of Calvary no longer had any meaning! One had only to read
the books written by the Jesuits—those by Father Escobar,[12] for example,
whose manual of moral theology was the casuists' guide! And Pascal would
quote—though not always accurately—extracts intended to cause horror
or laughter. His vehement criticism was not entirely untrue, however, and
the polemist's arrows, aimed at an obviously too facile moral outlook, did
not fail to reach their targets. But he implicated the whole of the Society of
Jesus, representing it as a monster of hypocrisy and laxity. This was a singu-
larly odd maneuver at the very moment when Fathers Isaac Jogues, Brebeuf,
Lallemant and Garnier had shed their blood in Canada, thus giving proof
of the heroism of the Jesuits. But in controversy adversaries frequently hit
below the belt, Pascal no less than others. Furthermore, he was not always
honest or self-consistent. In the last *Provinciale* he praised Thomism to the
skies (no doubt to win over the Dominicans), though he had jeered at it
in the first. On several occasions he was guilty of mental reservation, gar-
bled quotations and false innuendoes; all the faults, in fact, with which he
reproached "Jesuitism." The heat of battle alone cannot be offered as an
excuse for his attitude and some of the methods he adopted.

Was Pascal aware that he was going too far, that he was acting discredit-
ably and perhaps even doing injury to the Church?[13] Did he heed the advice
of Mother Angélique and M. Singlin, who considered the *Provinciales* too
spirited and too uncharitable? Did he perhaps experience an intellectual
and moral crisis of such a nature that the arguments he attributed to his
opponents found an echo in his own soul ceaselessly in torment? Replying
in the seventeenth *Provinciale* to Father Annat, who had described him as

12. Father Antonio Escobar y Mendoza (1589–1669) was a holy religious who, in 1630,
published a *Manual of Cases of Conscience*. The tenor of the work appeared so strict
that he was denounced to the Inquisition. No one was more surprised than he when
he learned that a French writer was accusing him of laxism!

13. Blondel has spoken very harshly of Pascal's role: "He makes a laughing-stock of theology; he exposes the sacred delicacy of the religious life to the mockery of a foolish
and corrupt world." Bremond expresses his judgment concisely: "Louis de Montalte
is guilty; Pascal is innocent."

454   the "Secretary of Port-Royal," he declared: "I do not belong to Port-Royal....
I have said nothing to support such impious propositions.... And even if
Port-Royal upheld them.... I am not attached to anything on earth but the
Catholic Roman and Apostolic Church alone, in which I desire to live and
die in communion with the Pope." He wrote a nineteenth and a twentieth
Provinciale, but he never published them. No doubt he regretted having
gone too far.[14]

Nevertheless Pascal had given valuable service to his masters' cause. If
ever the weapon of ridicule was used with deadly effect, this certainly was
the case in the battle of the *Provinciales*. Mazarin's laugh echoed throughout France. Such counterstrokes on the part of the Jesuits as *Entretiens de
Cléandre et d'Eudoxe*, by Father Daniel, and the *Bonne foi des Jansénistes*,
by Father Annat, fell flat. The ideas of Jansenius gained ground. The brisk
language of the *Provinciales* made much easier reading than the dry Latin
of *Augustinus*. Of course the Holy Office placed the famous letters on the
Index (September 6, 1657), and three years later the king commanded them
to be burned by the public executioner; but that delay itself and the severity
of the measures proved that the work was still very widely read. Perhaps it
was on account of the letters or the Miracle of the Holy Thorn that the persecution undertaken against Port-Royal was suspended in July 1656, that
the Little Schools, closed in February, were allowed to reopen, and that the
solitaries, dispersed after the condemnation of Arnauld, were permitted to

---

14. This attitude lends some support to the assertions of those who claim that Pascal
underwent a "third conversion," this time from Jansenism to complete Catholicism.
Facts and documents have been quoted to substantiate this theory; among them the
evidence of the parish priest of Sainte-Étienne-du-Mont, Father Beurrier, who was
Pascal's confessor in 1661, six weeks before Pascal's death. Father Beurrier's *Mémoires*
provide further evidence. But the strongest proof lies in the change that took place
towards the end of Pascal's life. He devoted himself to acts of charity and to the service
of the poor, and abandoned all forms of controversy. On the other hand Pascal never
signed the episcopal document formally rejecting Jansenism; he simply declared himself a Catholic subject absolutely to the Church. His family did not seem to think he
had retracted. Controversy over this aspect of his life appears to be endless. Such historians as A. Gazier, Father Petitot, as well as Faguet and Hallays, have argued *against*
a "third conversion," while others, among them E. Jovy, Henri Bremond, Father Yves
de la Briere and T. de Wyzews, have argued *for*.

return to their beloved solitude. Whatever the case might be, the climate   455
had changed.

9. LOUIS XIV AND PORT-ROYAL

BASICALLY, however, the problem remained unchanged. The preceding year it occurred to Pierre de Marca, Archbishop of Toulouse, to draw up a Formulary in which he explicitly condemned Jansenism, and called upon his priests to sign the declaration. In August 1656 the Assembly of the Clergy did likewise, modified the declaration a little and submitted it to Pope Alexander VII. The latter, when Cardinal Chigi, had been one of the commissioners charged by Innocent X to examine the "Five Propositions"; he was thus perfectly familiar with the situation, and gave formal approval to the text of the document. The Assembly of the Clergy therefore made it obligatory for all bishops to sign the Formulary, stating: "With heart and mouth I condemn the doctrine in the Five Propositions of Cornelius Jansenius contained in his book *Augustinus.* The problem of distinguishing between "law and fact" ceased to exist.

What were Arnauld and his friends to do now? The question at issue was no longer the holding of a simple theological opinion concerning grace and a strict or less strict moral attitude: it concerned the very authority of the Church. The Pope had now settled the problem of fact by stating that the five condemned propositions were indeed to be found in the work of Jansenius; to hold the contrary view was to question his authority. The danger of heresy, and even schism, was imminent. The more reasonable among the Jansenists, including Nicole, advised submission. Others suggested signing the Formulary with "mental reservation"; in other words, doing precisely what the Jansenists accused the Jesuits of doing so often. They would maintain a "respectful silence" without modifying their thoughts on the subject. The more impetuous Jansenists, who were the most numerous, demanded an out-and-out rejection. Among them were Pascal, his sister Jacqueline and the indomitable Mother Angélique de Saint-Jean. As for Arnauld, he

456   continued to write pamphlets and to approach the right people; in the name
of the Gallican freedoms he secured from the Parliament a refusal to register
Alexander VII's Constitution, and in the absence of Cardinal de Retz, the
Vicars-General in Paris published an ambiguous document reopening the
question of the distinction between "fact and law." It needed a *lit de justice*
to bring the Parliamentarians to heel, and strong threats to lead the Vicars General to rescind their publication. It was understandable that Mazarin became weary of all this uproar, more especially as the Jansenists had
struck up a friendship with his enemy Cardinal de Retz. When the latter
escaped from prison in Nantes the parish priests supporting Port-Royal had
the impudence to cause the *Te Deum* to be sung. And Retz himself, from
his exile in Rome, sent to the French clergy a letter (drafted by Arnauld)
in which he compared himself with St. Athanasius, St. John Chrysostom
and St. Thomas of Canterbury. He extolled the theories of Port-Royal and
posed as the defender of their doctrines concerning grace. It all seemed
rather comical coming from this "Cardinal Don Juan" who dispensed with
both sufficient grace and efficacious grace.[15] But Jansenism, having become
a sect, set itself up as a kind of ecclesiastical Fronde. Before Mazarin died
he advised Louis XIV to distrust that "refractory clique," and "no longer to
endure the Jansenist sect or even its name."

Undoubtedly the young King needed no encouragement in that direction. Anything which might cast a shadow over his power, and more especially anything which tended to remind him of the Fronde, horrified the
King. The gay young prince, busy trying to seduce his wife's maids of honour, was certainly not the man to perceive what was estimable, admirable
even, in the spirituality of Port-Royal. He introduced Pierre de Marca and
Father Annat into the "Council of Conscience," and instructed Port-Royal to dismiss its novices and boarders, which occasioned painful scenes
and a rather inordinate shedding of tears. M. Singlin had to leave to avoid
arrest, and Arnauld had to decamp once more. The old foundress, Mother

---

15. Moreover, having no very firm convictions, he made an offer to the Queen to "exterminate the Jansenists if she were to join forces with him"; that is to say, give him
Mazarin's post as first minister.

Angélique, died of grief, followed shortly afterwards by Jacqueline Pascal,   457
Sister Sainte-Euphémie. By the King's command a feeble attempt was made
to bring about a *rapprochement* between the Jesuits, through Father Ferri-
er, and the Jansenist leaders headed by Arnauld; but it came to nothing.
Jansenism remained stubbornly entrenched and prepared to give battle.
"Under the pretext of avenging the outrages perpetrated against God," said
the Protestant Jurieu, "these gentlemen appease their own particular passions"—which was certainly true.

Of the entire Jansenist clique the most determined in their resistance
were the nuns of Port-Royal du Saint-Sacrament in Paris,[16] of whom Mother Angélique de Saint-Jean was the mainspring. Despite a demand by the
court that they sign a declaration (a much more subdued document, in any
case, than the Formulary) submitting to the decision of Innocent X, they
remained obstinate, unresponsive, proud and grim. Heaven was theirs, and
everything tended to prove it. Sister Sainte-Suzanne, daughter of the great
painter Philippe de Champaigne, was miraculously cured of rheumatism.
More important still, the new Archbishop of Paris, Pierre de Marca, having
replaced Retz who had resigned, and from whom Port-Royal had everything to fear, died suddenly within three days of his having been appointed; an event which filled the holy women with uncharitable joy. De Marca
was replaced by the Bishop of Rodez, Hardouin de Péréfixe, a pleasant man
with a conciliatory disposition, but somewhat lacking in intellectual qualities. He was a good courtier, anxious to please the King, and he set about
"putting things in order." To that end he published a nonsensical instruction
in which he asserted that the question of law pertained to divine faith and
the question of fact to human faith. He then instructed the sisters to sign a
newly worded statement.

Mother Angélique de Saint-Jean was not the woman to be caught by
episcopal bombast of that kind. It seemed as though her ice-cold head had
suddenly become seized with some kind of vertigo, and that it had spread to
almost the whole community. Port-Royal of Paris began to play the martyr.

---

16. Henri de Montherlant's play *Port-Royal* stresses the convent's spirit of resistance.

458 Let the executioners come; the victims were ready! The good sisters looked upon Péréfixe as another Diocletian. In vain the archbishop pleaded with them through Lancelot to yield "to please the King." This clumsy phrase merely stimulated their courage. They pleaded liberty of conscience. To which the good archbishop, with all the grandeur and firmness of his vocation, replied that they confused "delicacy of conscience with obstinacy." And he was quite right.

The assertion by one of the most eminent theologians of the twentieth century[17] to the effect that objection on grounds of conscience is invalid against the Church points to the very root of the drama played at that time at Port-Royal. To resist in the name of conscience an order given in the name of the Church was to destroy the very foundations of the Church; and, because the Church is not merely a human society, it meant saying "No" to God. Did Mother Angélique's pious daughters appreciate that fact? The words of Archbishop Péréfixe—profound for once—described them perfectly: "As pure as angels and as proud as demons."

On June 9, 1664, the archbishop visited the convent for the first time, and questioned the nuns one after another. As he got no satisfaction, their stubbornness irritated him more and more, and he went so far as to tell some of them that they were mad. The interview with Mother Angélique de Saint-Jean was especially loud, tense and disappointing.

What was to be done? The archbishop had tried every possible means of conciliation. He had even sent the young Bossuet, a highly reputable preacher, to explain their duty to the nuns. They still held out. They considered it to be God's will that they should do so; and the proof lay in the fact that when Mother Agnès opened the New Testament to seek the answer she came upon these words of St. Luke: "this is your hour, and the power of darkness" (22:53)! This attitude verged on illuminism; they entered into the darkness with gloomy zeal. It was a dramatic episode well suited to inspire the playwright Henri de Montherlant.

---

17. Father de Montcheuil, a Jesuit, chaplain to the "Maquis" at Vercours in 1944; he was shot at Grenoble on August 8 of that year.

On August 26 the archbishop returned with police and armed men.   459
Twelve nuns were selected to be removed from Port-Royal and distributed
amongst other convents, and the order was carried out in deathly silence
broken only by stifled sobs. We can appreciate the "dreadful solemnity" of
the archbishop, compelled to resort to such measures and no longer acting like the simple, good-natured man that he was. Mother Angélique de
Saint-Jean was transferred to the Couvent des Annonciades; and the "Blue
Sisters" with five Visitandines settled in Port-Royal in company with the
new provisional superior. Mother Eugénie de Fontaine, a spiritual daughter of St. Francis de Sales. But the firm gentleness of the Bishop of Geneva
left these aggressive virgins unmoved. Those who remained of the original
Port-Royal nuns carried on an unbearable war of nerves against the hated
Visitandines, while those who had been banished to other convents continued silently stubborn, writing "accounts of their captivity" of which page
after page revealed the pride of the dark angel. It eventually became necessary to strike harder; the refractory nuns were regrouped at Port-Royal-des-
Champs, cut off from the world and completely deprived of sacramental
life. Yet they remained unconquered for four years.

10. THE "CLEMENTINE PEACE"

NOT only the nuns resisted. Some of the bishops did likewise, and their
resistance, though less spectacular, was more serious.[18] In the spring of 1644
Louis XIV instructed the Parliament to register a declaration under which
all priests were ordered to sign the Formulary under pain of losing their benefices. Four of the bishops, who were inclined towards Jansenism—Pavilion of Alet, Caulet of Pamiers, Choart de Buzenval of Beauvais and Henri
Arnauld of Angers—protested that the King had no right "to make canons
and laws within the Church." They probably imagined that the Gallicanism

---

18. "Since the women have shown the courage of bishops," said Jacqueline Pascal, "the
    bishops must have the courage of women."

460 of Louis XIV would restrain him from calling upon the Pope. The king, however, felt compelled to do so, and Alexander VIII replied to his request with the Bull *Regiminis apostolici*, making it obligatory for priests to sign a new Formulary expressed in more precise terms than the previous one. The outcome was rage and confusion in the Jansenist camp, some of their number pressing for submission while Arnauld and Nicole pressed for resistance. Once more the four Jansenist bishops adopted a definite attitude, instructing their flock to accept the Formulary as to law, but to maintain "a respectful silence" as to the question of fact. The Pope condemned this strange directive and, in agreement with Louis XIV, decided to set up a commission to sit in judgment on the rebels. The affair had begun to take a very serious turn when Alexander VIII died in 1667.

At once the atmosphere changed. The new Pope, Clement IX, was of a conciliatory disposition; so was Bargellini, his Nuncio in Paris. The friends of Port-Royal, especially the Duchesse de Longueville, who had a long arm, bestirred themselves to get the proceedings stopped. The three principal ministers of Louis XIV, Lionne, Le Tellier and Colbert, each hoped for different reasons that some kind of a settlement might be reached. The whole Gallican clique pointed out to the King that he himself had allowed Rome to intervene in a matter that strictly concerned France alone, and that his action had not perhaps been very shrewd. Arnauld, relying upon this decoy, addressed a circular to all the bishops of France in which he accused Rome of "demeaning episcopal dignity" and "overthrowing the holy canons" of the French Church. It was in this rather extraordinary atmosphere that ultrasecret negotiations were entered into without the knowledge of Péréfixe and the Council of Conscience. They were to terminate in 1669 with an official statement by Clement IX, announcing a general easing of the situation and the return of the lost sheep to the fold.

A close study of the "Clementine Peace" shows that it was founded on a host of misunderstandings; for the Jansenists continued to intensify their quibbles and reservations, while the Pope did not appear to have been kept fully informed. In France an idea became current which may be summed up as follows: "The Holy See does not claim that the signing of

the Formulary makes it obligatory to believe in the implicit or explicit pres-   461
ence of the five condemned propositions in the book by Jansenius, but only
that they should be regarded as condemned and heretical in whatever book
they might appear." But it is not at all certain that that was the meaning
Clement IX wished to attach to his declaration. The truth is that everybody, including Arnauld, was weary of so many squabbles, so much secrecy
and underhand dealing. Within the framework of the interpretation given
above the Jansenists, and even the nuns of Port-Royal, agreed to submit. The
bells rang out again in the valley of the Chevreuse; the candles were re-lit
in the chapel; the solitaries returned to their hermitages and a rousing *Te
Deum* was sung.

Then began an idyllic period during which men of goodwill were persuaded that the Jansenist problem was solved. *Giansenismo estinto* ("Jansenism is dead!"), the Nuncio Bargellini wrote to Rome. The Council of
State published a decree under which the king's subjects were forbidden to
discuss the question of grace or to accuse anyone of being a Jansenist. Le
Maître de Sacy was freed from the Bastille, and Arnauld de Pomponne, son
of Robert Arnauld d'Andilly, was made Secretary of State in the Department
of Foreign Affairs. Louis XIV received the Great Arnauld with extreme
politeness; and when Arnauld expressed his regret that he should have been
embroiled in so many controversies the king interrupted him: "All that is
over; we must not talk about it any more."

Bossuet had always maintained a guarded attitude towards the Jansenists. He had condemned their revolt and made short work of the question of "law and fact"; but he admired none the less their moral aspirations
and shared their aversion from laxism. He therefore decided to make use of
Arnauld's vigour in his struggle against Protestantism. There was even some
talk of making the leader of Port-Royal a cardinal. To commemorate this
happy hour in the history of the great reign a medal was struck depicting the
hand of Justice clasping the Keys of St. Peter over an altar—a symbol of the
union of the spiritual and temporal powers.

Giansenismo estinto, Bargellini had said. But Jansenism was by no means
dead. The period of the "Clementine Peace," which, for better or for worse,

lasted to the end of the century, was just another period of expansion for the movement; in fact, its third. During that time it reached its zenith. Once again Port-Royal became fashionable. The "charming friends" of the convent, Mme. de Longueville and Mlle. de Vertus, had small houses built for themselves in the vicinity. Mme. de Sévigné, Mme. de Sablé, Mme. de Liancourt and many other ladies visited the nuns very frequently. The roads in the valley were cluttered with the carriages of duchesses. The common people flocked there on foot from Paris as on pilgrimage. Well-to-do families contended for the honour of having their daughters educated by the famous nuns of Port-Royal. Even the dying asked to be buried near the holy house. All this, as Nicole, Mother Agnès and a few others wisely agreed, was going too far.

The solitaries returned and occupied the lodges they had built not far from the convent, and their numbers increased. The most outstanding among them were Lancelot, the gentle and industrious Le Nain de Tillemont, the scholarly Pierre Nicole and Doctor Hamon. None, however, was as brilliant as the early occupants. When Singlin died in 1664 Le Maistre de Sacy (1613–1684), nephew and contemporary of the Great Arnauld, became spiritual director of the group; a learned exegete, he also possessed a profound understanding of the human soul. De Sacy was succeeded by Claude de Sainte-Marthe. This third generation of Jansenists had an even greater passion for writing and publishing than their predecessors. The works of Saint-Cyran were published posthumously, and a collection of notes by Blaise Pascal, originally intended to form the basis of an apologetical work, were published in 1670 under the title *Les Pensées* and aroused widespread interest. Le Maistre de Sacy undertook the colossal task of translating the Bible (1672–1696), and his version, written in exquisite French, met with tremendous success. The Little Schools were unable to open officially after the crisis of 1661, but houses affiliated to Port-Royal sprang up everywhere; the Jansenist educational system, based upon their own works (e.g., *Grammaire*, *Logique* and *Règles pour l'éducation des enfants*) spread into many other schools, where it functioned during the whole of the eighteenth century. The excellence of their teaching methods was vindicated by the

famous pupils they produced; among them Jean Racine, nephew of the solitary M. Vitart and author of *Andromaque* and *Britannicus*. Racine had been
the much-loved pupil of M. Le Maistre, and at that time was winning glory
with his dramatic works. Other famous men of letters were also friends of
the movement. Nicolas Boileau, like Mme. de Sévigné, was something of an
"amateur Jansenist," though his brother Jacques, author of the *Traité contre
l'abus des nudités des gorges*, was militant; and even the worthy La Fontaine,
whose life was far removed from the austerity of the sect, agreed to back a
volume of *Poésies chrétiennes* composed at Port-Royal.

It was at this time that the Jansenist spirit really penetrated into French
Catholicism. Many Christians who were quite unmoved by theological
arguments allowed themselves to be influenced by those men and women
of Port-Royal whom Mme. de Sévigné described as "angels on earth," rivals
of the hermits of the desert, saints descended from heaven. Never before
had it been so easy and so defensible to confuse a movement towards general reform in the spirit of Trent with those equally austere tendencies that
concealed questionable doctrine. There is no question whatever that some
saintly souls did succeed in drawing from this well the pure waters of spiritual vitality; but the danger was no less positive. The Jansenist spirit insinu-
ated itself everywhere; it would soon be traced in Orders far removed from
Port-Royal, such as the Benedictines and even the Visitandines. It could be
detected also in new foundations, such as the Filles de l'Enfance, founded at
Toulouse by Mme. de Mondonville. The image of the crucified Christ with
the arms extended above the head became common among the clergy, even
in the most reliable circles. Many parishes adopted it, such as Saint-Jacques
and Saint-Maur in Paris, and others in Toulouse, Grenelle, Orleans, Alet,
Angers and Rouen. It was the period when the famous black wooden Cross
was to be found everywhere[19]; and today large numbers of these crucifixes

---

19. This type of Cross was not, however, of Jansenist origin. The museum at Cluny possesses one dating from the sixteenth century. The Crucifix was sculpted in bone, and
the position of the arms was generally as described above; but it became very popular
among the Jansenists. Pascal's Christ, however, which may be seen in Lafuma's large
edition of the *Pensées*, as well as on p. 174 of Albert Béguin's little book, *Pascal, par
lui-même*, certainly shows the arms stretched above the head.

with the body of Christ carved in bone or ivory, showing the arms stretched taut above the head, may still be found in antique shops. The same profound sentiments of the sect influenced painting, as is clear, for example, from the works of Philippe de Champaigne, father of the nun who was miraculously cured.

Outside France, Jansenism prospered in the Low Countries, both in the United Provinces and in the territories under the dominion of Spain. In the very regions where the movement was born its scope remained limited for a long time to theological circles. Jacob Boonen, Archbishop of Mechlin, Antoine Triest, Bishop of Ghent, and many of the doctors of Louvain University refused to accept the judgment against *Augustinus*. The success of the *Provinciales* helped to imbue the masses with Jansenist ideas. In 1671 Alphonsus de Bergh, who favoured the sect, succeeded to the archbishopric of Mechlin; he allowed the ideas of Saint-Cyran and Arnauld to be preached publicly, and his successor, William de Precipiano, tried in vain to combat them. Henceforward Belgium seemed to become a hotbed of Jansenism, and it was not long before Catholic Holland felt its influence, especially after the Great Arnauld finally sought refuge in that country. Utrecht, in fact, became a Jansenist headquarters.

All this tends to create an impression of enormous success, the triumph of Jansenism. Yet the more reasonable members of the sect knew that they had good cause for uneasiness. After all, what was the enthusiasm of the worldly minded worth? Was the spirit of the abbot of Saint-Cyran present in the carriages of the duchesses? Even the best of their adherents betrayed signs of weariness. Robert Arnauld d'Andilly was half-hearted in his wish to return to Port-Royal when peace had been restored. He seemed to be somewhat caught up in the attractions of the world. There was evidence of occasional friction within the group. Nicole began to work more and more alone. Were not the splendid years of Port-Royal, described by Sainte-Beuve as "the lovely hours of a soft autumn, of a rich and lazy sunset," rather years of apparent glory and hidden decline? And no one knew how long the "Clementine Peace" would last.

11. QUIETISM, THE HERESY OF DIVINE LOVE

A new controversy flared up shortly afterwards, causing a commotion among all sections of society, although it was not a subject calculated to excite the feelings of ordinary Christians. Although doctrinal deviation does occasionally result in real moral aberration, the finer points of heresy are generally perceptible only to the trained mind of the theologian. It is not a common occurrence to see two of the most famous bishops of the day engaged in such bitter controversy that one of them is brought to ruin. Quietism was a trifling matter in itself; but its historical importance was derived from the great conflict between Bossuet and Fénelon.

It has generally been assumed that this new type of deviation was essentially opposed to Jansenism; but this notion is too shallow. Some basis of Augustinianism existed in Quietism as well as in the theories of Jansenius, but in both cases they were exaggerated and distorted. The Quietist conception of man was not very much more optimistic than that of Saint-Cyran, Pascal and Arnauld. In the eyes of Catholics as a whole the emphasis was rather on the general attitude of the soul to moral practice and its conclusions. Jansenism bowed man to the ground before a dreadful God who, according to His whim, called some and rejected others. Jansenist morality clouded over and dried up the heart. Quietism reached conclusions much less pessimistic; we might say that the Quietists deviated in favour of *softness* as opposed to the *harshness* of Port-Royal.

The Quietist starting-point did not differ from the tenets held by the Jansenists and the most orthodox French school regarding the miserable state of man, this "nothing," as Cardinal de Bérulle said, "this most vile and useless creature," or, as Pascal put it, "this outcast of the universe." From such a concept the great spiritual leaders of the French school, Bérulle, St. Vincent de Paul and Olier, had educed that practical and mystical doctrine that raised man towards God through his own conquest of himself and the giving of his whole being to Love. The Jansenists, in their frantic contempt of human nature (although Pascal declared man to be the "glory" as well as the outcast of the universe), had merely emphasized the first aspect of spiritual experience, namely the ascetic. The Quietists overstressed the second aspect.

St. Francis de Sales in his great wisdom counselled a form of abandonment to God which consoled man in the midst of his many miseries. "I shall do my best," he said, "to avoid having sores on my face; but if I have them I shall love the humiliation it causes me." The idea of trusting in God and not "overrunning" grace might console troubled souls, but the true doctrine, as contained in the *Devout Life* of St. Francis, in the works of the great St. Teresa and St. John of the Cross, and even in *The Imitation of Christ*,[20] taught that God's infinite bounty bestows its gifts upon those who are wholly faithful, who progress heroically towards God's goodness, overcoming the temptations to which sinful nature is prone. Absolute abandonment, self-abasement by all means—but of our egoism, not of our spiritual faculties and the striving of the soul.

Confusion was all the easier because the doctrine of abandonment to God was linked with a tendency which has always existed in Christianity; it existed even among the ancients, in the *apatheia* of the Greeks, in the scepticism of Pyrrho and in the famous words of Seneca, *Deo non pareo, sed assentior* (I do not obey God; my desires are like his)—and we know that that concept is essentially Islamic. Looked at from a Christian point of view the doctrine of "indifference" had numerous supporters. Was St. Augustine really so very far from Seneca when he declared that those only have true liberty who submit entirely to God, to His will and to His law? The Alexandrian philosophers, together with Isaac the Syrian, St. John Climacus, author of *Scala Paradisi*, and St. Maximus of Constantinople—"Maximus Confessor"—all repeated in different ways that the first degree of contemplation consists in utter indifference to earthly passions. During the Middle Ages, and more so in the great mystical school of Flanders and the Rhine, indifference had become synonymous with the spirit of renunciation, which, according to Eckhart, Tauler, Blessed Henry Suso and even the author of *The Imitation of Christ*, is indispensable to the soul's impulse towards

---

20. *The Imitation of Christ*, Book III, chapter 39.

God. By the sixteenth century this idea had become universally accepted.
For St. Ignatius of Loyola total indifference was the means by which man renounced all inordinate affections and desires; for St. John of the Cross it was the point of departure of the soul's journey towards the mystic heights; for St. Francis de Sales indifference alone enabled the human will, having shed self though not yet resigned to accept everything, to abandon itself utterly to God, to love "nothing except for the love of God's will."

During the Middle Ages this state was described as *quies mentis*, "quiet of the mind." The expression itself suggests the danger contained in this doctrine if it were but slightly misunderstood. It is easy to drift from legitimate "quiet" towards a state of complacent sloth; and that facility exists not only in the psychical domain. Is it necessary for the soul, utterly abandoned to God and closely bound to Him, to continue to make any effort, to perform any act or to mortify itself? According to the Quietists it was sufficient that the soul rest in God, passive and indifferent to everything, even to the temptations that might assail it, and indeed indifferent to its own salvation. "My desire is to desire nothing," said Sister Marie-Rosette, a well-known Quietist; "my will is to will nothing, to remain attached to nothing.... But I do not even desire to desire nothing, because I think that would also be a desire." What a strange moral and spiritual world such a doctrine leads to! Is the soul still in a Christian climate, or has it attained some vague condition of *Nirvana*? It is very easy to "wait until God moves us," and to "do nothing and be led." But how do we know the devil is not leading us?

There had always been Quietists in the Church. St. Jerome had long ago denounced this tendency in the monk Evagrius. About the year one thousand the "Hesychasts" of Byzantium remained still and silent, with their eyes fixed on the navel, in order to arrive at the contemplation of the uncreated light of God. They considered that in this state the soul is altogether incapable of sin. In the twelfth century, in the West, the followers of Amaury Bène and Ortheb's "Brethren of the Free Spirit"[21] were Quietists; the Brethren,

---

21. See Henri Daniel-Rops, *The Church of Cathedral and Crusade* (Providence, RI: Cluny, 2023), Volume 2, pp. 654, 655.

468   on the plea of total renunciation, attained a condition of depravity that was anything but spiritual. Quietists also were the enigmatical Begards[22] among whom good and evil were to be found side by side. Even Luther in his youth, between 1515 and 1518 when he despaired of salvation, recommended total surrender to God, the suppression of all effort and every desire, the acceptance of everything, even hell; a doctrine so discouraging that he rejected it.

In the seventeenth century, especially in France, the lure of Quietism was noticeable even among the most lofty and sincere mystics, champions of the principle of Pure Love.[23] They rejected it instinctively, however, remaining within the bounds of a love of God which their prudence enabled them to understand and to which they endeavoured to remain loyally responsive. But it was always possible to misunderstand the counsels of spiritual leaders. M. Olier wrote to a nun: "You must purify yourself to please God alone." He advised priests to "so abase themselves in serving God that they no longer looked for a reward." Father de Condren counselled his penitents to leave themselves to God, abandoning all desire to live and to be. Jean-Pierre Camus, Bishop of Belley, the friend and biographer of St. Francis de Sales, preached that the soul should aim at a renunciation so perfect that it would be prepared to accept damnation instead of salvation if such were God's will—which, of course, it is not possible to imagine. Such precepts, so susceptible to misinterpretation, were plentiful. They were to be found in the writings and on the lips of such men as Father Surin and Father Nouet, Jesuits both; the celebrated Capuchin Benoit de Canfeld; the pious layman Jean de Bernières-Louvigny, author of *Chrétien intérieur*, his friend M. Bertot, spiritual director of the Benedictine nuns at Montmartre; and M. Boudon, the great archdeacon of Evreux and author of *Dieu Seul*. False mysticism lay in wait for those who lent a too willing ear to sincere calls to a holy indifference and surrender to the mystical impulse. By the light of the Molinosist conflagration the Church would perceive the danger more clearly.

---

22. See ibid., pp. 699, 746.
23. See Volume 1 of this work, Chapter II, p. 76.

12. THE ENIGMATICAL MIGUEL DE MOLINOS   469

IT was not only in the Church of France that the tendency existed to distort what Henri Bremond called the "Charter of Love, sublime and holy," on which religious life during the Great Century had been founded. The tendency itself consisted in regarding divine love as a kind of sensual pleasure, and prayer as a "vague celestial hashish." Similar views were held in Italy by Achille Cagliarde, author of *Breve compendio intorno alla perfezione cristiana*, and his penitent Isabella Bellinzaga—the "Milanese Lady"—a capable woman who in her youth had helped St. Charles Borromeo in the running of a hospital. In Spain also there were two very saintly men who thought along the same lines: Gregorio Lopez, who went to Mexico and lived the contemplative life of a hermit, and the Venerable John Falconi, author of *Alphabet pour apprendre à lire dans le Christ*. "The short way to perfection," wrote Falconi, "is to remain in peaceful and silent rest, in pure faith in God and total surrender to His holy will." The same, or in any case less orthodox, tendencies were to be found in less commendable spheres. In certain confraternities, called Schools of Christ, the "prayer of quiet" embraced a blend of ideas that originated in Islam and India; and the Illuminati, such as those who were condemned in Seville in 1625, practised a spirituality fairly closely related to it. Their counterparts also existed in Italy, notably among the "Lombardists" of Dom Giacomo Lombardi in the Italian region of the Marches and the devotees of St. Pelagia, who assembled in chapels dedicated to that saint. All these movements were eventually linked together and swept along by the violence of the tide.

History is far from having solved the secret of the strange Miguel de Molinos.[24] Prudent, learned and eminent men have disagreed as to whether he was a saint or an impostor. Some regard him as a kind of Rasputin who duped the papal court just as the famous monk later fooled the court

---

24. He is not to be confused with the Jesuit Luis de Molina whose sophistry has been much discussed. See *An Age of Renewal: The Catholic Reformation*, Volume 1, p. 44; Volume 2, p. 442; and the note on p. 419, below of the present work.

of Nicholas II. He seems to be condemned by his own admissions; yet the official judgment was surprisingly lenient in view of the crimes attributed to him. France and the world learned from the Dreyfus affair how difficult it is to see clearly in discussions of this nature in which a man becomes a symbol of contention.

Molinos was born near Saragossa in 1628 of poor parents, and studied under the Jesuits in Valencia. He received the degree of Doctor of Theology at Coimbra, and was ordained priest at the age of twenty-four. Intellectually he was brilliant; he radiated an air of authority which observers have described as "at first disconcerting, and then supercilious." At thirty years of age he was already the idol of religious circles in Valencia, a fashionable preacher, a confessor in demand in all the convents. His fellow townsmen sent him to Rome in 1664 as procurator in the beatification cause of Jerônimo Simon, who was dear to them; and Miguel Molinos met with the same success in the Eternal City. Whenever he said Mass those in search of the path towards mysticism gathered round him; even members of the Sacred College of Cardinals, and among them the future Pope St. Innocent XI, at that time Cardinal Odescalchi. Letters reached him from all over Italy, and above his signature he wrote: "Moved by the Holy Ghost," or "In the light of the Most High." He was at that time "submerged beneath a torrent of souls, though he remained as detached and solitary as a hermit." His triumph lasted unalloyed for ten years.

In 1675 Molinos published in Spanish, and subsequently in Italian, an account of his teaching; the work was entitled *Guia Espiritual*—"Spiritual Guide." Its success was enormous, not only in the two languages in which it was published but also in Latin, French and German. Less notice was given to his *Tradado de la Comunión quotidiana*. He received the most flattering tributes, and when his opponents dared to criticize his theories it was they whom the Holy Office condemned, including even Father Paolo Segneri, at that time the most famous among the Jesuit preachers and a renowned ascetic doctor. Meanwhile Molinos himself remained aloof from all this, and declared that "his one desire was to be annihilated for Jesus and contemned by all."

Molinosist doctrine was unqualified Quietism. Its spirituality culmi-
nated in two fundamental themes: absolute passivity and contemplation in
complete spiritual tranquility. The soul must aim at "mystic death," annihilation in God; allowing God to substitute Himself for the Ego and to
dominate the whole being. The soul should have no desire, should make no
act of love. In fact, every act is displeasing to God because it interrupts the
state of passive resignation. Devotion itself is harmful if it is addressed to the
visible, such as the humanity of the Man-Christ, the Blessed Virgin or the
saints. Thus one way only was offered to the mystical soul: the "inward way."
The "purgative way" was no longer necessary: away with asceticism!

Had Molinos meditated on the Gospel of St. John, in which Christ said:
"He that hath my commandments, and keepeth them, he it is that loveth
me" (John 14:21)? Not that he denied sin and man's falling into sin, but
he held that our very vices were acceptable to God, provided that the soul
humbled itself. When these onsets occurred it was because God allowed the
demon to use violence against the will of perfect souls, even to the point of
making them perform shameful acts. Under the doctrine of abandonment
it was harmful to resist.

What might have appeared to be serious faults were regarded by Molinos as simply miserable snares of the Spirit of Darkness. *Etiam peccata....*
That was carrying things far indeed.

That these theories were not condemned out of hand could only be
explained by the prestige Molinos enjoyed with Innocent XI, the Cardinals Ricci, Azzolini, Cybo, the Secretary of State, Capizucchi, who was
responsible for the *Imprimatur* granted to the *Guta Espiritual*, and Petruc-
ci, author of a book containing similar ideas; not to mention many of the
Roman princesses and ex-Queen Christina of Sweden. What is even harder
to understand is that opinion suddenly turned against him. There might
have been several reasons for this. A number of confessors drew attention
to the fact that some of their penitents—especially female penitents—were
giving anything but a moral interpretation to Molinosist ideas. Inigo Carac-
ciolo, Archbishop of Naples, declared that the "prayer of quiet" had oust-
ed all vocal prayer as well as confession, especially in convents. The elderly

472 Cardinal Albizzi of the Holy Office took a similar stand. Perhaps Quietism appeared to Innocent XI as the antithesis of the Jansenist error which had been condemned, and considered that it also should be stamped out in the general interest. Perhaps also the Pope's confessor, Father Maracchi, pressed for condemnation because he wished to show clearly that the Society of Jesus had no connection whatever with such doctrines, even though it had fought the myrmidons of Jansenius and the over-strict moral code of Port-Royal. Strange rumours were current in Rome, and accusations regarding the holy man's relations with his female penitents reached the Inquisition.

In 1685 he was arrested by the papal police. His household staff protested the absolute innocence of his life, and kissed his feet as he entered the carriage which took him to prison. Mabillon, who was then in Rome, noted in his diary that no one knew exactly why Molinos had been arrested: "No one believes that it is on account of the doctrine contained in his published writings, but rather on account of his letters, or at least the unfortunate interpretation put on his ideas by his followers." To defend the victim of the Inquisition pamphlets were posted up on the famous "Pasquino"—the mutilated statue to which lampoons were affixed. The mood of hostility developed rapidly, and many of the mystic's disciples were also thrown into the prisons of the Holy Office. It was proved beyond a shadow of doubt that Molinosism was working havoc not only among the women who strove to attain the Nirvana of imperturbable tranquility, but among others who sought joys of a less celestial nature. Molinos himself confessed to everything of which he was accused; he agreed with whatever his accuser wished to plead against him, whatever the demon, doing violence to his will, might have been able to make him do. His attitude was clearly that of a Christian who, under blows and insults, rejoiced at being like the outraged Christ. Sixty-eight propositions were extracted from his writings and condemned by Innocent XI. He submitted at once, and solemnly agreed to renounce his errors. This he did in the church of Santa Maria Sopra Minerva, on his knees between two *sbirri*, and holding in his bound hands a candle, while the crowd on the square shouted: "To the stake, to the stake!" He evinced a mysterious air of gaiety and imperturbability, possibly in that state of complete spiritual passivity in which "no glad tidings bring joy, and no misfortune brings sadness." Innocent XI flatly refused to allow him to be condemned to death, a fact which gave rise to doubt as to the truth of the moral turpitude of which Molinos had been accused, though he had admitted his guilt. He passed the last nine years of his life, until 1696, in prison, with every appearance of a life of mortification and prayer, if not of repentance.

13. MADAME GUYON

FROM the very beginning Molinosism penetrated into France, where, as we have seen, it found conditions favourable. Although, however, the French Quietists exaggerated the state of passivity and assimilation with God, they never adopted the extraordinary theory of evil and man's lack of responsibility embarked upon by Molinos. Thus, in 1664, the blind mystic Malaval, "the lay saint of Marseilles," as his fellow townsmen called him, published a practical manual on contemplation which achieved immense popularity; Father Segneri discovered seven "illusions" in the work but nothing more serious. With Father Lacombe and Madame Guyon, however, the deviation developed into something much more significant.

The circumstances surrounding these two personalities were very much on a par with those pertaining to Miguel Molinos. They were the centre of such a maelstrom of heated controversy and vehement quarrels, and were attacked with such violence, that the historian hesitates to accept at their face value indictments in which equity does not always appear to have been observed; or even to recognize confessions which may have resulted from their own fanatical, but Christian, humility.

Father Lacombe was born in Thonon in 1643. He does not appear to have been endowed with that very sound sense of proportion and practical wisdom normally recognizable in natives of Savoy. According to Mgr. Calvet he was "a simple man and a zealous missioner," but also "a pious visionary"; emotional and incapable of marshalling his ideas. He admitted: "I

474 make foolish blunders which I have to pay for soon afterwards...more often resulting from the painful reproaches I feel within me than from the punishments I bring down upon myself." A man of such temperament was inevitably exposed to the accidents of fortune. Having joined the Barnabites, an Order founded in the preceding century by St. Antony Maria Zaccaria, he became a teacher of theology in the motherhouse of the Order, and later Superior of the community at Thonon. In Rome he became acquainted with the theories of Molinos, and was on friendly terms with Augusto Ripa, Bishop of Vercelli and an ardent Molinosist. He explained his spiritual doctrine, very similar to that of Molinos, in two short works, one of which was written in Latin. They passed almost unnoticed, and perhaps the good father would have remained an obscure Quietist had not chance—or the demon—brought him into contact with Jeanne-Marie Bouvier de la Mothe, widow of Jacques Guyon de Chesnoy and sister of his provincial, Father Dominique Bouvier.

At Gex, facing Thonon across the Lake of Geneva, a house belonging to the organization "Nouvelles Catholiques" had been recently set up to guarantee the perseverance of Protestant converts. It was founded at the request of the Bishop of Geneva by a woman whom everyone regarded as an unusual person, and for whom Father Lacombe, the new spiritual director of the house, had boundless admiration. This little middle-class woman from Montargis certainly was extraordinary within the full meaning of the term. She was born in 1648. Even when very young she declared that she had "visions like those of St. Teresa"; she said that "with a large needle" she had sewn on her flesh a piece of paper bearing the name of Jesus! She was physically abnormal, a prey to strange swellings of the body when her skin became pitted with purple marks. She did not seem very much more balanced psychologically. At fifteen her reading of romantic works and a natural tendency towards day-dreaming created a queer tumult in a mind ceaselessly in a whirl. This explosive mixture led her into marriage with a good-natured cousin twenty-two years her senior. On the day after the wedding she declared amidst tears that marriage was to her a hateful sacrifice and that she would rather have been a nun. Though she had four children

she somehow (under a process which Freud has studied) transferred her 475
unsatisfied passion as a great lover to the religious plane, and lived in a mystical delight which made her forget her real life; she applied to herself all the
spiritual states the details of which she had read in books, and went so far as
to claim that the Child Jesus had placed on her finger the invisible ring of
mystical marriage.

In this unusual woman the features of mystical experience were amaz-
ingly blended, and hysteria undoubtedly exercised a stupendous influence
over her. As a young girl she was pretty and coquettish, with alluring lips
and the gentle eyes of a doe; but smallpox had left ugly marks upon her face
and she regarded them as an extraordinary grace. She had little need of the
everyday weapons required to charm and assert her personality. Her tremendous flow of words disconcerted even those who were most unamena-
ble to persuasive eloquence. She wrote with a speed that St. Jerome might
have envied. In a week she produced a commentary on the most difficult
of the biblical books, and wrote one on the Canticle of Canticles in twenty-four hours! When Jeanne-Marie Guyon became a widow she was at last
able to devote herself to her true vocation: the winning of souls. "Our Lord
has made it clear that He has destined me to be the mother of a great people!" she said. And she added: "Deep down I have a natural aptitude for
sound judgment, and it never fails me." In the matter of humility at least this
Christian evidently stood in awe of no one.

When this preposterous woman came in contact with Father Lacombe
their meeting put the finishing touches to her ardour. Entirely free from
material worries, thanks to an income of fifty thousand *livres* left to her by
Jacques Guyon, she could without hindrance abandon herself to an apostolic zeal continually inflamed by her interior voices. She dragged the worthy Barnabite along with her in that spiritual Odyssey into which he was
already inclined by temperament to plunge. It ended in a complete fusion of
souls, the mutual discovery "of a land entirely new to them both, so divine
as to be utterly inexpressible." There followed the ebb and flow of graces
interchanged; a supernatural silence in which their minds, independent of
words, were united. Which of the two controlled the other? It needed but

476   one word from the priest, the magnetic touch of his hand on the penitent's brow, to dispel a sick headache or a stubborn cough. But the Barnabite confessed that when he was away from her he felt bereft of a part of himself. Did their relationship develop into something rather less unearthly? At least Louis XIV, Mme. de Maintenon, Bossuet and Cardinal de Noailles thought so, and stated it publicly. Mme. Guyon herself never admitted to anything of a serious nature, apart from a few innocent kisses; but Father Lacombe later confessed to moral turpitude. That confession, however, occurred after he had become insane, when the truth of his admissions might have been regarded as open to doubt.[25] Whatever the case may be the mystico-sensuous nature of their relationship was sufficient to throw off balance two dispositions that were already on the threshold of error.

For a while Mme. Guyon took the habit of the Ursulines at Thonon. There, and at Gex, Marseilles, Lyons and Dijon, she conducted an apostolate, while she carried out the duties of a simple medical attendant at hospitals in Turin with admirable charity. There were no limits to the zeal of the visionary. The enthusiastic and ardent Father Lacombe followed her despite the warnings of his provincial, Mme. Guyon's brother, of his bishop, Jean d'Aranthon of Alex, who was very disturbed, and of Cardinal Le Camus, Bishop of Grenoble. They were surrounded by a fanatical nucleus of "devout" of both sexes; for them only was reserved the teaching of hidden ineffable truths, while the public was given the mere outline of their doctrine. In 1683, after a dreadful crisis, both physical and spiritual, during which Mme. Guyon knew not whether she was carrying the Child Jesus or tormented by the great dragon of the Apocalypse, she experienced a period of tranquility during which she drafted her *Moyen court et très facile de faire oraison.* It was published two years later and met with enormous success. In two leaflets—the *Torrents spirituels*—circulated secretly she formulated mystical theories for the initiated. This was intensified Quietism, unrestricted Molinosism: surrender, passivity, "recollection in God," the

---

25. Henri Bremond has clearly stated: "It is certain that Mme. Guyon was never proved guilty of the slightest fault with Father Lacombe or with anyone else."

mystical marriage, "unimaginable innocence" and indifference to human   477
acts. There was nothing new in it all. The only point in which Mme. Guyon
and Lacombe differed from Molinos was the matter of sin. They did not
refer to it as violence used by the demon, but they affirmed that "extreme
surrender" and detachment from self could lead the soul to commit faults;
"to commit a sin of which one had the greatest abhorrence" was to offer the
greatest sacrifice to God! Such statements confirmed the worst suspicions.

When Father Lacombe and his "soul-mate" arrived in Paris their doctrines found an immediate hearing. A number of society ladies went into
raptures over the visionary. They were anything but mad, but were, on the
contrary, souls sincerely in search of spiritual advancement. They included such ladies as the Duchesse de Charost, Colbert's three daughters, the
Duchesses of Chevreuse, Beauvilliers and Mortemart, Mme. de Miramion,
foundress of the Sisters of the Holy Family, known as the "Miramionnes,"
and Mlle. de la Maisonfort, Canoness of Saint-Cyr, who happened to be
Mme. de Maintenon's cousin. The mystic couple created such a stir that the
Archbishop of Paris became uneasy; in order to please Rome where, as a
matter of fact, Molinos had just been arrested, he secured an order from
the authorities to confine the Barnabite to the Bastille "on account of his
scandalous conduct,"—an action which gave rise to gossip and mirth, for
there was nothing edifying about the conduct of Archbishop Harlay de
Champvallon. Shortly afterwards Mme. Guyon was confined to the convent of the Visitandines in the Rue Saint-Antoine, a trial which she welcomed with great strength of mind, rejoicing to be "deemed infamous"; she
even talked of facing the scaffold, a fate with which she was not in the least
threatened.

Meanwhile her friends were indignant; they busied themselves trying to
secure her release, and Mme. de Maintenon, who was then at the height of
her influence, agreed to intervene. Poor Father Lacombe became more and
more absorbed in God, lost in a prayer of quiet which left him insensible to
trials. He went from prison to prison: from the Bastille to the île d'Oléron,
from the Fort in Lourdes to the one in Vincennes. In 1712 he died insane—
or so it is claimed—in the asylum at Charenton, and his penitent left the

convent of the Visitation to return in triumph to the fashionable circles. It was at the house of the Duchesse de Charost that she met a young bishop of thirty-five, whose irresistible charm and noble bearing seemed predisposed to inspire a spirit of mysticism, the surrender of the will, the annihilation of the being in divine love. His name was François de Salignac de la Mothe Fénelon. "They found each other's mind to their taste," said Saint-Simon, "and the sublime in each intermingled."

14. THE SEMI-QUIETISM OF FÉNELON

THAT remark of Saint-Simon's, like many of his witty sayings, was not quite true, for the sublime did not immediately blend in the two friends. At first Fénelon was reserved. After a good three hours' conversation with the mystical lady in the carriage which took them from the Château de Beynes to Paris the principles she discussed began to touch him. When at the end of the journey Mme. Guyon asked him if he accepted all she had said, he replied: "It has gone in by the coachman's door." In other words, he was almost won over.

Is it surprising that a man in whom burned the fire of genius should have allowed himself to be caught up in this way? There might have been many indications that the widow of Jacques Guyon was neurotic, and that "her mind was clouded over by subconscious dreams which she accepted as divine impulses," but she undoubtedly had within her also an ardent love of God and the conquering strength of an apostle. At the time Fénelon met her she was free from the cumbering influence of Father Lacombe. For the moment she appeared to be well balanced, and no one in the pious coterie frequenting Colbert's noble daughters (with whom Fénelon was on very close terms) had any doubt about her loftiness of purpose. Fénelon's prejudice against her was therefore bound to collapse. Furthermore, he had reached that stage in his life when a youngish but maturing man, laudably uneasy about his destiny, asks himself questions about the future life; he must also, despite his enjoyment of the full flavour of success, find in it a bitter taste, and to some extent be predisposed to heed as a messenger of Providence a woman who, in a burning voice, speaks to him of abandonment, an inner call and the prayer of simplicity. After all, what did it matter to be a celebrated preacher, the favourite pupil of the great Bossuet and the Superior of Nouvelles Catholiques at twenty-eight years of age? How important was it to be one of the missioners especially appointed by Louis XIV to convert the Protestant provinces, if he experienced an anguish, more intense because it was hidden, that the firmest faith was not sufficient to conquer? What Mme. Guyon told him was undoubtedly what Fénelon was waiting to hear.

From their very first meeting Mme. Guyon herself experienced, as she said, "an inexplicable urge to open her heart" to the young director. Without over-emphasizing the likeness between Fénelon and Ulyses, the hero of his book *Télémaque*—"his eyes full of fire, the look steady, the smile delicate, his movements casual, his speech soft, ingenuous and winning, and concealing behind his reserved manner a depth of charm and sparkle"—we may yet be permitted to think that Mme. Guyon had a sufficiently keen understanding of human nature to guess that Fénelon was an exceptional man in whom burned a mysterious flame. From her point of view it was a veritable venture of spiritual seduction, the lover feeling her soul "in perfect harmony" with the one she wishes to win, her soul "adhering to his as the soul of King David adhered to Jonathan's," and having but one aim: to render this sublime harmony fruitful. There is not the slightest doubt that their relations were chaste. Bossuet did not enhance his stature when he accused them of moral turpitude and compared their relationship with that of the heretic Montanus and his concubine Priscilla. Despite the obviously uncommon appearances which this type of mystical union assumed, theirs was the harmony of two souls in pure love, never departing from the bounds of the supernatural.

What we know of their relationship—and we do know a lot from their letters—certainly causes astonishment; even if we allow for the fact that the language of the day was different from our own (and in this respect we have only to compare the correspondence between St. Francis de Sales and St.

Jeanne de Chantal), and that words which may be ambiguous nowadays possessed at that time a delicate transparency. Though we may also agree with some writers that Fénelon had "a certain simplicity of soul, at once naïve and profound," we cannot but feel that the filial trust he evinced towards the woman he regarded as his spiritual mother led him to express himself in a manner distressingly puerile. It is embarrassing to see such a great man childishly stringing together doggerel lines to the tune of *Tai-sez-vous, musette*; lines which run: *Comme au maillot, je suis en grace...à peine je bégaie, je ne sais pas mon nom* ("I am in favour, like the baby in the cradle.... I can scarcely lisp a word, and I do not yet know my name"). It is even more distressing to read that he called the widow Guyon his "Maman Téton," and that she should reply by calling him "Bibi." How strong must have been the spirit of purity in the tender and passionate soul of the future "Swan of Cambrai" to ensure that all these sentiments did not develop into anything worse! "I experience no feelings towards you," he wrote to his spiritual mother, "and yet I am attached to no one more than I am to you. Nothing can be compared with my *cold, dry* fondness for you." The words in italics are important.

Mme. Guyon's influence over Fénelon was therefore beyond question. He thought and believed with all his strength that she had been placed by God along his path to guide him and provide him with the answer he sought. "My confidence in you is complete," he wrote, "because of the brilliance of the light you bring to bear on interior things and God's designs through you." And he never repudiated that trust and admiration; even when he was compelled to part company with his friend, and ceased to write to her. When she was defeated and rejected by all he remained faithful to her with the grace of the nobleman that he was. "Hold fast to what I have told you," she commanded; "it is of God!" Undoubtedly he obeyed her deep down in his heart to the end of his days.

Not that he accepted all Mme. Guyon's opinions and made her errors his own. When he wrote, "From you I receive my daily bread," he was presumably not referring to his correspondent's dogmatic assertions, but to the spiritual impulse she gave him, to the interior peace he had won back through his contact with her. Apart from that he meant to remain free. "You mistake your illusions for divine impulses," he wrote. "I have never doubted the honesty of your intentions, but I express no opinion as to the details of your doctrine. I believe in you without judging you, although it demands an effort not to judge you. You have often made a mistake in temporal matters...." Those are not the words of a man who adheres to a doctrine and follows a guide blindly.

Fénelon refused to agree with his friend on very many fundamental points in which Quietism proper deviated seriously and deserved to be condemned as a heresy. Mme. Guyon was not very sure of her ideas and her theological terms. She became entangled in the worst snares of Molinosism, accepting the theory that evil is imposed upon the innocent by the violence of the demon, and that God allows the innocent to become "stained" in the interest of their spiritual progress. She even maintained that a soul in a state of perfect passivity should be indifferent to its own salvation; she went so far as to declare that a soul in a state of imperturbable peace "would be content to live deprived entirely of the practice of religion"—which *ipso facto* would render the sacraments almost useless. Not for a moment did Fénelon recognize such reckless propositions. On the contrary, he strove to lead his friend to correct them, which she did to a great extent. In Fénelon's hands Mme. Guyon certainly grew to resemble less and less the Mme. Guyon of Father Lacombe—which suggests a somewhat feminine type of mimesis. Thus the spiritual son also exercised an influence over his "mother." "Guyonism" became "Fénelonized," as Mgr. Calvet has judiciously remarked.

Although the future Archbishop of Cambrai was not a Quietist in the heretical sense of the term, it is none the less true that from a doctrinal point of view, and especially from the standpoint of his profound aspirations— for he was never an ardent Schoolman—he was drawn very close to the basic doctrines of the "spirit of quiet." He was born and had developed in the atmosphere of "pure love." During his childhood at Cahors, where the memory of the Venerable Alain de Solminihac still lingered, he had read in Father Chastenet's book on the great bishop that he had extolled the virtue of being childlike and preached a love of God detached from all desire of heavenly reward. And in the Chartreuse, where he made his retreats, he had listened to Dom Beaucousin talking about Mme. Acarie, Marie de l'Incarnation, and her mysticism of love. His uncle, Salignac Fénelon, an influential member of the Company of the Blessed Sacrament, had brought him into contact with the ideas of M. de Bernières-Louvigny. Later at Saint-Sulpice the famous director M. Tronson taught him the pedagogics of divine love, and instilled into him the habit of the presence of God, introducing him to the bountiful source that originated with M. Olier, in which the Christian ideal begins with complete forgetfulness of self. All these influences operating in the same direction, combined with the doctrine of pure love and perfect surrender to God, were bound to bear fruit in a soul which, as Fénelon himself admitted, "bore the burden of itself" and awaited in torment an answer to its problems. What an antidote to the poison of doubt and scruple was this doctrine that counselled the rejection of all things, utter surrender to God and the whisperings of the silent voice! In the circle of his friends, the pious duchesses, Fénelon was able to sense the tendency to dryness in certain forms of asceticism of which Jansenism was the extreme example. Should the life of a Christian consist merely in fighting against sin? Did it not consist rather in living in God and in His love?

Thus Fénelon adhered not so much to Quietism as to that long tradition of spiritual *indifference* that permeated the whole history of Christianity; a sentiment intrinsically bound up with theocentric thought. He who seeks only the will of God is compelled to be indifferent to everything else. "Holy indifference," he wrote, "demands that we desire nothing for ourselves, but everything for God." Did St. Francis de Sales, M. Olier and Monsieur Vincent say otherwise? It was the alpha and the omega of what Bremond called "the metaphysics of the saints." There was no question of destroying the human will, but rather of delivering it from everything that fettered it, releasing it from *possessing* in order that it might tend towards *being*. The quintessence of this endeavour was the very experience of the mystics: complete renunciation, absorption in God. Holy indifference, the "Fénelonian" state of passivity, meant more than vague contemplation; it meant supreme submission to the divine will. To love God was to die to oneself; it implied

rejection of egoism, even of the selfish desire to be ultimately rewarded for   483
one's trust. Briefly, was it unorthodox to "dispossess" oneself? St. Augustine said much the same in other words; and Pascal said: "The one true virtue is to hate onself." The most admirable and profoundly Christian thing
about "Fénelonism" was its expectation of God, "an ever-present God who
envelops us and continually calls us; whom we often fail but who never fails
us."[26] Even when, in some of Fénelon's statements, his doctrine lends itself
to misinterpretation, it remains in keeping with the fundamental ideas of
Christian tradition; or, more precisely, to one of the two essentials of that
tradition.

For there are two Christian conceptions of the spiritual life, and the
Church has always striven to reconcile and fuse them. One views the spiritual life more especially from the theological standpoint, stressing its elements rather than the principles that ultimately draw the two conceptions
together on the highest levels; it considers above all dogma, the doctrinal
assertions to which faith adheres and the rules upon which life must be
ordered. The psychological aspects of human problems remain somewhat
outside this conception. But the other places religious experience in the
psychological sphere, and requires that faith consist primarily in a perfect
state of expectation, the reply to the *irrequietum cor nostrum* of which St.
Augustine speaks. When the soul knows definitely that it has been called,
that it has been pierced by the dart of love that quivers in the hearts of the
great mystics, then is everything else added to it: loyalty to dogma and obedience to the Commandments. In a word it is precisely this total merging
with God which is the goal of all genuine religious experience, the consum-
mation underlying St. Paul's words, "And I live, yet not I; but Christ liveth
in me"; providing always we do not forget that this fusion is possible only
at the cost of heroic mastery of self. There is not the slightest doubt that
Fénelon was the perfect embodiment of the second of these conceptions;
but he had to contend with Bossuet, who was the perfect embodiment of

---

26. Jean Lacroix, in *Le Monde* (February 23, 1957), with reference to J. M. Goré's book,
La notion d'indifférence chez Fénelon et ses sources.

the first. When Fénelon, thinking of those souls who aspired to the pleni-tude of the spiritual life, offered them his doctrine, his adversary, bearing in mind the needs of less ambitious souls who required safeguards rather than wings to soar to the heights, replied that all this mysticism was very danger-ous and might lead to serious doctrinal aberrations. From their own points of view both had cause to claim that religion was at stake; but both were wrong in not recognizing that true Christian experience results from the harmonious blending of these two conceptions, which are complementary. It was over this perplexing question that Fénelon came into conflict with his old friend and master Bossuet.

15. STORM AT SAINT-CYR

MEANWHILE the early success of the young prelate and the visionary Mme. Guyon gradually became a triumph; their most resplendent period being from 1689 to 1694. Fénelon had just been selected to be tutor to the king's grandson the Duc de Bourgogne, and he set about transform-ing this temperamental and quick-tempered boy (who was, however, steady and upright) into a prince pleasing to God, with the result that much was expected of him. His father, the Dauphin, was a remote nonentity living in his little court of Meudon. He knew nothing about France apart from what he read in the society columns of the *Gazette de France*. Fénelon devoted himself to training the future heir to be an exemplary king who would establish in France the reign of piety and the pure love of God. Fénelon felt within him "a disinterested urge to engage in the conduct of important affairs of State, a task for which he considered himself to have been born." Might he not become the Richelieu of this future Louis XV? Mme. Guyon prophesied that he would be the light of the realm, the star that would lead kings towards the Child Christ. Fénelon's novel *Télémaque*, which he began to write for his pupil the Duc de Bourgogne, set out his ideas of a policy founded entirely upon moral principles. He went so far as to address to the Great King himself an explosive letter worthy of the prophets of Israel, in which he cast the king's faults into his teeth and threatened him with the thunderbolt of divine justice.[27] It was all very beautiful.

A little group gathered round the mystical couple creating something of the atmosphere of a secret society—a community of saintly souls, the Order of "Michelins," who, like the archangel of old, would conquer "Baraquin," the devil. It had a general, assistants, a master of novices, a secretary, even brother porters and brother gardeners; there was no task which the Order did not provide for. It was a childishly mystical scheme to which were added one or two more worldly aims; for, after all, the Duc de Bourgogne was destined one day to rule France. Mme. de Maintenon, the queen without a crown, was kept well informed, and she approved these pious endeavours which she hoped would bring about the complete conversion of her husband and the spiritual rebirth of society.

Yet it was through Mme. de Maintenon that the troubles began. To begin with she confided utterly in Mme. Guyon, "hoping to find joy and consolation in the sweetness of her intercourse." But all that changed. Mme. de Maintenon had recently founded Saint-Cyr, where she intended to educate young society ladies who would become the élite of French womanhood. Fénelon lectured there, pointing out the way that lay open to the little children of God. He spoke eloquently on the pure love of God, mental prayer and the suppression of methods based on reason. It did not take Mme. Guyon long to find her way into Saint-Cyr, where she spoke with equal ardour. The new institution, having no religious tradition, was literally seized by a wave of fervour and joy. About that time Racine was putting on his plays *Esther* and *Athalie* at Saint-Cyr. The king himself watched them at the door of the theatre, and Mme. de Sévigné was in raptures over them. Mme. Guyon had a staunch supporter at Saint-Cyr in her cousin the bewitching Mlle. de la Maisonfort, even more of a Guyonist than herself, who disseminated strange doctrines among the students: there was no further need for prayers or good works; no need to practise virtue and perform acts of penance; the way of union and passive purification

---

27. See above, Chapter IV, p. 244 and note 1.

was sufficient. It was indeed a strange doctrine. Mme. de Maintenon might have been influenced by subconscious jealousy at seeing another woman exercise so much sway over the young ladies, and she opened her heart to the Bishop of Chartres and her spiritual director Godet des Marais. The latter, perhaps also subconsciously, might not have been very happy about Fénelon's success. An inquiry was instituted among the students, and it was found that they were all more or less Quietist in outlook. When the king was informed he expressed a desire to read some of Mme. Guyon's writings and those of her great friend, with the result that he found all this spirituality too fanciful for his taste. A group of theologians was secretly consulted, and all, except Tronson and Bourdaloue, had some very definite comments to make. Father Joly, Superior of the Lazarists, even went so far as to use the word heresy. Mme. de Maintenon decided to submit the matter to an adjudicator, and she chose Bossuet.

This choice, which Fénelon accepted with great marks of respect, was sufficient in itself to cause the Saint-Cyr incident to miscarry. Though Bossuet was an excellent theologian and very well acquainted with patristic studies, he was not really familiar with the mystical writers of the previous two centuries, even St. Teresa and St. Francis de Sales; he was therefore instinctively suspicious. Thus his approach to mysticism was through the writings of an unbalanced woman concerning whom the most unpleasant rumours were current; and he was expected to express an opinion. All this was sufficient to cause him to confuse to some extent true mysticism with the false, Fénelonism with Guyonism, Quietism and moral decadence. As he read the works of Mme. Guyon, and especially her autobiography, and after several interviews with her—or rather cross-examinations to which he subjected her at the Visitation convent in Meaux, where the visionary had agreed to settle—he became more and more convinced that he had to deal with a madwoman. This may have been a rather drastic conclusion, but he was not entirely wrong. In any case he looked upon her as a very dangerous woman.

Thinking herself lost Mme. Guyon asked for two other judges in addition to the terrible bishop to be appointed to consider the matter. This

request was granted her, and the commission of three members met at Issy 487
in a country house belonging to the seminary of Saint-Sulpice. The members were Bossuet, M. Tronson and Noailles, who was at that time Bishop
of Chalons. The inquiry lasted eight months, much to the disgust of Mme.
de Maintenon, who hoped for a speedy settlement. Mme. Guyon defended herself with the help of enormous volumes, and endeavoured to prove
that she was vindicated by the Fathers of the Church and the spiritual writers. Fénelon discreetly lent her his support. The attitude of the three judges was not altogether similar. Bossuet arrived at Issy in a carriage loaded
with books, determined to prove that he was right beyond the shadow of a
doubt. Tronson was more subtle; he feared that an out-and-out condemnation might harm the cause of genuine mysticism. Noailles kept in mind the
court of Versailles. And the Archbishop of Paris, Harlay de Champvallon,
aware of the general opinion, once more condemned poor Father Lacombe
and Mme. Guyon's *Moyen Court* in order to steal a march on the commission. A draft judgment was eventually prepared. It condemned a number of
"articles" extracted from the works of Mme. Guyon without mentioning the
author's name. Mme. Guyon still had many friends, and there was no desire
to discredit publicly one who had been so prominent at Saint-Cyr; besides,
the noble Fénelon had powerful connections.

During the course of the discussions at Issy, Fénelon's personal position
in the matter had not been questioned; he remained in the background, but
stated openly that he was ready to agree in advance with the decisions of the
three judges. In February 1695 he was appointed Archbishop of Cambrai,
which Saint-Simon contemptuously described as "a country diocese." However, it brought in an income of two hundred thousand *livres*. This may have
been a reward for Fénelon's attitude at the inquiry, or a means of removing
him from the court at Versailles; it might even have been the outcome of
skillful maneuvers on the part of his friends the duchesses. He immediately took advantage of his new appointment to make himself a member
of the committee of judges and to add a number of clauses which toned
down the verdict. Mme. Guyon agreed to retract publicly and it seemed
that everything would be settled satisfactorily. Bossuet consecrated the new

archbishop in the chapel at Saint-Cyr, in the presence of Mme. de Maintenon and the Duc de Bourgogne. The problem of Quietism appeared to have been solved; but it had only just begun.

16. BOSSUET VERSUS FÉNELON

WHY was the controversy resumed? Why should these two great men who had so far not opposed each other openly engage in a duel from which neither would emerge with enhanced reputation? No one knows precisely, but the causes were certainly complex. Bremond held the rather romantic view that the Jansenists planned to discredit the Church which had condemned them; but that is pure hypothesis. It seems more likely that the motives were psychological.[28] It is quite possible that Fénelon, whose submission was sincere when he assured Bossuet that henceforward he would hold no opinion that differed from his, changed his mind in one of those spasms of conscience that were habitual with him. In certain respects he was unstable. He admitted: "I could not say anything that might strike me as false a moment afterwards." His friends may have reproached him with having given in and betrayed the cause of Pure Love and true mysticism. Perhaps also those who had staked everything on him, and dreamed of attaining high office through the "Michelin" scheme, were thinking along the same lines. Mme. Guyon stood as a living sign of contradiction. Bossuet kept her within arm's reach in the convent of the Visitation at Meaux, in the hope of bringing about a more complete conversion. Unable to bear it any longer she escaped and fled to Paris, where she was arrested by the police and imprisoned in Vincennes. The extremely tactless manner in which she was interrogated concerning her relationship with Fénelon ended quite rightly by ruffling the Archbishop of Cambrai. His dismissal from Saint-Cyr and his replacement

---

28. To some extent they may also have been political, as R. Schmittlein has indicated in his book, *L'aspect politique du différend Bossuet-Fénelon* (Baden-Baden, 1954). It was in the field of Quietism that Bossuet's support of the king's authority and Fénelon's attitude of reserve in regard to absolutism clashed.

by Bossuet really hurt the sensitive archbishop. Even Mlle. de la Maison- 489
fort turned anti-Quietist. Bossuet probably suspected his onetime protégé
of playing a double game, but his reaction to Fénelon's courageous loyalty
towards his harassed friend may have been too harsh. Did Bossuet view with
displeasure the fact that Fénelon had become his equal, even his superior, in
ecclesiastical dignity? Certain rather tactless words used by the Bishop of
Meaux in a pastoral letter weighed heavily upon the heart of the Archbishop of Cambrai.

These two men were really so different in disposition that their antagonism appeared almost natural. One cause of the trouble was the difference in
their ages. Bossuet was nearly seventy, and the ardent forty-year-old Fénelon
was in the prime of life. Then there was the clash of temperaments between
the proud peer from the south, so easily offended, quick and unsophisti-
cated into the bargain, and the son of middle-class Burgundian parents,
with his feet firmly on the ground, little inclined to dreams, more sound
than subtle. But the greatest difference between them lay in their spiritual
outlook. And we have seen how closely this was in keeping with the particular genius of each. Finally the conflict between these two extraordinary
men was based on their doctrinal concepts, each being convinced that he
was upholding the rights of God and the Holy Spirit: the one defending
the integrity of dogma and morality against dangerous innovation, and the
other striving for the liberty of the interior life against religious conform-
ism and its deadening effects. This controversy between two geniuses concerning problems of such magnitude was indeed a great controversy, even
though human frailty led both antagonists to make use of weapons that did
them little credit.

In July 1696 Bossuet wrote a second *Instruction pastorale sur les états
d'oraison*,[29] and when it was finished he sent the manuscript to Fénelon seeking his approval. Undoubtedly his intention in doing so was to establish

---

29. Bremond remarked shrewdly, and perhaps with a touch of irony, that the best pages
Bossuet ever wrote were precisely those in which, without knowing it, he upheld the
theories of pure love (*Bossuet, maître d'oraison*).

the fact that they were in perfect agreement on the clauses set out during the inquiry at Issy. But Fénelon was suspicious, and scented a trap. When he opened the manuscript he noticed that quotations from Mme. Guyon's *Moyen Court* had been made in the work without any attempt to be lenient. He put away the work indignantly. Was he expected to be so dishonourable as to overwhelm his defeated friend? Was he being asked to repudiate what he held most dear? At the end of three weeks he returned the work without having read it, still less approving it. Then, taking pen and paper, he wrote at top speed his *Explications des Maximes des Saints sur la vie intérieure*, in which he explained his doctrine on religious experience, and in addition showed how easy it was to turn true mystics into heretics by distorting their ideas. When reading these two books today we do not see as much opposition in the views expressed as did their authors. There is great beauty in both books, especially in Bossuet's; and if Fénelon had only studied it a little more calmly he might have found grounds for agreement. But at the back of their minds they already felt bitter towards each other. As soon as Fénelon finished his book he sent the manuscript to his friends. The Duc de Chevreuse took it to the publisher at once without apparently obtaining Fénelon's clear approval. Everything moved so quickly that the *Maximes des Saints* was published (in 1697) a month before Bossuet's *États d'Oraison*. Bossuet's pride as an author was wounded and, not without good reason, he regarded Fénelon's behaviour as discourteous.

This brought about the final rupture. Bossuet was furious against the "perfect hypocrite," as he described Fénelon, and threw himself at the king's feet to beg his pardon "for not having revealed earlier the heresy of Monsieur de Cambrai." He knew what he was doing. A strong anti-Fénelon group existed at the court of Versailles: those who were jealous of his success, those who envied his appointment as tutor to the king's grandson, those who hated the Jesuits—well disposed towards Fénelon but opposed to Quietism. There was Noailles, the new Archbishop of Paris, and Mme. de Maintenon, who could not forget the trouble at Saint-Cyr. As for the king, his feelings towards Fénelon were uncertain. He admired him, but regarded him as "a chimerical person," which, coming from the king, was a severe censure. Perhaps he was also aware of Fénelon's criticisms, albeit discreet, of his morals, his policy and his costly wars. All that was quite sufficient to destroy the "Swan of Cambrai."

The *Maximes des Saints* was violently attacked as soon as it was published, and frequently by people who had never read the work and who were indeed utterly incapable of understanding it. The most unkind rumours were current in the court and throughout the capital. It was claimed that the book was nothing more than an attempt by the archbishop to plead the case of Mme. Guyon; what sort of a relationship must therefore exist between them? Generally speaking, the theologians who read the work were extremely hostile; even the prudent M. Tronson dealt cautiously with it. When the stern Abbé de Rancé, the reformer of La Trappe, was consulted, he replied that, "If M. de Cambrai was right the Gospels should be burned; and one might complain that Christ had come into the world only to deceive us." Fénelon was kept aware of all this fuss, the ill-natured gossip and the pamphlets,[30] and he knew that his enemies deliberately confused his ideas not only with Guyonism but even with Molinosism, of which he disapproved. But he committed one tactical error. He refused to participate in any discussion of his book if Bossuet were to be present; and he added that he would not retract, in any case, as his conscience told him that he was right. The outcome was open war.

One would prefer to pass over the various episodes of the quarrel, not only for the sake of the honour of the Church, but on account of our admiration for these two great men. They hurled numerous pamphlets at each other, which were a mixture of theology and polemics, and their methods were sometimes unsavoury. As far as ideas went it was, said Cardinal Grente, "a magnificent contest" lasting two years, the indignant Bossuet "riding full tilt" against his adversary, and Fénelon "parrying swiftly and brilliantly, remaining ever courteous, and assuming, with devastating elegance, an air

---

30. The echo of this campaign against Fénelon is reflected even in La Bruyère's *Dialogues*; in the seventh dialogue, for instance—the account of the "Spiritual Nuptials"—where a young penitent is shocked, and exclaims, "Fancy talking like that, Father, before a girl of my age!" Fléchier also refuted Quietism in verse.

492 of injured innocence."[31] But their conduct towards each was shabby. Their intrigues involved the palace and the police; there were thefts of correspondence, abuse and slander, both in private and public. Everything was done to render the business "unfortunate and lamentable," as Innocent XII described it.

Indeed the Pope was drawn into the controversy despite himself. Fénelon refused to submit to the judgment of his peers: he appealed to the Pope, saying that he recognized but one judge, the Vicar of Christ. It was a bold stroke, and as far as Rome was concerned a clever move which pleased everyone. But the appeal was a blunder in so far as it affected his relations with the king, who regarded his action as a betrayal of the rights of the Gallican Church. And all this was taking place fifteen years after the business of the "Four Articles"! The Great King's reaction was swift, and rendered all the more forceful by the fact that extracts from Fénelon's *Télémaque* had been circulated in secret, together with a number of political comments which were later to constitute the *Tables de Chaulnes*. Louis XIV did not relish being told how to rule. The king gave an order that Fénelon should leave the court, return to Cambrai and remain there. The Duc de Bourgogne pleaded for his former tutor, but to no avail. Fénelon left Versailles "under a deluge of affronts." He was refused permission to be present at the marriage between his pupil and Marie-Adélaide of Savoy, and even to visit his niece who was very ill. His brother, his family and his friends were all swallowed up in his disgrace, which endured for the rest of his life; for the premature death of his pupil in 1711 removed all hope of reinstatement. Even after Fénelon's death the canons of his chapter dared not pronounce a funeral oration, and his successor in the French Academy hurried through the traditional panegyric, in which the *Télémaque* was not even mentioned.[32]

Disgraced and defeated, exposed to innumerable attacks, Fénelon put on a bold front. With a sad touch of humour he warned those of his friends who still had the courage to remain faithful to him: "Be careful; I have the

---

31. See the article entitled "Fénelon," in the *Dictionnaire des Lettres, XVII siècle*.
32. This suggests that politics were not entirely excluded from the French Academy.

plague." He fenced so dexterously, however, that Bossuet was nettled on 493
many occasions. Pamphlets followed each other week after week, and their
tone became more and more bitter. The dispute reached a climax with the
publication in June 1698 of Bossuet's *Relation sur le Quiétisme*, a veritable
lampoon equal in literary quality to the *Provinciales*; the bishop of Meaux
adopted the same methods as Pascal, transferring the controversy from the
field of ideas to the field of facts, accusing his opponent of dishonourable
intentions and buttressing the weakness of some of his arguments by the
violence of his abuse. It was a masterpiece of style and insincerity. Worse
still, by making use of the original documents concerning the relations
between Fénelon and Mme. Guyon he went so far as to make all kinds of
scurrilous insinuations, comparing them both with Montanus and Priscilla—an imputation which, however, he was later to regret. Fénelon was
able to profit from the very violence of the attack, and with such subtlety
that his rival exclaimed: "That man *is* clever! The power of his intellect is
frightening." One retort especially struck home. Without exactly accusing
Bossuet in precise terms, Fénelon hinted that his former master and friend
had used a written confession he had made to him in confidence and out of
the fullness of his heart before the Issy discussions took place. There is no
doubt that, strictly speaking, this was not a sacramental confession, but it
constituted a glaring indiscretion on Bossuet's part, and did him no credit.

The affray continued just as briskly in Rome, and the methods adopted were no less shameful. Both camps had their supporters and agents. On
Fénelon's side stood the ambassador, Cardinal de Bouillon, nephew of the
great Turenne, who detested the Noailles family; the Jesuits, who wrongly
suspected the Bishop of Meaux of Jansenism. He also had the support of
several cardinals who feared that his condemnation might be regarded as
an attack on true mysticism. Furthermore, Fénelon's appeal had pleased the
Pope and the Roman Curia, who were well acquainted with the virtuous
life of the Archbishop of Cambrai. His own agent was the Abbé de Chanterac, a highly respected priest. Bossuet sent his nephew, the Abbé Bossuet,
to the Eternal City. He was a dubious character, but wily and an excellent
theologian. He had the backing of all who had fought Molinos, and his

personal prestige was considerable. Two rather contemptible incidents give some idea of the extent to which the power of influence was utilized in the controversy. The "Bossuetists" communicated to the Holy Office the record of the cross-examination during which the unhappy Father Lacombe, who was half mad, had confessed to a guilty relationship with Mme. Guyon. The "Cambraisians" for their part cast a slur on the Bishop of Meaux by saying that he was merely influenced by jealousy; they circulated the distressing story of the love affairs of his nephew the Abbé Bossuet, whom the flunkeys of Duke Cesarini had soundly thrashed for having tried to seduce their master's daughter. Zeal for the Pure Love of God was lost sight of in all these squabbles.

Considering all this mud-slinging one feels almost grateful to the King of France for having intervened to ask the Pope to put an end to the quarrel as soon as possible. If Innocent XII had resembled Julius II or Paul IV, or even Innocent XI, the king's interference might have induced him to act energetically, and he might have confined in the Castel Sant' Angelo the insolent Abbé Bossuet who, like a true Gallican, told the Pope what to do, and suggested that he should word his Bull to the satisfaction of the French bishops! In fact the Pope gave in and agreed to sign a condemnation, but he did so in subdued terms to the effect that Fénelon's book was prone to "lead the faithful imperceptibly into errors already condemned by the Church," and that it contained propositions which were "rash, offensive to the ear and discreditable." The condemnation made no mention whatsoever of heresy.

It did, however, mean repudiation and defeat for Fénelon, but he accepted it with dignity. On March 25, 1699, he received the news of his condemnation just as he was entering the pulpit. Putting aside the subject of the sermon he had prepared, he improvised a sublime discourse on obedience to the authority of the Holy See and the virtues of submission. Two weeks later he published the papal brief declaring his adherence to it "simply, absolutely and without the shadow of reservation." Perhaps he experienced a sort of bitter joy at feeling himself "held in low esteem and an object of pity," and remaining, as Chanterac told him, "steady and calm at the foot of his Cross." For all that his attitude was worthy of admiration, and gave him a strange grandeur. The fact that in one of those sudden spasms of moodiness which were common with him he subsequently wrote to some of his friends that he had been condemned for expounding theories which he had never held, or that he may sometimes have given the impression that he adopted the attitude of 'respectful silence" with which he had so often reproached the Jansenists, made little difference to the general dignity of his behaviour. Neither should we attach importance to the fact that he rejected a vague gesture of reconciliation by Bossuet—a rejection which the embittered bishop countered with a desperate attempt to secure yet another formal condemnation. Fénelon's submission brought the affair to a close. Mme. Guyon ended her days in 1717 in exile at Blois, at the home of one of her daughters. Her spiritual son's letters had become fewer and fewer. Quietism was dead.

But what were the consequences of the crisis? Considered objectively the literature that was born of the crisis might have fostered a greater knowledge of the spiritual life; it might have led to a fuller and more grandiose definition of the role of the mystic impulse, of reason and of the soul's activity. But there existed an atmosphere of emotion that impeded such a favourable outcome. To compensate for this, however, some of the effects of the crisis were beneficial though less ostentatious. By justly condemning the Quietism of Molinos, Father Lacombe and Mme. Guyon, as well as the semi-Quietism of Fénelon, Rome undoubtedly warded off grave perils— the perils of an easygoing morality. But at the same time did it not have a detrimental effect on true mysticism, as Innocent XII feared it might do? And was this not so in France especially, where a certain rationalist tendency had begun to develop which sought out motives for distrusting every inner impulse and denouncing those "possessed of God"? This tendency was one of the factors that gave rise to a narrowing-down of the Catholic mind. On the other hand, by insisting on the play of sentiment and interior experience did not the followers of Fénelon open the flood-gates to that tide of romantic egoism which in the next century found expression in the works of Jean-Jacques Rousseau? Again, the ruthless controversy between the two heads of the French Church gave encouragement to free-thinkers: the cruel language used by the Bishop of Meaux against the Archbishop of Cambrai made them shake with laughter! At that time a song was being sung in the streets of Paris, for everything that happens in France is eventually turned into song:

> *Dans ces combats où deux prélats de France*
> *Semblent chercher la verité,*
> *L'un dit qu'on détruit l'espérance,*
> *L'autre soutient que c'est la charité:*
> *C'est la foi qu'on détruit et personne n'y pense.*[33]

Such is the wisdom of the people.

Was it really wise to provide malignant tongues with an opportunity to turn Pure Love into an object of jest?

Another outcome of the Quietist controversy, but on a different plane, was soon apparent: once again the Jansenist threat became grave, and at the very moment when Rome had settled the bishop's quarrel. Bossuet was perhaps so carried away by his zeal to fight false mysticism that he remained blind to the imminent revival of Jansenism. He may have regarded the *Réflexions morales* of Father Quesnel as a sort of antidote to the errors of Fénelonism. His distrust of Pure Love seems to have provoked him into defending theses which, by crushing love under the weight of fear, resulted in keeping the faithful away from the sacraments, and prepared the way for irreligion. As often happens in violent controversies, it is Christ's truth, and especially Christ's charity, which emerges battered. Strictly speaking, only the Pope was victorious. The controversy was brought to an end through the appeal made to his authority; by the same token it was he who emerged triumphant from the great Jansenist contest. But from a spiritual point of view was not the whole Church the loser?

---

33. "In the conflict in which two French bishops appear to be seeking the truth, one says that hope is being destroyed, while the other maintains that it is charity. No one seems to know that faith itself is being destroyed."

17. RESUMPTION OF THE
JANSENIST CONTROVERSY: RACINE

SCARCELY ten years after the pious Clement IX thought he had put an end to the Jansenist heresy it appeared to be on the point of revival. Indeed the Jansenists displayed an utter lack of prudence. The popularity of Port-Royal, the fuss that was made over the convent and Antoine Arnauld were bound to arouse the king's suspicions: Louis XIV did not like anything to become fashionable which might deprive him of the limelight. The most zealous champions of the sect went about declaring that they had never been condemned or conquered, and that they had therefore never submitted. The Jansenist bishops, led by Henri Arnauld, Bishop of Angers, continued to rebel against the *Formulaire*, so that once again, in 1676, the king had to publish a decree to bring them to heel. At that time a new factor was introduced which greatly aggravated the situation.

In 1673 the Gallican crisis[34] had just blown up as a result of the *régale* affair. The conciliatory attitude of Clement X failed to check it. When the energetic Innocent XI followed him to the Chair of St. Peter in 1676, it became evident that the struggle was about to take a decisive turn. Who would triumph, the Pope or the Most Christian King? To aggravate the situation further the two bishops—Pavilion, of Alet, and Caulet, of Pamiers—who had protested against the government's claim to extend the right of *régale* to the whole country, were well-known Jansenists. Collusion between the friends of Port-Royal and the king's enemies appeared obvious. As a matter of fact, the Roman Curia had been extremely lenient towards Arnauld's supporters, and everyone was convinced that the Pope had promised Arnauld the cardinal's hat and had asked him to formulate a broad scheme of Church reform. In Jesuit circles Innocent XI was being discreetly referred to as "the Jansenist Pope." And did not the Probabilism affair seem to confirm these suspicions?

---

34. See above, Chapter IV, p. 273ff.

Arnauld and his friends had not forgiven the Jesuits, and they sought to get their own back. Pascal had shown them the Society's weak spot.

That indefatigable polemist had gleaned inspiration from various casuistic treatises, even among Jesuit writings, and found no less than sixty-five propositions which he regarded as responsible for moral laxity. Many of them proceeded from a "Probabilist" doctrine, a weak variety of laxism. It allowed that everything not formally rejected by the Church, or condemned by one of the Commandments, might be regarded as probable.[35] The sixty-five propositions were condemned by the Pope in 1679, and the Assembly of the Clergy at Bossuet's instigation reiterated the condemnation. The Society of Jesus was not mentioned by name, but it was the object of the attack. Innocent XI made a formal request that Father Tirso Gonzalez, a well-known anti-laxist, be appointed the Society's General. Thus public opinion came to regard the Jansenists as the real defenders of Christian morals which had been jeopardized by the detestable defects of laxism. Consequently, Jansenism immediately began to forge ahead in various provinces of religious life, in Italy and Holland as well as in France. It was a practical form of Jansenism, having very little in common with Jansenius and the problems of grace, but very much concerned with moral austerity. Innocent XI had certainly not intended that; he desired simply to preserve doctrinal integrity against the laxists, as he intended later against Molinos and the Quietists. But his action ended by making Louis XIV apprehensive, for the king regarded it as an admission of an alliance between Rome and Port-Royal.

The atmosphere became oppressive. In the spring of 1679 the Duchesse de Longueville died—a loyal friend of Port-Royal and one of the very few people whom Louis XIV permitted to speak frankly to him. For the last ten years of her life she had spent six months in every year at Port-Royal-des-Champs. The good-natured Péréfixe had been succeeded in the episcopal

---

35. Probabilism went a long way towards moral laxity. For instance, it argued that "when opposite parties in a lawsuit are supported by opinions that are equally probable, the judge may quite rightly accept money to persuade him to give a verdict in favour of one party rather than the other."

See of Paris by Harlay de Champvallon, to whose part in the Quietist affair we have already referred. His private life was not very edifying, and he aimed at high office, an ambition he was not to fulfil. He distrusted the Society of Jesus, which had the king's ear through Father La Chaise, the king's confessor. At the same time, in lending its support to the revelations which Margaret Mary Alacoque had had four years earlier and to the new devotion to the Sacred Heart, the Society was promoting a form of piety radically opposed to the harsh Jansenist observance. The whole business made Bossuet uneasy.

It was Archbishop Harlay de Champvallon who, having learned how to please the king, initiated new coercive measures. On May 17, 1679, he visited Port-Royal; he was polite and all smiles, but implacable. He ordered all the postulants, the young boarders and the priests to leave forthwith. The convent was forbidden to accept novices, and the number of nuns was not to exceed fifty. Port-Royal was condemned to death by extinction.

At the same time Antoine Arnauld was asked to drop the spiritual reunions that he held in the suburb of Saint-Jacques. Imagining himself threatened he fled to Flanders and then to Holland, and the gentle Nicole was persuaded to do likewise. Not that the great fighter had laid down his arms: he refused to return to France despite the fact that his safety was assured (though Nicole did take advantage of the offer), and continued to produce polemic writings to the end—more and more of his "machine-gun theology." He remained firmer than ever in his conviction that his trials were his guarantee of right, and that he was one of God's elect.

Before leaving France for ever the Great Arnauld had one consolation: Jean Racine, the most brilliant of the students issuing from the Little Schools, returned to the fold. Arnauld and his friends had considered him for ever lost to heaven, a slave to the world and the disastrous passions which his plays portrayed. After his marriage and the comparative failure of *Phèdre* (1677) Racine began to reflect. The Abbé Jacques Boileau, brother of the "lawgiver of Parnassus," reconciled him with Nicole and subsequently, though not without difficulty, with Arnauld himself. In a famous speech before the whole Areopagus of the Jansenist élite the dramatist demonstrated that his play *Phèdre* was not immoral, and at the end the great Antoine took him in his arms. From that moment Port-Royal had no better friend than Racine. When he described the persecution of the Jews by Haman, in his play *Esther*, was he not depicting the persecution of Jansenism? In any case Mordechai made a good portrait of Arnauld, and Esther's maidens bore an extraordinary resemblance to the nuns of the valley of the Chevreuse. He went further: courageously taking the part of the persecuted, he took upon himself the task of writing a history of Port-Royal; and in his will he asked to be buried among the "Solitaries" in the cemetery of Port-Royal-des-Champs, at the feet of M. Hamon.

18. THE AGONY OF PORT-ROYAL

IN 1698 Jean Racine died. Arnauld had died four years earlier, but just as he had taken the torch from the hands of Saint-Cyran, he left behind him another to take it up: Pasquier Quesnel (1634–1719), an Oratorian. It will be remembered that when Jansenius and his friend developed their first plans they dreamed of making the spiritual sons of Bérulle the shock troops of their great offensive. But that did not happen; the Oratory never became Jansenist *en bloc*, though its members regarded the Port-Royalist movement with less animosity than hitherto. Some manifested an attitude of benevolent neutrality because they recognized the undeniable qualities of Port-Royal, and feared that a sweeping condemnation of its principles of austerity might simply foster a tendency towards a soft spirituality. Pasquier Quesnel was among those who held this view. While Director of the Paris Oratory he did not intervene in the Jansenist quarrels. He was a pious priest who was certainly not on a par intellectually with Arnauld and Saint-Cyran, as suggested by his dull look and ovine cast of features; but morally he was among the most upright. In 1671 he published a small book entitled *Réflexions morales sur le Nouveau Testament* which competent judges deemed to be an excellent spiritual treatise, severe in tone but containing nothing suspect. To the moderns it has a Pascalian flavour, and many of the ideas expressed read very much like Pascal's *Pensées*.

Father Quesnel became the victim of a circumstance fairly frequent
in his day but which we of this age find surprising: some of his personal
notes were published without his permission, and they proved to be very
much more Jansenist in tone than his former work. It was useless for him
to disclaim publication; he was still held to some extent responsible. When,
therefore, his friend Father Abel de Sainte-Mardie, General of the Oratory,
was forced to resign his office in 1681 on account of his friendship with
Arnauld, Father Quesnel was involved in his downfall. Various incidents
aggravated the dispute between him and his congregation; he left and settled in Brussels near the Jansenist leader.

In the meantime the *Réflexions morales* met with success, and went into
several editions. In the manner of La Bruyère, Quesnel went on adding to
his work with each new edition; so much so that it eventually appeared to
be a book altogether different from the original edition, and infinitely more
Jansenist in tone. Moreover, a number of very pious people had approved
the first edition, notably Félix Vialart de Herse, Bishop of Châlons-sur-
Marne, who had even recommended it to his clergy. Both Father La Chaise
and the Bishop of Meaux had praised it, and it was known that the Pope
himself had read it. But did the succeeding editions warrant such commen-
dation? And were the episcopal prefaces which Father Quesnel retained at
the head of succeeding editions still valid? The alert opponents of Jansenism
could not risk letting such trickery pass unheeded. They began a campaign
against Quesnel, who was accused of being Arnauld's lieutenant, and in
1694 the *Réflexions morales* was denounced to the Sorbonne and the Holy
Office simultaneously.

It was about this time that Louis-Antoine de Noailles, bishop and later cardinal, appeared on the scene of this unending drama of Jansenism.
One hesitates to judge this pious and kindly prelate too harshly; his morals
were perfect, his life austere and his intentions absolutely beyond reproach;
none the less the part he played was an unfortunate one. It is sufficient to
study his portrait painted by Largillière to recognize that this man, with
his expressionless face, ungainly red nose and kindly smile, had nothing of
that quality of shrewdness and authority required for the position he held.

502   He succeeded Vialart de Herse to the See of Chalons and, as we have seen,
        played a prominent though ambiguous role in the Quietist affair, acting as
        judge with Tronson and Bossuet of Mme. Guyon's writings. When Harlay
        de Champvallon died in 1695 several preachers refused to pronounce his
        funeral oration—"prevented equally," as one of them said, "by the manner of
        his life and his death." Mme. de Maintenon then had Noailles nominated to
        the See of Paris that he might break with the past, but also because Noailles
        was a friend of Bossuet's and his selection would definitely bar the way to
        Fénelon, whom she pursued with her resentment. "He was a man of limited
        understanding and a confused mind, and he was weak and soft-hearted. He
        said white to one and black to another. It was useless to seek his opinion,
        for he had none." Such was the description of him given by the "Swan of
        Cambrai"; it was hardly flattering, but not untrue.

        One of the first things Noailles did was to devote a pastoral letter to
        Father Quesnel's book, redoubling the praises bestowed upon it by his pre-
        decessor. "This book is as good as a whole library," he told his priests. The
        Jansenists hailed the appointment of Noailles to the See of Paris as a great
        victory, whereas their opponents suspected him at once. An incident that
        occurred shortly afterwards amused the gallery. The Jansenists had repub-
        lished an old book propounding their ideas; it was entitled *Exposition de la
        foi touchant la Grace*, by Barcos, a nephew of Saint-Cyran. The Jesuits asked
        the archbishop to censure it, and this embarrassed Noailles. To approve
        Quesnel and condemn Barcos appeared to involve a contradiction, even to
        "a man of limited understanding." He called on Bossuet to help him, and
        the bishop got him out of the difficulty by drafting for him a statement
        repudiating Barcos but extolling St. Augustine! Shortly afterwards a small
        leaflet appeared under the title *Problème ecclésiastique*, and it caused much
        amusement. Its anonymous authors (two Benedictines of Saint-Maur) pre-
        tended to ask innocently if the Noailles who had disapproved of Barcos was
        the same bishop who had so warmly recommended the *Réflexions morales*.

        Bossuet then attempted to put things right. It occurred to him to pre-
        pare a new edition of Father Quesnel's book, after pruning it of everything
        that might be deemed suspect. He did even better: he wrote a *Justification des*

Réflexions morales expressed in the warmest terms. "We oppose the *Réflex-*
ions," he wrote, "purely in a spirit of contention"; but, went on Bossuet, "we
cannot find anything in it but good advice and instruction." He went so far
as to add: "Is it not manifest calumny to upbraid the author of the *Réflexions*
for having spoken as so many saints have done? If his language is suspect...
we shall have to be continually on our guard against the words of the Gospel, lest some quibbler comes along and accuses us of being Jansenists." On
this last point at least Bossuet was quite right; a frenzied anti-Jansenist attitude could do a great deal of harm. But there is no doubt at all that in his
desire to plead a cause the great bishop did more or less delude himself in the
matter of the *Réflexions*, and failed to discern the other danger—the imminent revival of Jansenism. He did not publish his treatise,[36] but informed
Quesnel of its contents. At that time Quesnel was living in Belgian Flanders
and, considering himself safe from attack, absolutely refused to make the
corrections suggested by Bossuet. He published yet another edition of his
book emphasizing his attitude.

Fénelon was the one man who did not permit himself to be misled by
Quesnel's ideas. The Quietist conflict during which he had been made to
bite the dust had just come to an end. Fénelon has very often been accused
of wishing to get his own back on Bossuet and Noailles, whose embroil-
ment in the new controversy was causing them embarrassment. We cannot
entirely discountenance the theory, for Fénelon was a man of complex character, and he might well have entertained the notion side by side with the
more praiseworthy desire to re-establish his good name with the Pope and
the king. But undoubtedly his conscience and a sense of duty impelled him
to resist Jansenism. His diocese of Cambrai swarmed with Jansenists. Their
gloomy doctrine could only horrify him, for he had never ceased to proclaim that "we must not approach God with the respectful fear of a slave,
but with the surrender and trusting tenderness of a son." He conducted a

---

36. It did not appear until 1710, six years after Bossuet's death; it preceded a new edi-
    tion, more Jansenist than ever, of the *Réflexions morales*. In consequence Quesnel was
    accused of yet another breach of faith.

considerable correspondence from his retirement in Cambrai, and his letters warned his friends of the dangers of Jansenism and the increasing harm the heresy was doing to souls. As a result of his efforts Godet des Marais, Bishop of Chartres, who was among those who first attacked Quietism, also became concerned. At the Assembly of the Clergy in 1700 it was the influence of Fénelon and Godet des Marais which predominated, not that of Bossuet and Noailles. On that occasion the Assembly condemned a posthumous work by Arnauld in which the old fighter had endeavoured to prove that Jansenism was a mere phantom invented by his opponents. He claimed that laxism, to which the observance of Port-Royal was the antidote, was indeed the real heresy.

These battles between theologians and bishops did not lend a great deal of excitement to the discussion, yet it suddenly became violent. The Jansenist leaders, aware of the temperament of Noailles, endeavoured to persuade him to take a definite stand on their behalf. They presented him and his mentor the Bishop of Meaux with a particular "case of conscience." Father Gay, superior of the seminary at Clermont-Ferrand, refused absolution to a Father Fréhel, parish priest of Notre-Dame du Port, because he himself had given absolution to the Abbé Perier, Pascal's nephew, a hardened Jansenist who had always adhered to the principle of "respectful silence" on the question of "law and fact." Had Father Gay the right to refuse absolution? Forty doctors of the Sorbonne declared that he had. A pamphlet dealing with the case was being read all over France, and Bossuet was furious at being unable to hush up this new quarrel. He sent a strongly worded protest to Noailles. Clement XI condemned both the pamphlet and the forty doctors of the Sorbonne. In four pastoral letters Fénelon returned to the condemnation of all "so-called Augustinians." Bossuet himself, unhappy at the way matters were going, made known to the king the danger "evident in innumerable writings emanating from the Low Countries." A kind of Holy League was developing against the "phantom" of Jansenism, which still seemed very much alive.

Louis XIV had become weary of all this commotion. The older he grew the more he detested non-conformists, especially the Jansenists. He

said that he regarded them as republicans and, according to Saint-Simon,
he deemed them to be just as heretical as the Protestants.[37] He asked for
details of recent incidents, and decided that the person really responsible for
the whole trouble was Father Quesnel. It was quite an easy matter for him
to obtain from his grandson, Philippe V, the new King of Spain, a promise to have the former Oratorian arrested in Brussels. The Spanish police
were so accommodating that they sent to Versailles all the documents they
had seized. The "Quesnel Papers" were decoded, broken down, commented
upon, and read to the king by his confessor every evening over a period of
ten years in the presence of Mme. de Maintenon. Since the introduction
of *Pilmot* the Jansenists had always retained a mania for assumed names
and disguised expressions. Consequently there was no doubt whatever in
the old king's mind that Jansenism was anything but a phantom; it was an
intrigue and a public danger.

He then asked Clement XI to publish another Bull condemning the
sect and especially the "Case of Conscience." Clement XI agreed, but not
without some hesitation, for he suspected a flavour of Gallicanism. The Bull
Vineam Domini was published in 1703, registered by the Paris Parliament
and approved by the Assembly of the Clergy—which alone made the Gallicans regard it as valid; it was even accepted by Cardinal de Noailles in an
involved pastoral letter. Fénelon was unpretentious in his triumph. Briefly
the Bull declared that it was not sufficient to sign the *Formulaire*, without
believing that Jansenism was a heresy—"as though it were permissible to
deceive the Church by an oath, and to say what she says without thinking
what she thinks." Henceforward there was no possible means of evasion, no
way of playing with the idea of "law and fact"; there was no longer even any
chance of hiding behind "Gallican freedoms" since the king had no desire
to quarrel with Rome.

---

37. His hatred of the sect reached such a pitch that it bordered on the ridiculous. An
army general whom the king took to task for having appointed to his general staff a
Jansenist notary, replied that the officer in question was a complete atheist. "Is that
so?" replied the king. "Can you vouch for it? If it is true there is no harm done, and
you can keep him." The Duc d'Orléans almost died with laughter when relating this
story to Saint-Simon!

It was easy for their opponents to drive the Jansenists to the wall: at least those who were unskilled at the game of mental reservations, implications and misrepresentations. Among these were the nuns of Port-Royal-des-Champs. The valley very quickly ceased to be fashionable. The nuns had grown old; they were less numerous than formerly for they no longer took novices. They remained firm, however, in their austere piety, very much attached to their memories of a great past, and on the whole very much out of touch with recent squabbles. Who was the enemy of Noailles who thought of using them to strike at the archbishop? The nuns of Port-Royal-des-Champs[38] were invited to sign a formal acceptance of the Bull. It was a clever stroke because everyone expected a refusal. If then the archbishop agreed to take the stern measures demanded of him he would become an object of loathing to the Jansenists; but if he refused to be co-operative he would be acknowledging that he was a Jansenist. And Bossuet was no longer alive to disentangle him! This backhanded stratagem occasioned one of the most famous and dramatic episodes in the whole ghastly business.

The nuns suspected a trap but agreed to sign, adding simply the words: "Without prejudice to the Clementine Peace." The Pope would have been content to accept this conditional submission; but the king's new confessor, the Jesuit Father Le Tellier, pointed out to him that these stubborn old ladies were defying his authority. Louis XIV then went a step further; he asked for a bull of suppression. For a long time no decision was reached; partly because the religious, as worthy heirs of Arnauld, appealed again and again; but also because the Pope was reluctant to be too severe. Noailles groaned; he reproached the nuns with ingratitude for refusing to listen to him and not striking out their restrictive clause. As of old Port-Royal-des-Champs became the symbol of Jansenist resistance to every form of authority. September 25, 1709, marked exactly one hundred years since the "Day of the Grating"—when the young Mother Angélique closed the door of her monastery against her father.

---

38 Port-Royal de Paris had become little more than a convent for ladies of fashion.

On Tuesday, October 29, d'Argenson, the chief of police, entered the convent with the constable of the watch and his patrol. The community was made to assemble in the chapter room and d'Argenson, courteous, frigid and formidable, read out the royal decree. To carry out the provisions of the Bull the nuns, numbering twenty-two, were to be dispersed. Twenty-two carriages had been brought for that purpose. Each nun entered a carriage and, accompanied by an old woman, set off for the convent allocated to her—Autun, Rouen, Nantes, Amiens and so on, all over France. Each was also accompanied by a military escort on horseback, as though they were dangerous criminals. The convent remained empty, and left to be looted by the soldiers charged to guard it.

"Such a way of exercising authority," said the Duc de Chevreuse, "can arouse only pity for these poor women and indignation against their persecutors." And that was precisely what the Pope had feared. Supporters of Jansenism all over France, many of whom were people of sincere faith and truly Christian hearts, longed to make a pilgrimage to the beloved valley and its deserted convent. Disconsolate women came to weep and pray in the deserted cloisters.

These demonstrations exasperated Louis XIV, and he decided to put an end to them: he gave orders that Port-Royal was to be demolished. In January 1710, during a dreadful winter of national famine, distress and defeats on the battlefield, gangs of workmen proceeded to raze to the ground the convent, the houses and even the church; only Les Granges des Solitaires was spared. But the cemetery remained, and again pilgrims flocked to it. An order was given to destroy that also. Influential families were authorized to remove the remains of their own dead. Saint-Etienne-du-Mont, in Paris, where Pascal's body lay, received the remains of Racine, Saint-Médard those of Nicole, and Saint-Jacques-du-Haut-Pas those of Saint-Cyran. As for the others, the poor and the unknown, and all who had wished to lie near the nuns and the "Solitaries," they were disinterred and cast into paupers' graves. Saint-Simon and later Sainte-Beuve, whose pens were perhaps more vindictive than veridical, have described the dreadful scene—the drunken grave-diggers at work in the cemetery, while the dogs fought over the remains that had not yet decayed.

508 It was not only a shocking decision but a ghastly blunder. To make martyrs of twenty-two stubborn, elderly nuns was anything but clever. "For the stones thereof have pleased thy servants: and they have pity on the earth thereof." Henceforward the Psalmist's words would be whispered in prayer by countless souls moved by so much injustice. One day when the unhappy Noailles was bewailing the straits into which Jansenism continued to plunge him, a witty woman replied: "What can you expect, my Lord? God is just, and the stones of Port-Royal are falling on your head."

19. THE BULL "UNIGENITUS"

IT was an easy matter to disperse a few nuns, to raze a convent to the ground and throw bodies into a common grave; much easier than to eradicate Jansenism from people's souls. Glaring signs of its vitality existed everywhere. Jansenist convents still survived. At the convent of Gif in the Île de France, the young nuns headed by Françoise de Ségur tried to persuade the abbess to take up the standard of Port-Royal; in Toulouse the Daughters of the Holy Childhood were so openly Jansenist that they had to be suppressed. The behaviour of the Sisters of Saint Martha, recently founded by the widow of the sculptor Théodon, was more moderate; they worked as peasants, and sustained the spirit of the sect in their humble life of prayer without aspiring to any connection with the great Cistercian Order. Bishops did not conceal their Jansenist outlook, and there were innumerable sympathizers in the lower ranks of the clergy. The three parishes which had welcomed the remains of the famous men whose bodies had been disinterred remained the bastions of resistance in Paris. Jansenist schools continued to function in the capital and in several provincial towns, and eventually the link-up between Gallicanism and Jansenism became complete; for those who had regarded the king's reconciliation with Rome in 1693[39] as a betrayal of Gallican freedoms made common cause with those overtaken by the agreement

---

39. See above, Chapter IV, p. 284.

between Pope and king. They counted many supporters in legal circles and
among the foremost politicians; even among high Church dignitaries who
considered that the authority wielded by the Holy See was excessive and its
demands exorbitant.

It was Father Quesnel who fired the powder magazine. The *Réflexions
morales* were condemned by the Holy See in 1708 after fourteen years of discussion. Instead of abiding by the decision the one-time Oratorian replied
with a cleverly written pamphlet entitled *Entretiens sur le décret de Rome.*
The Gallicans who were members of the King's Council, Chancellor Pontchartrain, Torcy, Foreign Affairs Secretary, and d'Aguesseau, Procurator
General, opposed France's acceptance of the papal brief on the grounds that
the carrying out of the sentence was, as stated in the document, entrusted
to the Inquisition. Emboldened by this Quesnel republished his *Réflexions*,
very much enlarged and rendered all the more discreditable by the fact that
the work was prefaced by Bossuet's famous *Justification*, which had obviously not been written for this enlarged version. The "Eagle of Meaux" had died
in 1704, and could have no say in the matter!

The result was a violent outburst against the Jansenists and their supporters. Fénelon forewarned his friends, and Father Le Tellier brought the
whole weight of his influence to bear. A certain student of the Archbishop
of Cambrai named Chalmet persuaded Champflour, Bishop of La Rochelle,
and Valderies de Lescure, Bishop of Luçon, to sign a directive that had been
prepared for them, under which they associated themselves with the papal
condemnation and described those who had approved the pernicious work as
"abettors of heresy." But to make quite sure that there should be no doubt as
to the identity of the person alluded to, young seminarists from Saint-Sulpice
were sent to post the pamphlet on the very walls of the archbishop's palace! At
the same time Fénelon denounced Percin de Montgaillard, the elderly Bishop
of Saint-Pons and a well-known Jansenist, in a pastoral letter. Rome congratulated the authors of the directive and condemned the unhappy Percin.

Cardinal de Noailles grasped the purport of this salvo perfectly well.
Tired and old, less capable than ever of governing the largest diocese in
France, his reaction to the attack was extraordinarily clumsy. He was, as

510   Fénelon somewhat ironically remarked, "exceedingly scrupulous where honour was concerned, and very particular about his reputation." He became cross and obstinate. "He made the great mistake," wrote Saint-Simon, "of imitating the dog that bites the stone instead of the hand that threw it." The first thing he did was to dismiss from Saint-Sulpice the nephews of the authors of the directive; this resulted in complaints to the king and to Rome, backed by several bishops and Mme. de Maintenon. Next, recognizing that he had made a tactical error, he openly attacked the Society of Jesus, which he accused of being the instigator of the whole affair; he deprived its priests of the authority to preach within his diocese and to hear confessions, and publicly deprecated their complacent attitude towards "the superstitions and idolatries of China."[40] He even went so far as to write a letter to Mme. de Maintenon, asking her to persuade the king to dismiss Father Le Tellier.

    The reaction was swift. Father Le Tellier, Cardinal de Rohan (who had succeeded Bossuet to the See of Meaux) and Cardinal de Bissy, taking the advice of Fénelon, who was supported by his staunch friends Chevreuse and Beauvilliers, suggested to the king that the Pope be asked to pronounce a formal condemnation of Quesnel's book, on the king's promise to compel all the bishops to abide by the decision. It was just as bitter a defeat for the Gallicans as for the Jansenists. Clement XI knew that he was doing them a great honour by issuing a Bull against the *Réflexions morales*, but he was careful not to throw away such an opportunity which the king offered him to exercise his authority. A committee was set up to examine the work once more; the extraordinary thing was that only one of its members was well acquainted with French. Several months had elapsed before the Pope, pressed by the king, promulgated, on September 8, 1713, the Bull *Unigenitus*, which began: "When the Only Begotten Son of God, who became man..." The Bull made history. The condemnation of Quesnel's work and, in a wider sense, Jansenism itself, was categorical. Quesnel was described as "a ravening wolf, a false prophet, a teacher of lies, a knave, a hypocrite and a poisoner of souls."

---

40.   The distressing Rites controversy was at that time being hotly debated. See *The Church of the Classical Age: The Era of Great Splintering*, Volume 1, Chapter II.

THE GREAT CENTURY OF SOULS: *Volume 2*

It contained nine lines of similar adjectives describing the ex-Oratorian, and 511 there were some who thought he did not deserve either the distinction or the humiliation. From a doctrinal point of view the Bull merely confirmed and emphasized previous condemnations. Among the hundred and one propositions condemned Rome did, however, slip in a few which were not Jansenist but Gallican; and they were taken word for word from Richer.

It now remained to fulfil the second part of the programme: to enforce acceptance of the papal ordinance throughout every diocese in France. Would the bishops agree? Fénelon immediately made himself the "guardian angel" of the Bull. He wrote a memorandum on the way in which it should be dealt with, and the Assembly of the Clergy gave its verdict accordingly. Subsequently a hundred and seventeen bishops accepted the Bull "purely and simply." About fifteen, however, qualified their acceptance. Eight openly rejected it, declaring that they intended to appeal to the Pope for further details. The Bull *Unigenitus* thus divided the French clergy into two camps, those who opposed it being backed absolutely by the whole Gallican party. Threatened with a command under the king's seal the Parliament decided to register the Bull, and the Sorbonne was induced to submit when it saw seven or eight doctors shut out. Events appeared to be moving towards a schism. Cardinal de Noailles's own brother, who succeeded him at Châlons, wrote: "If the Pope is in error in straying from the traditions of his See, it is he who is parting company with the Church."

As for Noailles, at first the blow took him by surprise and left him dumbfounded. For a moment he spoke of accepting the Bull, and suggested that the Pope be asked to *forbid* Quesnel's book, not to *condemn* it! Subsequently he endeavoured to draw closer to Versailles. The people of Paris called him "Our back-sliding Eminence," and they sang:

> "*Et Noailles jusqu'au bout*
> *Sera semblable au pendule*
> *Qui vient, revient et recule...*"[41]

---

41. "To the end Noailles will resemble a pendulum swinging to and fro."

512   Suddenly the pendulum stood still. In a magniloquent, but not entirely lucid, pastoral letter he forbade his priests under pain of suspension to
recognize the Bull because, he said, the papal decision was irregular as to
procedure and offensive to French bishops. At the same time, however, he
condemned Quesnel's book.

The king was furious and intervened. Would there be no end to this
Jansenist hydra, these conspirators and republicans? Books containing
noxious ideas, such as the widely read *Hexaples*, which claimed to demonstrate the complete orthodoxy of Quesnel's theories, continued to appear.
The king's attention was drawn to the unrest among the lower ranks of the
clergy. D'Aguesseau openly declared that the Bull, having been registered
under pressure, certainly did not possess the force of law in France. The old
king, more jealous than ever of his authority, brought the weight of his fury
down upon the Cardinal Archbishop of Paris. He was denied access to the
Assembly of the Clergy, forbidden to go to Rome to plead his case, and
was treated "almost like a heretic." There was even talk of "decardinalizing"
him! Amelot, the councillor of state in Rome, lent his support to the idea,
and it was suggested to the Pope that a national council be assembled to
depose the archbishop. To this Clement XI replied with a touch of defi-
ance that he did not mind if he and his Bull were "thrown as fodder to the
bears."

Father Le Tellier then advised Louis XIV to get Parliament to register a
straightforward declaration that they adhered to the Bull and that it should
be signed by all the bishops. Whereupon the king summoned the president,
the procurator and the advocates general; but he was unable to overcome
their resistance. The rumour went around Paris that when d'Aguesseau was
leaving for Versailles his wife said to him: "Go. Forget your wife and children
when in the presence of the king. Throw away everything—but not your
honour." It was considered that a *lit de justice* should be convened to compel the "Parliamentarians" to agree, but the aged king was sick and lacking
in strength. Meanwhile, however, the police arrested about two thousand
Jansenists and their associates, and interrogated about ten thousand more.
Fénelon remained calm, relishing his revenge. Before he died he dealt some

well-directed blows against the hostile sect with his *Instructions en forme de* 513
dialogues. The crisis appeared to have reached its climax. The pope yielded,
and agreed to assemble a council; but thoughtful men wondered what good
he hoped to achieve. Then, on September 1, 1715, the Great King died.

20. HOPES AND DISAPPOINTMENTS OF THE JANSENIST PARTY

THE reign of the little Louis XV began with the Regency. It also saw the
rise of "that eighteenth-century type of Jansenism" of which Sainte-Beuve
said: "Not all the gold in the world nor all the promises of heaven could
move it." Indeed, it was a type of Jansenism that became more and more
pernicious, drifting further and further away from the ideals of the early
Port-Royalists. It took the shape of a "party" pure and simple, not in the
seventeenth-century meaning of the word, but in the political sense of the
present day. The famous words of Péguy—"Everything has its origin in the
mystical and ends in the political"—were never more pertinent than in the
present instance.

The "Jansenist Party" would therefore assert itself under the direction
and management of high ecclesiastical Gallicans, gentlemen of the Robe
and politicians hostile to Rome who, as we have seen, were supporters of
the sect. As was natural, the mass of militant Jansenists hardly counted; they
were honest people who could no more understand Gallican theories than
they could the arguments relative to grace. However, a sort of "Catholic
Presbyterianism" was seen to develop and make its influence felt, deriving
its inspiration both from Richer and Jansenius's concepts of the priesthood;
and demanding that the lower ranks of the clergy be granted privileges
equivalent to those exercised by the wealthy incumbents. This was the first
sign of that antagonism which became so painfully evident during the Revolution. More disturbing still was the fact that certain elements, who made an
absolute mockery of grace of any kind, whether "efficacious" or "sufficient,"
also joined the "Party." Such were the free-thinkers, sceptics, men inimical

to religion. Their numbers grew, for they saw in the diverse episodes of the long Jansenist dispute an easy method of attacking the Throne and the Altar. This species of support given to the descendants of Saint-Cyran, Pascal and Arnauld by such unworthy allies was just retribution for their sectarian outlook and rejection of authority. Cardinal de Forbin-Janson had said of Cardinal de Noailles: "One day he will be the leader of a party without intending or knowing it." And that is precisely what happened.

When the body of the Great King had been laid in the church of Saint-Denis to the almost unanimous relief of the whole of France, weary of that long reign of seventy-two years, the Jansenists made merry. It did not seem, however, that the austere ideal of Port-Royal was destined to turn to account the succeeding period, which Voltaire described as "the pleasant period of the Regency, when Folly jingled its bells and skipped light-footed throughout France, and people did anything and everything except penance." But it was only necessary for Jansenism to stand as an opposition party against the ideas of the late reign for it to gain the sympathy of the new groups, and especially of the Regent, Philippe d'Orléans. The fact that this vice-monger showed goodwill towards the spiritual descendants of Mother Angélique should have been sufficient to open their eyes. But the party was too overjoyed at seeing their new master overhaul all the orders issued under the late king's seal, set free the imprisoned Jansenists and withdraw the Journal of Benefices from Father Le Tellier, whom the Regent sent to La Flèche. Bishops forbade the Jesuits to preach and hear confessions in their dioceses, and Cardinal de Noailles was made president of the Council of Conscience. The courtiers, previously so devout, loudly applauded these measures—Tartuffe was being transformed into an unscrupulous Turcaret, but claimed kinship with Quesnel!

Resistance to the Bull immediately stiffened. It was not popular with Catholics generally, for they were unable to understand why propositions that had every appearance of being orthodox had been condemned. The Sorbonne announced that it had accepted the Bull purely under duress, and the faculties of Rheims and Nantes followed suit. Twenty-five bishops took advantage of the new political situation to announce that they "had accepted the Bull only conditionally." Once again Cardinal de Noailles shifted his position; he stated that on the whole the papal text appeared to be acceptable subject to a few modifications. His clergy begged him to keep quiet, and a deputation from the Sorbonne asked him not to yield. By the end of 1716 the Parliaments of six cities including Paris had revoked their former acceptance.

Before long all this fuss began to annoy the Regent. He had more serious troubles on his hands; the most important was his attempt, with the aid of the brilliant Scotsman John Law, to avoid financial bankruptcy. He had also to guard against the intrigues of the wily Spanish minister Alberoni. His one desire was to be left in peace and free from all politico-religious troubles. These were legitimate aims, in which he was assisted by his personal secretary and former tutor Guillaume Dubois (1657–1723), who was popularly known as "The Abbé" although he was not a priest. Furthermore, Dubois was not the contemptible, intriguing, hypocritical monster portrayed by the famous Saint-Simon, whose ducal pride was hurt at seeing "this commoner...from the dregs of the people rise to power," and succeeding "by sheer force of Greek and Latin." This "thin, weasel-faced little man with the intellectual air" was above all clear-sighted and ambitious; his purpose was to become first minister and cardinal, and he required a springboard from which to attain his ambition.

It was the affair of the "Jansenist Appeals" that offered him his opportunity. Four bishops—Soanen of Sénez, Colbert of Montpellier, de la Broux of Mirepoix and de Langle of Boulogne—appealed to the Council against the Bull. Their appeal was supported by the Sorbonne and twelve other bishops, of whom Noailles was one. As a matter of fact these "appellants," as they were called, represented a very small proportion of the Church in France; not more than sixteen bishops out of thirty-three, and three thousand priests out of a hundred thousand. Languet de Gergy, Bishop of Soissons, the most spirited defender of the Bull, was quite right when he declared in his ardent epistles that they were but a weak minority. They constituted, however, a turbulent minority, backed by the entire Jansenist party. The Regent charged Cardinal de Rohan to negotiate with the agitators;

but nothing came of it.[42] The Jansenists' resistance provoked Clement XI beyond measure. He wished to "decardinalize" Noailles, an action which the Regent opposed through sheer Gallican pride. The "appellants" were condemned by a Holy Office decree and subsequently by the Bull *Pastoralis Officii*; they were even excommunicated. In the meantime Noailles, carried away by his determination to resist, appealed against the new Bull as he had done against the *Unigenitus*. Schism was openly discussed; a Gallican Church would be established independent of Rome, and the Archbishop of Paris would be its head. The situation was pregnant with possibilities.

At that moment Dubois acted, and with supreme skill. He let it be known in Rome that he was in a position to bring the two hostile factions together. On his advice the Regent intimidated the diehards by having Jansenist writings publicly burned and insisting that the Sorbonne expunge from its records an offensive resolution regarding papal infallibility. He persuaded Noailles to preside with Cardinals de Rohan and de Bissy over a committee of bishops to prepare a vaguely worded form of acceptance of the Bull satisfactory to everyone; and the king signed an edict to the effect that no one should publish any attack on the Bull—all of which soothed the feelings of its over-enthusiastic defender, M. Languet. Thus in 1720 a settlement was reached known as the *Accommodement*. After much hesitation Noailles to sign it. As for Dubois, he reaped the reward of his zeal: he was given the revenue of the See of Cambrai, and received Holy Orders a week later; Cardinal de Rohan consecrated him bishop, and a year later the Pope made him cardinal. In the meantime he had become Secretary of State for Foreign Affairs, was nominated to the King's Council, and eventually became first minister. The shrewd Dubois had succeeded.[43]

---

42. An amusing scene took place at the church of Saint-Léger, in Soissons, when the Vicar-General came to read Bishop Languet de Gergy's pastoral letter condemning the "appellants," and it gives some idea of the intense feeling prevalent at the time. The parish priest, who was a Jansenist, first ordered the congregation to leave, and then instructed the cantors to drown the Vicar-General's voice with a loud singing of the Canticles. Finally he ordered the church bells to be rung!

43. Cf. also Carreyre's *Le Jansénisme durant la Régence* (1932), where the facts are given in detail and which also has an account of the part played by Bishop Languet de Gergy.

2 1. "NO MIRACLES, BY THE KING'S COMMAND"

IN actual fact the *Accommodement* served no useful purpose. A rumour was current that Cardinal de Noailles had prepared two versions of his directive: the first, expressed in compliant terms, was sent to the Pope; the second one contained mental reservations, and was dispatched secretly to his most reliable supporters. As a result the whole party felt strengthened in its resistance. Yet 1720 marked the final turning-point in the history of Jansenism. Quesnel died at Amsterdam on December 2, 1719, after having stated in his will, which contained some fine sentiments, that he had "never intended to say, write or think anything contrary to the beliefs and teachings of the Holy Catholic Church." With him ended the third season, as it were, in the Jansenist story—a troubled and declining autumn. Saint-Cyran had heralded in the mild spring, which was followed by the sizzling summer of the Great Arnauld; what now remained was a dreary winter, laden with darkness and heavy storms. Jansenism was entering upon its agony, becoming more and more political, a prey to internal squabbles and secessions, buffeted even by a wave of madness.

During the entire pontificate of Innocent XIII (1721–1724) chaotic negotiations were undertaken, but without result. The new Pope, Benedict XIII, a Dominican of the Thomist school, was determined to have done with the matter. A council held in Rome declared the Bull *Unigenitus* to be an article of faith. Noailles's attempts to formulate a compromise doctrine in four articles were repudiated. Colbert, Bishop of Montpellier, invoked the Clementine Peace in order to bolster up the Jansenist position, and the government, with the agreement of Rome, appropriated his benefice. The Soanen affair created an even greater disturbance. Soanen was bishop of the unimportant diocese of Sénez in Haute-Provence. He was a pious priest, but fiery and obstinate. In 1726 he published a pastoral letter in which he retracted his submission to the *Accommodement*, praised the "appellant" bishops as "the sole defenders of truth," and without beating about the bush pressed for open revolt and schism. The Government instructed Archbishop de Tencin, of Embrun, to assemble a provincial council to try the refractory bishop. De Tencin was not a happy choice, for he was far from worthy of the task. Furthermore, the interference of the civil authorities could only irritate the bishops, who by no means approved of Soanen. Thirty-one bishops supported him, and he himself appealed again and again, basing his case on legal quibbles. Finally the little Bishop of Sénez was suspended by the Council. He took refuge in the monastery of Chaise-Dieu, where he died in 1740 at ninety-three years of age, without having made the vaguest gesture of submission. The Jansenists described the council as "a band of brigands," and fifty Parisian advocates signed a legal document declaring its decision null and void.

There followed a violent outburst of Jansenism in Paris and in various other parts of France, and Soanen was treated as a martyr. Anybody who at all criticized authority was susceptible to the influence of Quesnel, whether they were parish priests, magistrates, intellectuals, middle class or lower class. Cardinal de Noailles assumed the leadership of this Jansenist revival. But suddenly he changed his mind again; feeling the approach of death and influenced by his niece, the Marquise de Gramont, and Fleury, the shrewd first minister, he decided to submit and become reconciled with Rome. This he did in precise terms in July 1728. He withdrew all the directives he had issued, condemned Quesnel and the *Réflexions morales*, and affirmed his acceptance of the Bull. Shortly afterwards he died, and the people of Paris sang an ironical epitaph:

> "*Ci-gît, Louis Cahin-Caha*
> *Qui dévotement 'appela'*
> *De oui, de non s'entortilla*
> *Perdit la tête et s'en alla.*"[44]

Only the poor mourned him, for throughout his life he had relieved their misery; so much so that he sold his silver to provide them with bread. He may have had a small mind, but he had a large heart.

---

44. "Here lies Louis the Muddler who piously made his 'appeal.' In a maze of Yeses and Noes he lost his head and departed."

It naturally followed that immediately after his death letters of his were published in which he repudiated his submission. But they carried no weight; episcopal Jansenism died more or less with him. His successor, Mgr. de Vintimille, accepted the Bull without reservation. Most of the theologians in Paris did likewise, and only three refractory bishops remained. The king then decreed (in 1730) that all ecclesiastics who did not sign a straightforward acceptance would be deprived of their livings, which could be appropriated by law. The threat was quite sufficient to cool the ardour of the bulk of the party.

Not that Jansenism was by any means crushed. Its resistance hardened in three domains: amongst the lower clergy, where "Presbyterian" ideas developed side by side with the growing antagonism of the higher clergy; among parish priests and vicars with their *portion congrue*, who to some extent supported Jansenism on the assumption that by opposing the bishops as ecclesiastics of dubious morals and minions of the temporal power they were defending true Christianity, the Church's freedom and their own rights. Thirdly, resistance was strong in parliamentary circles, which seized every opportunity to stand up to authority. When parliamentarians attacked the Bull in defence of the rights of the Gallican Church, their activities acquired a political significance; in 1730 the Paris Parliament went so far as to publish a memorandum to the effect that "the ecclesiastical power acquired the exercise of its jurisdiction through the secular power," and also that "the authority of the Crown is not above that of Parliaments, for the latter are the Senate and the Supreme Tribunal of the nation"—and that was a revolutionary declaration. Obviously such statements immensely gratified the "progressive intellectuals" who were sceptical and anti-religion in outlook, and were already being described as "the philosophers." Ever since 1727 a weekly news-sheet called *Nouvelles ecclésiastiques* had been secretly produced by two brothers from Vendée who were priests—Etemare and François de la Roche. It was printed in the deep forest of Puisaye, in the country around Vitry-le-François, and distributed in the back streets of Paris. It vigorously denounced the scandals, great and small, of the clergy; railed against the Jesuits and lampooned the obsequious bishops of the court and

520 the cardinal ministers.[45] All this was, of course, very far removed from the ideals of the "Solitaries" of Port-Royal. In any case those of the party who desired to remain loyal to the traditional spirit had other misfortunes to put up with. First there was the alleged "Letter to Monsieur Nicole," followed by a treatise by a certain Petitpied on the subject of "fear and trust." The movement's spiritual leaders fought desperately among themselves, and there was no Arnauld to patch up their quarrels. The situation became ever more confused.

And then some very surprising things happened. For three or four years the Jansenists had been saying that God had revealed Himself, and had come to their help as He had done in the past with the Miracle of the Holy Thorn. Indeed there was an abundance of miracles. In the parish of Sainte-Marguerite a paralytic was cured by a parish priest, a well-known "appellant"; in the diocese of Rheims two other unaccountable cures took place at the tomb of a "Quesnelian" canon. But all that was nothing compared with the miracles that occurred in the cemetery of Saint-Médard at the tomb of a pious young deacon named François de Paris. He was the son of a magistrate and, out of humility, became a weaver. On his deathbed he cursed the Bull and all who had accepted it. He accounted for no less than eight miracles in a year: a case of dropsy, a woman suffering from cancer, three paralytics, two cases of blindness and an eighth not clearly defined! The extraordinary nature of these cures was officially recognized in due course.

But once the story began to spread the cemetery of Saint-Médard was besieged by a swarm of sick, blind, the bandy-legged, the deaf and dumb and, which was more distressing, people who were mad or half mad. They all declared that as soon as they stepped inside the cemetery they were seized by an irresistible power which shook them, threw them to the ground and dragged them to the tomb, upon which they rolled; and all this took place amidst cries and shouting. "One could hear groaning, shouting, whistling,

45. *Les Nouvelles ecclésiastiques* continued to appear in France until 1794, and was for a long time published at the abbey of Hautefontaine, near Vitry-le-François. It survived until 1803 in Holland.

prophesying and caterwauling," a chronicler relates. "But above all they dance; they dance until they are breathless." Men were to be seen swallowing pebbles, or slashing their flesh with glass; women "twisting and throwing themselves about" in a frenzy, and adopting attitudes that could hardly be described as decent. The "convulsionaries of Saint-Médard" were the talk of Paris.

A report of these "strange goings-on" came to the ears of the king and his former tutor, the Cardinal de Fleury (1653–1743), whom he had just made his first minister—and a very autocratic minister he was. This baby-faced man of sixty-three with the calm, blue eyes was discreet and peaceable. His greatest wish was that his ministry might be uneventful. He reacted immediately to the Saint-Médard affair by ordering the police to close the cemetery. Paris composed a couplet which became very popular:

De par le Roi, defense à Dieu
de faire miracle en ce lieu.[46]

But the "convulsionaries" continued their activities. They assembled in private houses, in the countryside, in cellars and attics. "Sisters" began to prophesy; others went off to heal the blind by using a paste made of spittle and dust. There were "Figuristes" who proclaimed the revival of the Church by means of their antics and through the conversion of the Jews. There were also the "Secouristes" who gave first aid to the sick, especially to the neurotic, whom they treated by beating them soundly with a stick. There were even "Augustinists" who confused Molinos with Quesnel, and authorized illicit relations between men and women on the grounds that by yielding to divine impulse they could commit no sin.

All these foolish pranks discredited Jansenism, which the "convulsionaries" claimed to profess. It is true that the early "miracles" were received with enthusiasm, even by such bishops as Soanen and Colbert; and the Jansenist Abbé d'Asfeld went so far as to compare them with the miracles

---

46. "By royal decree God must not work any miracles on this spot."

of Christ! But the madness and hysteria that were seen at Saint-Médard created consternation. Certain doctors belonging to the sect endeavoured to explain the convulsions, but the majority wisely repudiated them; this resulted in bickering. Fleury took advantage of the occasion to exercise a little authority; the insolent memorandum issued by the Paris Parliament was annulled by the King's Council, and, when the advocates replied by walking out, Fleury had ten of them arrested, a move which induced the remainder to adopt a more reasonable attitude.

22. JANSENISM OUTSIDE FRANCE

OPPORTUNITIES for the expansion and permanent development of Jansenism did not exist outside France to the extent which had enabled various forms of Protestantism to become firmly rooted beyond the countries of their origin. The austerity of Jansenism did, of course, reach out beyond France; in some countries it even exercised a profound influence, but it evinced nothing like the conquering force of Lutheranism and Calvinism. Nowhere in Europe did the struggle to impose Jansenist ideas assume the vigour it had displayed in the country of Saint-Cyran and Arnauld; not even in Belgium where Saint-Cyran had lived.

Yet the movement did at first seem to have taken deep root in Belgium during the Port-Royal days, when Alphonse de Bergh, Archbishop of Mechlin, authorized the preaching of the new ideas. Though his successor, William de Precipiano, gave all his support to the Jesuits—so much so that Innocent XII had to urge moderation—large bands of theologians hostile to the Society and to Molinosism rallied around Ruth d'Ans, and conducted a campaign that was more or less Jansenist in scope. The Collège du Faucon, which exercised a great influence on the University of Louvain, openly set up as a Jansenist centre. But when Philippe V, grandson of Louis XIV, succeeded Charles V, a violent reaction set in. Philippe was not satisfied with arresting Quesnel; he exiled Ruth d'Ans and his friends, and so they remained until the Spanish regime, overwhelmed by the combined armies of Protestant England and Holland, eventually collapsed. Canon Van Espen of Louvain then took over the leadership of the movement, and published a series of pamphlets violently Erastian and anti-Roman. Ruth d'Ans returned, and many of the bishops rejected the Bull *Unigenitus*; but it was a mere flash in the pan, for they received very little support from the bulk of the clergy. When the Austrian administrators arrived they hastened to publish the Bull, and the regent, Marie-Elizabeth, together with Philippe d'Alsace (1716–1750), Archbishop of Mechlin, began a systematic war against Jansenism, so that it disappeared leaving scarcely any trace. Van Espen went to Holland and remained there until his death.

Jansenism therefore made its greatest stride forward in the Low Countries to the north, secure from Spanish and Austrian interference. There it was that the Great Arnauld had sought refuge, and that Quesnel had fled to escape the episcopal prisons of Mechlin. Several of the vicars apostolic charged by Rome to supervise the small band of Catholics, including the heroic Rovenius,[47] living amidst a Calvinist majority, had shown great sympathy with the theories of Port-Royal. One of these, a certain Peter Kodde, went even further: having refused to sign the *Formulaire* in 1699 he was declared suspended by Rome, but continued to govern his church. Thus the way to schism was opened, and it had been reached by the time the Bull *Unigenitus* was published. A group of "appellants," acting independently, revived the Cathedral Chapter of Utrecht without informing Rome, and, in 1732, elected Cornelius Steenhoven archbishop. Varlet, a French priest from the foreign missions, having recently been consecrated Coadjutor Bishop of Ispaham, agreed to consecrate the new archbishop; he had been assured that the French bishops, among them Soanen, approved their action. This was schism indeed. A Jansenist Church was thus established in Utrecht, flouting condemnation by Rome, but in very good odour with the Calvinist authorities, who had cause to be elated over this dissension among Catholics. Varlet retired to Holland, and on the death of Steenhoven he was available to consecrate his successor. In a very

---

47. See Volume 1 of this work, Chapter III, p. 195.

short time the suffragan dioceses of Haarlem and Deventer were linked to the See of Utrecht.

Yet this schismatic church meant very little. Its position was ambiguous, for while it professed to be anti-Jansenist and condemned the Five Propositions, it rejected *Unigenitus*. It proclaimed emphatically that it had not separated from Rome, but that Rome had become separated from the true Church! Despite the contribution made by French emigrants the schismatic church had at the most fifteen thousand adherents. Furthermore, they were far from agreeing among themselves. The arrival in Utrecht of the "convulsionary" Pierre Le Clerc and the violence of his teaching contributed to create confusion in their ranks. One of his books dealt with the theme that Rome had become worse than pagan. In 1763 the Synod of Utrecht split the sect in twain, and one section gradually returned to the bosom of the Roman Church. At the beginning of the French Revolution the schism of Utrecht numbered scarcely eight or nine thousand adherents, thirty of whom were priests. It has managed to survive until the present day, but its importance has dwindled.

Elsewhere Jansenist penetration was moderate because it lacked support. The minds of men no longer enthused over the metaphysics of grace or the morality of Port-Royal; they were concerned rather with the virulent anti-papism with which Jansenism seemed to have become identified. In the Austrian states Maria-Theresa, followed by Joseph II, endeavoured to keep the Church under control,[48] and gave their support to all anti-Roman elements; the empress's confessor and doctors were members of the Church of Utrecht. But really sincere Jansenists were very rare; the Austrian temperament did not readily lend itself to excessive austerity. In Germany, where the works of Nicole and Quesnel were translated, together with Racine's *Histoire de Port-Royal*, interest did not extend beyond the limits of curiosity, combined with a little ridiculing of Rome. In Portugal a small Jansenist nucleus gathered around the Oratorian Father Pereira, and provided the

---

48. See See *The Church of the Classical Age: The Era of Great Splintering*, Volume 2, Chapter V.

famous minister Pombal with arguments in his struggle against the Jesuits
and the Holy See. In Savoy and Piedmont, where "convulsionaries" and a
few followers of Quesnel had taken refuge, Jansenism merely took the form
of a type of anti-papism; the same thing occurred in Venice, where Jansenist
canonists urged His Most Serene Highness to demand, from the popes, privileges modelled upon those which were the pride of the Gallican Church.

In all this dissension politics rather than the spiritual life of the soul
were the issue. There were exceptions, however: in Hungary, for example,
where the pious Francis II Rákóczy led a life comparable with that of the
"Solitaries"; and in Italy, where the sect gained many adherents because
the stern morality of Port-Royal, freed from condemned doctrinal errors,
savoured of the spirituality of the great reformers of the early part of the
century. They included Mgr. Bottari, the librarian at the Vatican, the famous
scholar Muratori, who was rector of the seminary at Pistoia, and even the
secretary of the Congregation of Propaganda. But as far as all these well-intentioned "Romans" were concerned there was definitely no question of
encouraging a sectarian movement, although their leniency unconsciously
brought about a similar result. The Abbé Grégoire wrote that "Italy was perhaps the one country in which Port-Royal contained the greatest number
of genuine admirers." Port-Royal itself most certainly, but not the political
movement that Jansenism had become.

23. THE END OF THE STRUGGLE: THE "BILLETS DE CONFESSION"

FRANCE was to witness the passage of a few more incidents before the
Jansenist controversy ceased to be of any further interest. They occurred in
an atmosphere very different from that with which men like Saint-Cyran,
Arnauld and Quesnel had to contend.

It was literally a pre-revolutionary atmosphere. The questions at issue
concerned the distribution of the sacraments, the recognition and condemnation of devotions. Something very different altogether was at stake.

526   Henceforward convinced Jansenists, the "appellant" type, became fewer and fewer; hardly any of them really believed that the Bull *Unigenitus* threatened the doctrine and morals of Catholicism, or that the Bull represented an attempt by Rome to "domesticate" the Church in France. But there emerged an increasing number of wily and intriguing persons, bent on taking advantage for purposes anything but spiritual of the extraordinary passion the public continued to show in such questions.

Faced with the ever-increasing failure of authority and a rapidly deteriorating financial and social situation, the Parliaments of the main cities, without any mandate whatsoever (for their members were not elected as in England, but functioned rather as courts of justice), took it upon themselves to stand up to king and government. In doing so they gratified public opinion because they appeared to be safeguarding national privileges. The La Chalotais affair illustrated the limit to which the overbearing insolence of the magistrates could lead them in the pursuit of their ambitions.[49] Jansenism's full collusion with parliamentary circles was transparent: a glaring instance of this lay in the refusal of the Paris Parliament in 1738 to register the Bull of canonization of St. Vincent de Paul on the grounds that the document dealt severely with Jansenism! By associating itself with every incident created by the sect, and from the contents of its 1730 memorandum, the magistracy made abundantly clear that it aimed at nothing less than complete control of Church and State and the imposition of its will on the regime itself.

But the parish priests who rebelled against their bishops, and declared that "the humblest priest possessed full power and jurisdiction," that he held direct from Christ his spiritual authority, that the bishops had no right either to empower priests to hear confessions or to withhold that licence — all these priests were indeed real revolutionaries, whether they recognized

---

49. La Chalotais was the parliamentary representative of Rennes. He quarrelled with the Duc d'Aiguillon, second in command to the governor of Brittany, over some new taxes which the government wished to impose. The incident was the starting-point of an attempt, which unfortunately failed, by the chancellor de Maupéou to reform justice and abolish the sale of public appointments.

the fact or not. These "Presbyterian" ideas were developed by a parish priest named Nicolas Travers, who managed to exercise a great deal of influence despite the fact that he spent his life either in prison or in hiding. All these activities constituted a definite attempt to aid the "appellant" priests and secure for the Jansenists authority to administer the sacraments. But this wave of independence went to many people's heads: these so-called "presbyterians" bore such hatred towards the Bull *Unigenitus* and the episcopate which had accepted its provisions that they were prepared to envisage a Church independent of Rome, no longer hierarchic but democratic, Gallican and equalitarian. This dream did materialize later on and became known as the Civil Constitution of the Clergy.

No event brings to light more clearly the collusion between these various forces than the circumstances surrounding the "Billets de Confession." In itself it was a trivial matter affecting ecclesiastical discipline, but wantonly exaggerated and over-coloured by the Parliaments, with the object of asserting their rights and embarrassing the Government. In 1746 Christophe de Beaumont became Archbishop of Paris. He was a pious, charitable and upright man, but lacked tact and skill in the handling of difficult situations. He was known to be aggressively anti-Jansenist; on several occasions he had belauded the Bull, and from the moment of his consecration as archbishop he became the butt of the Jansenist party. Everything he said and did was systematically distorted, and slanderous rumours were spread abroad regarding his relations with a nun whom he had placed in charge of the Paris hospital Hôtel Dieu. Even his charity was criticized.

The archbishop discovered that Paris was full of priests who were not empowered to administer the sacraments though they continued to hear confessions and give absolutions which were invalid, and sometimes even sacrilegious. He therefore directed his parish priests to require from the dying who wished to receive Extreme Unction a Billet de Confession, signed by a priest approved by the diocese, in default of which burial in sacred ground would be refused. This administrative measure was a severe blow to the Jansenists, for no priest was "approved" who had not declared his acceptance of the provisions of *Unigenitus*. It was, therefore, not long

528 before incidents occurred. Father Bouettin, parish priest of Saint-Etienne-du-Mont, began by refusing the last sacraments to Father Coffin, former rector of the university, and then to an aged priest named Lemerre, both of whom had refused to produce the precious Billet de Confession. Every Quesnelian priest in France rose up against Archbishop Beaumont. The Paris Parliament, to whom families appealed, three times instructed Bouettin to administer the sacraments—in other words, to disobey his archbishop. As he persisted in his refusal his living was seized. The king annulled the verdict, but Parliament replied by issuing a viciously worded decree forbidding parish priests to demand Billets de Confession or to attack Jansenism from the pulpit under pain of being prosecuted as disturbers of the peace! A few months later they proceeded even further, and labelled the Archbishop an "abettor of schism."

Extremely annoyed by these quarrels, Louis XV forbade by letters patent that anyone should be prosecuted for refusing to administer the sacraments; whereupon Parliament sent the king such an insolently worded protest that he dispatched his musketeers to the magistracy with an order under his private seal exiling its members to the provinces. A few months later, assuming that the storm had blown over, he allowed them to return, and published a *Déclaration* (1754) in which he imposed silence on both camps. At the same time he advised Beaumont to be a little more moderate.[50] But it was useless. When an elderly Jansenist woman refused to produce a Billet de Confession the archbishop instructed her parish priest to remain firm; this resulted in further proceedings and another verdict. This time, however, the archbishop was exiled for infringing the "law of silence" imposed by the king's *Déclaration*, and his pastoral letter was burned by the public executioner.

---

50. The following extract from a letter written by Mme. de Pompadour to Archbishop Christophe Beaumont is interesting in that it lacks neither wisdom nor Christian sentiments: "I should wish that some prelates, instead of regarding themselves as kings of the Church and writing pastoral letters which Parliament merely burns and the nation scorns, might be disposed to give us an example of moderation and a love of peace. What I mean is that your Billet de Confession may be an excellent thing in itself, but charity is worth much more."

The controversy became increasingly violent. Encouraged by their victory the magistracy and their supporters let loose their wrath. A pamphlet
by Voltaire on the subject of the "precious Billets which the dead took with
them to hell" was disseminated throughout France. In the towns of various
provinces, in Amiens and Troyes, for instance, pastoral letters were forbidden, and if published were burned by the Parliaments; in some cases the
revenue of the bishops was seized by officers of the law. Neither the court
nor the Government did anything to put matters right. One bishop was
very near the truth when he said: "We have been abandoned to the rough
treatment of Parlements." At the same time in the lower ranks of the clergy
refractory priests formed teams to move by night, taking the sacraments to
those at the point of death who were known to be hostile to the principle
of the Billets.

Indeed many bishops thought Christophe de Beaumont was carrying
matters too far, and that it was quite unnecessary to be more Roman than
Rome herself; the Bull contained no reference to Billets de Confession, why
then should the archbishop demand them? While the Assembly of the Clergy vigorously and unanimously opposed lay interference in religious matters, they were divided on the fundamental question, and asked the Pope to
decide the issue. Benedict XIV replied with the brief *Ex omnibus* (1756),
which decided in favour of the moderates. Only those who were notorious-
ly insubordinate, and had expressly stated their opposition to *Unigenitus*,
were to be refused the sacraments. The matter of the Billets de Confession
was not even mentioned.

Thus ended an episode which derived its importance solely from the
fact that, much to the amusement of the gallery, it had brought into relief
the conflict between the Church and the Parliaments. There were other less
boisterous disputes, during which the intractable Mgr. de Beaumont went
into exile no less than three times. Other sources of trouble between the
archbishop and the unfriendly Parliamentarians were his censure of a community of Jansenist nuns and his publication of a pastoral letter without
stating the name of the printer and quoting the authority for publication.
More unpleasant, though in a sense rather amusing, was the incident which

530 occurred in 1765, when the ageing archbishop proposed to the Assembly of the Clergy that the feast of the Sacred Heart, already recognized in many dioceses, be extended to the whole of France. There followed an outburst of protests against the "visions" of Margaret Mary Alacoque (whom her enemies referred to as *Marie à la coque*!) and against those who had a devotion to the Sacred Heart. A number of melodramatic demonstrations took place. For instance, on the day on which the archbishop went to his cathedral to celebrate the new feast he found that all the vestments required for the service had disappeared. No doubt some Jansenist sacristan had made away with them.

But interest in the whole business was on the wane. The number of Jansenist leaders was diminished following the publication of royal decrees, and the party's importance grew ever less. It existed in one or two dioceses, where a few "appellants" took advantage of an occasional indulgent attitude towards them which was more or less deliberate; and in Paris, where the really zealous militant Jansenists lived in hiding. The climate of the age was growing ever less favourable to religious controversy on a grand scale. Jansenist morality had long ceased to have anything in common with the easy-going morals of the period. Lack of restraint in matters of sex and an unbridled taste for speculative thought could scarcely be expected to accord with Jansenism's stern precepts. Rousseau, despite Mgr. de Beaumont, who had condemned his *Émile*, wrote of the benevolence of nature, life and human activities; all of which absolutely ran counter to Jansenist theories of grace and the miserable state of man. In the midst of general indifference[51] Jansenism was beginning to sink into the sands of time. But before disappearing altogether it witnessed its supreme victory when its parliamentary supporters imposed judicial interdiction on the Society of Jesus, whose crime had been its constant and fearless opposition to Jansenism. In 1773

51. It should also be mentioned that Jansenism had to contend with the indomitable spiritual influence of elements that still remained Christian, and were diametrically opposed to Jansenist tendencies. Especially important was the influence of St. Alphonsus of Liguori (see *The Church of the Classical Age: The Era of Great Splintering*, Volume 2, Chapter VI).

Pope Clement XIV was weak enough to yield to those governments which   531
demanded the Society's dissolution.[52]

During the worst moments of the trouble over the Billets de Confession
Voltaire wrote to his friend d'Argental: "Jesuits and Jansenists continue to
tear each other to shreds; we must fire on them while they are biting each
other." And a little later he wrote to Helvetius: "Would it not be fair and
reasonable to suggest that by strangling the last Jesuit with the intestines of
the last Jansenist the whole matter would have been brought to a satisfactory conclusion?" These flashes of wit, accompanied no doubt by a Voltairian
burst of laughter, point clearly to the moral in the story, and show the harm
done to the cause of Christ in the long run by this interminable Jansenist
quarrel.

24. THE AFTERMATH OF JANSENISM

BY the eve of the French Revolution Jansenism had had its day, both as
a great spiritual movement and as a political party. What remained of it
after the crisis was insignificant. In Holland the small schismatic church of
Utrecht has remained until our time,[53] but growing ever smaller; although
its vehement hostility to the principle of Papal Infallibility led it in 1872
to absorb some old Catholic elements equally hostile to the newly defined
dogma. Its present tendency towards allowing the marriage of priests draws
it closer to Protestantism pure and simple. In other countries there remained
nothing but tiny cells of Jansenism secretly linked together and feeding
a common relief fund called "La Boîte à Perrette,"[54] into which the living
gathered the legacies of the dead. Even today, lost amidst the countless sects

52. See *The Church of the Classical Age: The Era of Great Splintering*, Volume 2, Chapter
    V.
53. See Erich Kunhelt Leddin's article in the December 1954 issue of *La Table Ronde*,
    entitled "Les foyers jansénistes contemporains en Hollande."
54. We might call it in English "the money box." Perrette was the name of Nicole's ser-
    vant—the Jansenists always had a taste for cryptic nicknames.

and small churches that abound in Paris there exists a "Jansenist" Church, canonically dependent upon the Bishop of Utrecht; its centre is near Saint-Jacques-du-Haut-Pas, formerly one of the three strongholds of Jansenism in the capital. Religious Orders directly descended from Port-Royal have survived to the present day; the Sisters of St. Martha, although condemned by Mgr. Affre, continued to a limited extent. It was not until 1918 that the white head-dress of those pious women, who by then had had the wisdom to submit to their bishop, ceased to be seen in the village of Magny, near Chartreuse, where they had conducted a welfare centre.[55] The "Frères Tabourin" was founded in 1709 by Charles Tabourin to carry on the teaching work of Port-Royal. After a short period of modest success, especially in the Saint-Antoine district of Paris, their schools—more or less contemporary with those of St. Jean-Baptiste de la Salle and his spiritual sons—foundered in 1887 through financial difficulties.

All that meant very little. Much more important were the scars left by Jansenism upon the Christian conscience, the halo that still envelops the great figures of Jansenism and the continued interest that exists in the vast issues they raised. A shoal of books has been written on Port-Royal; scholars continue to confront each other supported by copious documents, almost as in the days of the *Formulaire*, and the Bull *Unigenitus*. A veritable cult has grown up around the illustrious memory of the nuns and the Solitaries, the flame of which is kept alive by the "Friends of Port-Royal."[56] The success in 1838 of Sainte-Beuve's six volumes and the recent play by Montherlant are equally significant of that attitude of mind which continues to present problems. The French have a weak spot for those who stand out against

---

55. When they were condemned, about the year 1840, another institution—the "Soeurs de Sainte-Marie"—sprang from them. It was a perfectly orthodox organization, subject to the Church, engaged in teaching and nursing the sick. Today it is a flourishing community which has spread beyond France, even as far as Mexico. (For further information relating to Orders descended from Jansenism, see Le Moign-Klippfel's "Les derniers Jansénistes," in the September 1956 issue of *Ecclesia*; S. M. d'Erceville's book, *De Port-Royal à Rome* [Paris, 1956] and, of course, Gazier's *Histoire générale du mouvement janséniste*, mentioned in the bibliographical notes.)

56. For a long time, Henry Jaudon, Counsellor of the Supreme Court of Appeal, has been their president.

established authority; they are easily moved to pity the persecuted and the vanquished, and they have a sneaking dislike for excessive solemnity and an admiration for those really worthy of admiration, strong characters, men deserving of a better cause. A blend of all these sentiments lies at the root of that lingering veneration of Jansenism, or more precisely of Port-Royal; for its eighteenth-century successors are very much less famous and less admired—as though one could praise the source and scorn the river that flows from it!

Jansenism undoubtedly introduced new elements into Christian experience, incessantly varied down through the centuries, giving a new resonance to the eternal message. Literature and art themselves testify to this. It may not be quite true that Pascal and Racine owe everything to Port-Royal, as certain materialist historians[57] try to prove by parading these two writers as the product of the social-religious cellule of the valley of the Chevreuse; but their genius would never have developed in the way that it did had they not been nourished on the ideas of Saint-Cyran and the "Gentlemen of Port-Royal." And there is no doubt whatever that the pathetic contrast of grief and supernatural light portrayed in the features created by the brush of Philippe de Champaigne is just as much the fruit of the mournful doctrine of the *Augustinus* as of the stern morality which he practised as a Jansenist.

It would be unjust to ignore the role played by Jansenism in the rebuilding of Catholicism, especially in France and Italy. The raising of moral standards during the seventeenth century, the stricter—even ascetic—tendency in the practice of religion, owes something, as we have seen, to the influence of those men and women of Port-Royal who offered such splendid examples. But only to a certain extent; for after all the Port-Royalist movement was not entirely divorced from all those institutions which stirred the Christian conscience during the great century—the Oratory, Saint-Lazare, Saint-Sulpice. Their methods were different, but they laboured towards the same

---

57. Cf. Lucien Goldmann's *Le Dieu caché* (Paris, 1955), and, concerning that work, A. Blanchet's article "Pascal est-il le précurseur de Karl Marx?" *Etudes* (March 1957).

end without drifting into rebellion. It may be justly claimed that Jansenism, through its books and its schools, succeeded in penetrating the masses with a certain spiritual gravity, a respect for holy things which may be discerned in Catholicism today. The practice of standing during the reading of the Gospel, though it existed in the Middle Ages, was not always adhered to in the early part of the seventeenth century; but the Jansenists enforced it in their parishes. Similarly they revived the custom of rising during the saying of the *Credo.* An effort made by the Jansenists to induce the faithful to participate more actively in the liturgy has left its mark; the most noticeable instance is the reading of the Gospel in the vernacular.[58]

Though such positive contributions[59] were considerable they could not compensate for the losses and the injury which Jansenism inflicted on Catholicism and the Church. In the strictly spiritual sphere its responsibility appears overwhelming. It is quite certain that the work of such saints as Jean-Baptiste de la Salle and Louis-Marie Grignion de Montfort was frequently thwarted by sectarians whose conception of holiness was based on their own standards and, in their opinion, it did not exist outside their own ranks. More serious still, it was the Jansenists and their followers, led by Nicole, who began, and continued with dreadful zeal, the action taken against the mystics; we cannot attribute to the Quietist trouble alone those proceedings which eventually stifled the mighty impulse sweeping so many souls towards God at the beginning of the seventeenth century. Even the solid doctrine of St. Teresa and St. John of the Cross did not emerge altogether unscathed from their attacks. Mystical union appeared to many Catholics as a state so rare as to be inaccessible; it was not, in any case, considered either meritorious or tending towards spiritual perfection. Beneath

---

58. "Under the influence of Port-Royal a new tendency developed during the second half of the seventeenth century: the faithful were urged not to be content with extracts or paraphrased versions of the Scriptures, but to become acquainted with the sacred text itself." (From the article entitled "Écriture," by Father du Chesnay, in the *Dictionnaire de Spiritualité*.)

59. We must also include the contributions made to Christian scholarship and learning in general. Le Nain de Tillemont was a master in this branch of instruction, and historical criticism owes a great debt to the Jansenist Launoy.

the anti-mysticism of Nicole and his friends lurked a religion of command-ments and precepts and the threat of formalism.

Such a tendency was all the more disturbing because, at the same time, Jansenism was conducing to a decline in the practice of religion; that is to say, it was robbing souls of the support of the sacraments. By virtue of the scruples that arose, as we have seen, from an absolutely false notion of what the sacraments really are, confessors, in the manner of Saint-Cyran, turned the faithful from confession and Communion. Innumerable documents tes-tify to this attitude of mind and its consequences. At the beginning of the eighteenth century a priest of the diocese of Auxerre was recorded as being proud of the fact that he made some of his parishioners wait up to ten years before giving them absolution and Holy Communion. In Dauphine a par-ish priest proudly told his bishop: "I am sure that there has not been a single sacrilegious Communion in my parish during the last year, because no one has been to Communion." It was only at the end of the eighteenth century that, under the influence of St. Alphonsus of Liguori, another path was dis-tinctly mapped out, as far removed from laxism as it was from austerity; a path to which Pius X in 1905 would direct the whole Church. But, in the meantime, how many souls must have lost their way to the confessional and to the Sacred Banquet!

Just as serious were the consequences of Jansenism's approach to dis-cipline. Their refusal to submit unhesitatingly to authority, their caviling, their arguments and, in short, their revolt, dealt the Church some heavy blows. If we can also establish that Jansenius's theories constituted a definite heresy in relation to grace, then it cannot be denied that the behaviour of the sect resulted in a heresy against the Church itself, as it questioned the very authority of the Sovereign Pontiff and his legitimate claims. In addi-tion the "Presbyterianism" which Jansenism encouraged in the eighteenth century undermined the authority of the bishops and the very structure of religious society; the "subordination of the lower ranks of the clergy," to use the words of the regent in 1717, was at stake, and with it the entire structure of the Church. The Civil Constitution of the Clergy would show where this democratization would lead. And there is scarcely any need to add that the frenzied attacks conducted since Pascal's time against the Society of Jesus by every Jansenist capable of wielding a stinging pen finally discredited for a while an institution which might have had its faults, but nevertheless remained one of the strongest supports of the Church. The Jansenists threw down the pillars of the Temple.

But that was not all. In very many other ways the Jansenist crisis did great harm to the cause of Christianity. It will be remembered that, when the Port-Royalist movement began, it appeared as the vanguard of the saintly company set on their way by the Council of Trent; many excellent Catholics made no distinction whatever between St. Francis de Sales, Bérulle, Condren and Saint-Cyran. All were equally animated by the spirit of reform. When Jansenism became a doctrinal deviation, and then a revolt against the Church, and when the Church was forced to condemn it, an atmosphere of uncertainty hovered over the Tridentine reform and all that proceeded from it. A long time elapsed—even to our own day—before Catholics really appreciated the work of the Council and ceased to mistake the counterfeit for the true message of holiness.

Furthermore, the obvious consequence of these repeated dissensions among themselves in which Catholics engaged so readily occasioned a loss of prestige affecting Catholicism generally. In the Quietist controversy contemporary Catholics were well aware of the worsening effect and the dangers underlying such conflicts. "The free-thinkers owe their success to them," wrote Bossuet. "They seized the opportunity to turn piety into hypocrisy and to deride everything pertaining to the Church." As for the "convulsions" and other antics that took place in the Saint-Médard cemetery, there is scarcely any need to mention that they shocked sincere men, who were puzzled by this kind of Christianity.

To say that Jansenism was the harbinger of incredulity may be a harsh accusation, but it is in a large measure true. If the Church in the eighteenth century was, as Sainte-Beuve has said, "so powerless, so defenceless, that it was straightway riddled by the arrows of Montesquieu's *Lettres persanes*," not all the blame can be laid upon Port-Royal and its heirs, but they must bear a great deal of the responsibility; and not merely on account of their censures and their insubordination. The excessive austerity which they 537 wished to impose alienated from Christianity the average man, the general run of Christians who felt ill at ease under a religious system in which, as Father Bonal said, "Nothing was virtuous unless it was heroic, nothing Christian unless miraculous and nothing tolerable unless inimitable." Yet it was the most illustrious of the Port-Royalists who has told us that by trying to be angels we run the risk of becoming animals. By dint of repeating that man's state of sin is so frightful that nothing moves him but his passions, we are liable to force him to conclude that it is much simpler to deliver himself up to his instinct for pleasure. By continually "denying school and Church a say in theological matters, and leaving decisions on doctrine to the laymen," are we not serving the cause of rationalism? Surely by stressing the transcendence of God, rendering Him more and more inaccessible, we are in danger of discouraging man from ever attaining Him; or, as a writer with Marxist tendencies[60] has observed, man lays himself open to replacing, as happens today, the transcendence of a superhuman God by that of mankind, "both of which are at once outside the individual and within him." If the enemies of Port-Royal, by exaggerating the role of nature and reason, encouraged Rousseau and the philosophers, it is beyond question that Jansenism immensely contributed to the crisis of minds and consciences which proceeded side by side with the shattering episodes of that interminable controversy. "Through the open crack," to quote Sainte-Beuve once more, "Saint-Évremond, La Fontaine and Bayle entered"—and many others besides.

"Pascal paved the way for Voltaire," wrote Lanson, and the reflection is not as paradoxical as it sounds. But it was certainly not the purpose of those profound believers of Port-Royal, or of Pascal, the hero of the "night of fire."

---

60. Goldman, *Le Dieu caché*. Father Blanchet, reviewing *Le Maistre de Sacy et son temps*, the extremely erudite work of Geneviève Delassault, in the April 1958 issue of *Etudes*, remarks that in these days many people who are not by any means Christian pose as the champions of an uncompromisingly strict Jansenism.

SELECT BIBLIOGRAPHY

THE following are the principal works to which the author refers in his extensive bibliographical notes.

CHAPTER IV. LOUIS XIV: "MOST CHRISTIAN KING"

E. Michaud, *Louis XIV et Innocent XI*, 1883.

C. Gérin, *Louis XIV et le Saint Siège*, 1893-1894.

G. Lacour-Gayet, *L'Éducation politique de Louis XIV*, 1898.

A. DuCasne, *La guerre des Camisards*, 1946.

P. Gaxotte, *La France de Louis XIV*, 1946.

T. Orcibal, *Louis XIV contre Innocent XI*, 1949; *Louis XIV et les protestants*, 1951.

F. Gousseau, "Religion fondement de l'ordre social au Grand Siècle," in *Verbe*, May–July 1954.

Duc de la Force, *Louis XIV et sa cour*, 1956.

540 CHAPTER V. CHRISTIANS OF THE CLASSICAL PERIOD

J. Baruzi, *Leibniz et l'organisation religieuse de la terre*, 1907.

Mgr. Gauthey, *Marguerite Marie Alacoque*, 1915.

Crousaz-Cretet, *Paris sous Louis XIV*, 2 vols., 1921.

H. Bremond, *L'Abbé Tempête* (Rancé), 1929.

G. Truc, *Bossuet et le classicisme religieux*, 1934.

M. Denis, *Art chrétien*, 1939.

Gillet, *L'éloquence sacrée*, 1943.

L. Le Crum, *S. Louis-Marie Grignion de Montfort*, 1946.

A. M. Carré, *L'Église va-t-elle se reconcilier avec le théâtre?*, 1956.

P. Varillon, *Fénelon et le pur amour*, 1957.

V.-L. Tapie, *Baroque et classicisme*, 1957.

CHAPTER VI. THE DOCTRINAL CRISES OF JANSENISM AND QUIETISM

L. Seche, *Les derniers jansénistes*, 1891.

Ch. Vincent, *Malaval*, 1893.

J. Pasquier, *Quest-ce que le Quiétisme?*, 1910.

H. Bremond, *Apologie pour Fénelon*, 1910.

P. Dudon, *Le Quiétisme espagnol, Michel de Molinos*, 1921.

Sainte-Beuve, *Port-Royal*, 8th ed., 1923.

A. Gazier, *L'Histoire générale du mouvement janséniste*, 1924.

J. Laporte, *La Doctrine de Port-Royal*, 1925.

G. Hardy, *Le Cardinal de Fleury et le mouvement janséniste*, 1926.

J. Chaix-Ruy, *Pascal et Port-Royal*, 1930.

L. Carreyre, *Le Jansénisme pendant la Régence*, 1929-1932.

J. Orcibal, *Origines du Jansénisme*, 1947.

J. F. Thomas, *La Querelle de l'Unigenitus*, 1949.

L. Cognet, *La Réforme de Port-Royal*, 1950.

ENGLISH SUPPLEMENT

H. S. Lear, *Priestly Life in France in the Seventeenth Century*, 1873.

L. von Pastor et al., *History of the Popes*, 20 vols., 1929-1950.

H. Belloc, *Richelieu*, 1930.

A. Luddy, *The Real De Rancé*, 1931.

542   N. Abercrombie, *The Origins of Jansenism*, 1936.

C. Bartz, *Louis XIV* (translation), 1937.

Sir C. A. Petrie, *Louis XIV*, 1938.

T. Maynard, *Apostle of Charity: St. Vincent de Paul*, 1940.

A. Huxley, *Grey Eminence*, 1941.

Voltaire, *The Age of Louis XIV*, 1751 (M. P. Pollack translation).

Cardinal de Retz, *Memoirs*, 1717 (P. Davall translation).

Designed by Fiona Cecile Clarke, the CLUNY MEDIA logo
depicts a monk at work in the scriptorium,
with a cat sitting at his feet.

The monk represents our mission to emulate
the invaluable contributions of the monks
of Cluny in preserving the libraries of the West,
our strivings to know and love the truth.

The cat at the monk's feet is Pangur Bán, from the
eponymous Irish poem of the 9th century.
The anonymous poet compares his scholarly
pursuit of truth with the cat's happy hunting of mice.
The depiction of Pangur Bán is an homage to the work
of the monks of Irish monasteries and a sign
of the joy we at Cluny take in our trade.

"Messe ocus Pangur Bán,
cechtar nathar fria saindan:
bíth a menmasam fri seilgg,
mu memna céin im saincheirdd."

www.ingramcontent.com/pod-product-compliance
Lightning Source LLC
Chambersburg PA
CBHW020339100426
42812CB00029B/3180/J